Stuff
BRITS
Like

FRASER McALPINE

Stuff BRITS Like

A Guide to What's Great About Great Britain

Berkley Books, New York

BERKLEY

An imprint of Penguin Random House LLC
375 Hudson Street, New York, New York 10014

This book is an original publication of Penguin Random House LLC.

Library of Congress Cataloging-in-Publication Data

McAlpine, Fraser.
Stuff Brits like : a guide to what's great about Great Britain /
Fraser McAlpine.—Berkley Trade paperback edition
p. cm.
ISBN 978-0-425-27841-3 (paperback)
1. Great Britain—Humor.   2. Great Britain—Social life and customs—Humor.
3. Great Britain—Anecdotes.   4. National characteristics, British—Humor.   I. Title.
DA115.M43   2015
941—dc23   2014045469

PUBLISHING HISTORY
Berkley trade paperback edition / July 2015

PRINTED IN THE UNITED STATES OF AMERICA

10 9 8 7 6 5 4 3 2 1

Cover art: Brtish Flag © Andrey_Kuzmin / Shutterstock;
English Bulldog © Eric Isselee / Shutterstock; Crown © Katsiaryna Pleshakova / Shutterstock.
Cover design by Diana Kolsky.
Interior text design by Ellen Cipriano.
Interior images by Fraser McAlpine.

Penguin
Random
House

Stuff
BRITS
Like

Introduction ■

Let us start this preposterous journey in the most British way imaginable: with a series of meandering apologies and caveats. I don't know what it is about a book like this, but it seems you can't make huge, sweeping, lawn-mower generalizations about the likes and loves of an entire nation without slicing up the odd precious and unique orchid here and there, and for that, I am truly sorry.

It would probably have been easier to write a book called *Stuff Brits Don't Like*. That would have taken no time to compile and run to several volumes, such is the national zeal for complaining and taking things to task, but it's not as if the Internet is short of people showing their displeasure, so it's probably best to leave them to it.

And while we're shutting doors in people's faces, this book can only be a personal journey. It wasn't subject to a public vote and there won't be a chance to suggest subsequent chapters. People born and bred in the British Isles won't always recognize themselves on every page; there will be lots of points along the way where, if this were a blog, the comments section would blaze with outrage and correction (see: Pedantry). But that's because one book cannot hope to convey the full range of enthusiasms in a nation as endlessly and joyfully provincial as the United Kingdom.

Heck, I can't even get them to agree on a list of favorite movies (excluding *Star Wars*, which is, ah, universal). So I've picked just five popular cinematic experiences, the ones that say something about how British people like to think about themselves. That is, if they would ever settle down and think of themselves as British in the first place.

By which I mean we need to get our definitions straight. For the purposes of brevity, if not painstaking accuracy, "Britain" and "the United Kingdom" have been used interchangeably to describe the same place (the full title is the United Kingdom of Great Britain and Northern Ireland). However, the United Kingdom is made up of four countries—England, Scotland, Wales, and Northern Ireland—and Cornwall, which does not currently have nation status (it's actually a duchy). The Cornish have been identified by the European Union as a recognized minority; they are, in other words, their own people.

Then there are the island communities: the Isles of Scilly, the Orkneys, the Shetlands, the Isle of Wight, and so on. On some islands cars are welcome, and on others they are not allowed and the taxis all float. This must make watching *Top Gear* there an entirely different experience from what it is in landlocked Birmingham. So again, sweeping generalizations are hard to pull off.

Also, Britain and England are so often conflated that Welsh, Scottish, and Northern Irish (and Cornish) residents tend to feel left out. Make a list of British things that are principally English things and you're sure to get on someone's nerves.

Then again (again), you can't ignore the English either, not least because they made such a fuss about being in charge of everything in the first place. But which England? The north is a very different place from the south. As is the east from the west. And that's before you consider the dividing influence of class—still a hugely influential factor in British tastes—and the various experiences of people from different ethnic groups too.

In fact, the only thing British people will definitely all agree on with regard to this book is that it is hugely flawed in almost every respect. I can only offer sympathy with that view, and my humble apologies. Ideally a balance can be struck between compiling the common clichés of bowler hats and stiff upper lips and writing a huge list of things that everyone likes, delivered as if no one has ever noticed them, like saying, "Hey, this oxygen stuff isn't bad, is it?"

Oh, and while we're on definitions, here's a brief list of potentially confusing terms:

- If I say *football* I mean *soccer* (see: Football).
- If I say *fags* I mean *cigarettes*.
- If I say *chips* I mean *fries*.
- If I say *crisps* I mean *chips*.
- If I say *biscuits* I mean *cookies*.

Everything else, bar an eccentric glossary at the end, is yours to puzzle over and investigate further. Good luck!

FRASER McALPINE, CORNWALL, 2014

Pedantry ■

Let's be honest, we all knew this was going to be the first chapter. The British have many international reputations to uphold, but the most fondly held is that of the uptight gentleman in an immaculate suit waiting politely for his turn to explain that you've just done something wrong. Even in the act of putting together ideas for a book about things that British people tend to enjoy—not a controversial or damning theme—I started to worry about the kindly meant corrections, the outrage at having left something out. Y'know, the pedants' revolt.

Now I'm fretting that I've put the apostrophe in the wrong place just there. Do I mean it's a revolt of a single pedant or a group of pedants? Does it belong to them? Do people get that the phrase is a pun on the Peasants' Revolt of 1381? Should I explain that or does it ruin the joke? It's all very stressful.

There's also the fact that the only people who refer to the Brits as the Brits are not Brits. Regional pride runs strong and deep in the United Kingdom, a state of affairs that is only intensified by the fragmented nature of Britain as a combined nation. As there's a certain amount of cultural antagonism between the five nationalities involved—or, more accurately, between the other four nationalities and England—any reference to British people will draw the Pavlovian response that Britain is not England, that the two terms are not interchangeable. And that's before we've even started to take into account the significant differences between individual counties, districts, and villages, some of which really do not get on well.

You can pin this intense desire for subjective accuracy down to a need to create order out of chaos—using unimprovably impatient phrases like "Why don't you just . . ." or "Surely you'd be better off . . ." as a preface—but the British and their high standards manage to find chaos everywhere, even in places that look pretty ordered already, thank you very much.

By which I mean the Brits won't forgive the rest of the world for driving on the right-hand side of the road, much less America for taking so many letters out of British English words—colour, catalogue, axe—just to make spellings easier.

Naturally the online environment has only intensified this state of affairs. Create any kind of Web list—Five Best Tea Shops in Rhyl, Nine Greatest Achievements of Clement Attlee, Seven Greatest Beatles Songs—and the first comment afterward will be "You forgot Liffy's caff" or "You forgot maintaining government order in a cabinet of strong personalities" or "You forgot 'Nowhere Man,'" as if the omission of one runner-up deprives the whole enterprise of merit. That's largely why people create these online lists, of course—to encourage pedants to read, snort, and comment—and it's incredibly effective.

But there are also blogs and Twitter feeds devoted to the search for spelling mistakes on handwritten signs: patiently explaining why speech marks are not used for emphasis, impatiently yelling at the poor greengrocer and his "potatoe's," and generally channeling the sadistic English teacher from the writer's past who made tiny tears well up every time she read the student's homework out loud to the class. And of course those blog posts and tweets will also contain mistakes— whether made by fat fingertips on a smartphone screen, autocorrect larking about, or genuine human error—and this will provoke more snarky comments, which will also contain basic spelling mistakes or missed punctuation, betraying the glee and speed with which pedantry is applied. To be the second to point out a mistake is an unbearable shame. To have made a mistake while in the act of pointing out someone else's, well, that's grounds for immediate deportation from life itself.

Celebrities are invited to join the cause. Stephen Fry, as a fan of discourse and generally bashing words together to see the pretty sparks, is often encouraged to speak out against declining standards in grammar and the rising tide of neologisms. He stoutly refuses to do so, pointing out that language is a fluid thing. English teachers are wonderful, inspiring people, even the scary ones, but they only relay the basic rules of punctuation and grammar as they understand them at the time. To say the English language—something the Brits are quietly rather proud of—is on the wane because of *LOL* or *textspeak* is simply to echo the same view expressed in the 1950s with *daddy-o* and *cool*, and in the 1960s with *groovy* and *heavy*. Shakespeare coined hundreds of new words and expressions, from *barefaced* to *courtship* to *puking*, and you can bet that the first few times they were used, there was an unimpressed puritan within earshot, ready with a withering rebuke. And they had proper puritans in those days.

The nation's best-known film critic is Mark Kermode. He's a man of strong passions, very principled in his approach and firm in his point of view. And one of the reasons he is so popular is that he's a terrific pedant. Whether he's picking apart tiny flaws in the films he is reviewing or he's listening to comments from his radio listeners and correcting their grammar, his endless need to correct and improve is symptomatic of a particular outlook, one that is so popular that even when he makes a mistake—and let's be entirely honest here, there is no one so sure of their linguistic powers that they are above a little grammatical polish here and there—people rush to correct him.

The interesting thing is, these corrections still happen even when the perceived error is something that doesn't even really exist as a rule. A lot of people have been taught that sentences should not end with a preposition, for example. So the question "Which chair shall I sit on?" is a prime target for pedants to leap at and suggest "On which chair shall I sit?" as the correct alternative. This will then provoke other pedants to point out that the preposition rule is actually a myth, that it gets in the way of conversational speech, and that people should be less persnickety about grammar in general, so long as the meaning is understood. This will then provoke a further point of pedantry, because in Britain the word is *pernickety*. And that's when everyone realizes there are no more chairs.

WHAT TO SAY: "And you forgot you're manners, sir."

WHAT NOT TO SAY: "Gah! *Your* means *belonging to you*. *You're* means *you are*. Its so easy!"

Talking About the Weather ■

Hooray for Brollywood.

Making small talk is hard work. It's bad enough when a companion-able silence has descended between two complete strangers in a lift or in a doctor's waiting room, but what if they sort of know each other? What if they've met once or twice, just enough to be aware of the other, but not enough to have shared any personal details that could spur a decent conversation? How, in a nation that prides itself on decorum and social niceties, shall we endure the pain of not knowing what to say?

Time to dig out the British cure for all awkwardness: a quick chat about the weather. This is one of the most commonly observed quirks of British social interaction; from Land's End upward, the British are world renowned for striking up conversations that, to external ears, sound worryingly like banal observations about temperature and rainfall. They know this about themselves too and yet, in the absence of a better option, seem powerless to hold back. Where two British people are gathered together, there will be some talk about the weather.

And this goes back for years and years. George Formby, the beloved wartime entertainer, with his ribald songs and cheeky wink, had for a catchphrase the opening gambit of most weather-based conversations: "turned out nice again."

Of course, the reason the Brits are so wedded to meteorological matters is simple: there's a lot of weather in the British Isles, it changes often, and some of the changes are quite subtle. The mist rolls in from the sea, the clouds appear as if by magic, the wind shakes the spiraling keys from the sycamore trees, the sun cooks the clouds away, hailstones pelt down upon pensioners in the bus queue, the rain drenches the topsoil and creates a sudden stream across the zebra crossing, soaking the feet of children on their way to school, who laugh delightedly and jump up and down while their parents huddle under brollies and despair at their sodden socks.

There is always something going on, weatherwise. Even overcast days have their own color: a gray sky bleeding the bright greens from the grass and trees, a white sky that lends a forensic sharpness to an autumn morning, even a low and purple sky that demands that everyone get inside before the rain begins. It's all so very noticeable, you can't really blame the people that live in this kaleidoscope climate for paying attention to what is going on. They store up tiny details for later, make microcomparisons between what is happening now and what was happening earlier. So when the opportunity arises, whether in a queue at the supermarket or while matching stride with a fellow dog walker in the park, a summary of recent meteorological changes can be brought to mind right away.

These will go in one of two directions: getting better or getting worse. The getting-better conversation goes something like this:

"Glad that rain stopped, aren't you?"

"Oh, yes, it was miserable out here a couple of hours ago."

"Hopefully it'll hold off for the weekend. I want to get out in the garden."

The getting-worse conversation is more of a lament:

"What happened to all that sunshine, eh?"

"I know! It was lovely yesterday and now look!"

"I was checking the forecast and they say it's going to be like this for a couple of days."

"Oh, well, I might just stay under my blanket for the duration."

So it's not so much a summary of how things are as a kind of prediction of the future, a way to read significance into signs from on high, but on a beautifully banal and yet entirely practical level.

Every nation's people believe they are in some way favored by their creator, and the British like to use the weather as a litmus test to see how acidic (or otherwise) that relationship has become.

WHAT TO SAY: "Ooh, listen to that rain!"

WHAT NOT TO SAY: "I notice there is a dense layer of cumulonimbus clouds over Salisbury; this means an increased likelihood of precipitation."

Keep Calm and Carry On ■

It's a mug's game (etc).

There aren't many meme crazes that start with the threat of invasion and death raining from the sky on a nightly basis and end with oven gloves. But then, Keep Calm and Carry On is not like other meme crazes.

In spring of 1939, a few months before the outbreak of the Second World War, the British government commissioned a special poster, knowing that dark times were ahead. The slogan "Keep Calm and Carry On" appeared in white on a regal red background, set in a specially commissioned typeface to prevent forgery and with a Tudor crown above. The intention was to put the posters up in areas where German bombers would do the most damage, in order to encourage the population not to lose heart. But despite printing around two and a half million copies, the British government kept them in storage, caught between a concern that the slogan would be taken as patronizing—or even frustratingly obvious—and waiting for a moment of sufficiently dire need, such as a full invasion.

This never transpired, and so the posters were eventually destroyed, apart from a few exceptions. In 2000, one survivor made its way, in a dusty box of old books, to a magical secondhand bookshop in Alnwick, Northumberland, owned by Stuart and Mary Manley. They framed it and put it behind their till, to the delight and curiosity of their customers, who began to inquire if they could buy a poster like it. Eventually the Manleys decided to print their own copies, and slowly the design and slogan began to spread, that special font proving to be no deterrent whatsoever.

Now there are Keep Calm and Carry On mugs and notebooks, coasters and T-shirts in almost every gift shop in Britain, in all the colors of the rainbow and with constant variations to the slogan to serve some marketing need or other. Keep Calm has become an iconic British thing in an astonishingly short space of time. And yet, if you talk to anyone British about it, the most likely response is eye-rolling frustration that it remains quite as popular as it is.

They'll bemoan the fact that most of the hilarious phrases don't make sense—"Keep Calm and Cupcake," "Keep Calm and Swag," and even one that says "Keep Calm and Eventually the Keep Calm Epidemic Will Die Out"—and that you can't walk past a gift shop without seeing that regal branding and the big white letters of officialdom plastered across everything from teapots to toilet seats.

But despite becoming a target for sneers, the reason all these items exist is simple: secretly, the British *love* Keep Calm. There is something quintessential in the way the posters do not say "Don't Panic" or "We Will Prevail" or anything about duty, insubordination, or cold, dead hands. They say "Keep Calm," and what that means is, "We may be suffering something of an invasion at the moment, but that's no reason to start acting in a rash and hot-headed manner. We may be a subjugated nation—temporarily—but we are not about to start acting like savages."

And what of "Carry On"? It's a world of subtle insubordination in just two words: "The Germans may take over our towns, ruin our cricket pitches, enforce the chilling of the ale in our pubs, put cabbage in with the pickled eggs, but we shall not pay them the slightest mind. As a nation, we have been trained to look past the bad behavior of our rudest guests, especially the uninvited ones, and rather than cause a scene, we shall just go about our daily business as if nothing has happened."

Granted, if you take either of these sentiments out of that specific context and apply them to the modern world, they very quickly become meaningless, and if you start mucking about with them to make comedy screen savers, it's not surprising that some Brits claim to find the whole affair reductive, witless, and exasperating.

But deep down they also love that so much historical information and national identity can be wrung out of five short words and a crown. It's the very model of British reserve, even in the face of total annihilation.

WHAT TO SAY: "Oh, these things are everywhere, how ghastly."

WHAT NOT TO SAY: "Wait, I've got one . . . 'Keep Calm and *Doughnuts!*'"

British History ■

The important thing to realize about the way the British view their history is that while opinions about the significance of various events may be wildly different, the method of justification for having those opinions is exactly the same. When seeking to prove a point, British thought takes the legal view: if you can cite precedence—point to a thing that has happened before that suits your argument—then you're in the right.

And the great thing about the broad buckshot spray of British historical events is that there is almost always a precedent for any opinion, if you go back far enough. Not keen on the royal family? There was a civil war that ended with the execution of Charles I. Keen on the royal family? His son Charles II was eventually restored to the throne. Seeking proof that British women have always been strong enough to hold their own against the oppressive forces of patriarchy? I give you Boudicca, Queen Elizabeth I, Emmeline Pankhurst, Queen Victoria, and Margaret Thatcher. Need to identify an essential pluckiness of British society that binds everyone together for the common good in times of trouble, no matter how bleak things may appear to be? The phrase you want is "spirit of the Blitz."

You'll find people using the legal-precedent trick for all manner of reasons: to prove their right to call themselves local, to justify their support for a football team that hasn't won a championship in years, and to make fashion decisions based on crazy ideas from the past—polka dots, beards, mustache wax (the Brylcreem revival is surely only a few months away).

People used to believe Richard III had a deformed spine and a withered hand and was a rotten king, largely because Shakespeare said so and there wasn't enough evidence to disprove him. Then they believed that this was actually Tudor propaganda, designed to bolster the dynasty's claim to the throne, and that he was a fairly decent king with a fully working body after all, because that also made sense according to the scant records of the time. And then Richard's actual skeleton was found under a car park in Leicester and guess what? He had scoliosis as an adolescent (but his arms were fine), so his back *was* bent, and this was reported on the national news. Naturally, now people are arguing over whether it's really him or not, despite some compelling DNA evidence.

Then there are all the ruined castles—and former monasteries—left lying about the landscape like burst pimples. In parts of Cumbria you can still see the remains of the great wall the Roman emperor Hadrian built to keep the indomitable Scottish out of his face. Can you imagine the kind of psychological mark it leaves upon a nation to have been put on the wrong side of the Roman VIP rope for almost two thousand years? United, y'say? Kingdom? Aye, well, we'll see about that, pal.

Small wonder cultural traditions and regional pride have grown as intertwined as they have, not just in local and eccentric events (see: Weird Traditions) but also in the big statements of national identity. There are the eisteddfods, festivals that celebrate Welsh culture, literature, and music, keeping alive centuries of tradition and maintaining the Welsh language for future generations; there are also the Highland games in Scotland, which do exactly the same thing for Scottish literature and arts (and allow beefy men to throw a big stick in case Nessie wants to play fetch). And as you can't ever separate the cultural from the political in British folk history, it's probably worth adding that the Highland games in particular took on their modern form in Victorian times, after a highly unpopular campaign to drive small-time farm holders off the hills, in order to use the land to rear sheep. Nothing fuses communities together like adversity.

Then of course there are the commemorative customs, most notably the wearing of a paper poppy in the days preceding the annual Remembrance Day service—which takes place on the Sunday nearest to November 11—and observing two minutes of silence at 11.00 A.M. on the day itself. A constant interest remains in those wartime years, particularly the first and the second world wars, because it's unthinkable now that such events could ever have happened in so short a space of time. Or that only twenty years passed between V-E Day—the heyday of the Andrews Sisters and Glenn Miller—and the release of *Help!*, the Beatles' fifth LP.

The past is well served by British TV too. Costume dramas are a sure ratings winner, especially if they bring out an all-star cast of highly regarded thespians in nightshirts and starched collars—particularly if they are disheveled and a bit damp, like Colin Firth in *Pride and Prejudice*. And thanks to the work of the National Trust, these dramas are never short of an immaculately kept location for whichever era they are attempting to re-create.

Not that all of British history is given equal billing. In fact, if you were to go purely by TV drama alone, the complete history of England would go something like this: Roman times—King Arthur times—Medieval times—Robin Hood times—Tudor times—Jane Austen times—Charles Dickens times—Downton Abbey times—Charleston times—Blitz times—Rock 'n' Roll times—Yuppie times—Pre-Internet times—Nowadays.

Or if you were hoping to find out what the Scots were up to in all that time, it goes: Pictish times—Jacobean times—Today.

WHAT TO SAY: "Is there a historical drama about Welsh times?"

WHAT NOT TO SAY: "Whatever did happen to those princes in the Tower?"

Offal ■

These are the only British people to whom one could put the question "Do you like offal?" and expect an honest response:

1. Vegetarians and vegans

2. People who like offal

Everyone else is probably fibbing to a greater or lesser degree, and they probably don't even know it. Put the blanket suggestion that the British love offal to a decent majority of British people and they will almost certainly argue the toss. However, the sheer availability of the unprime cuts of various commonly eaten animals in everyday British meals would seem to suggest otherwise.

And this isn't even necessarily a sepia-toned jaunt down memory lane to a time when the Brits regularly ate tripe and sweetbreads—bits of cow stomach and various internal glands, respectively—although that wasn't as far back as you may like to imagine. It is also not a searing Jamie Oliver–style comment on the processes involved in making the average burger or chicken nugget. Let's just say that more than a few British meat dishes make use of the bits of the animal that are not commonly used for a roast dinner.

Like sausages, for example. The Brits love a banger. They love them sticking out of mashed potatoes and dripping with gravy (bangers 'n' mash); they love them providing a perimeter wall for the beans in a fry-up (see: The Great British Fry-Up); they love them encased in batter and roasted (toad in the hole); and they love them mineralized black on the outside and raw in the middle, in a badly cut finger-roll at a rainy-day weekend barbecue in August. And while there's a strong market for the kind that are made with only the finest meats, hand ground and delicately spiced, there's also a lot of love out there for the kind that you don't ask too many questions about.

Then there's the glorious steak and kidney pie. It's a pie; a delicious pie with steak and onions and gravy in it. And kidneys. So widely adored a combination of flavors that it is also available as a steamed pudding. The classic Melton Mowbray pork pie may contain the very best meat available, hand shaped and baked to perfection, but it is encased in a jelly made from the pig's trotters. And not every pork pie is a Melton Mowbray, if you get my drift.

A steak & kidney pudding for one.

In the Midlands and South Wales, there's a lot of schoolboy fun to be had in the unfortunate but very traditional name of meatballs made of minced pork offal (liver, lungs, and spleen, principally) and served with gravy and peas. They're called faggots. They just are. Let's not be childish or offensive about this.

To add extra offal value (and keep the balls round), each faggot is wrapped in caul fat, which is the membrane found around the pig's internal organs. Not so funny now, eh?

And how about oxtail soup? You'll never, ever guess what oxtail soup is made from. And even if you did, while it's safe to assume that the beef tails in soups served by high-end organic restaurants are of the highest quality, just imagine the kind of stringy bovine wagglers that go in the cheaper tins on the supermarket shelves.

The dish that probably looms largest in the popular imagination when talking about Britain and offal is haggis, Scotland's culinary masterpiece. People get peculiar about haggis in a way that they never would about sausages—although the reaction to black pudding comes close. They harp on about the ingredients—the minced heart, liver, lungs, and rolled oats; they gag over the sheep stomach into which the haggis is traditionally encased (although it tends to come wrapped in a sausage skin these days); and they make terrible retching noises without so much as trying a mouthful. Which seems a shame, given that haggis is actually not unlike a peppery meat loaf.

Still, you'd be hard put to convince a good deal of the Brits who live south of the Scottish border that haggis is a stuff Brits like, but it remains hugely popular in Scotland—you can even get it in fish and chip shops, deep-fried in batter—and in January, when Hogmanay rolls on toward Burns Night, you can get haggis in supermarkets from Inverness to Penzance, so it's clearly more popular than anyone is prepared to admit.

Scotland is also home of the fish dish crappit heid (no, really, it's food), in which the descaled head of a large cod or haddock is stuffed with a mixture of oats, suet, onion, and fish liver. And while we're on fish: jellied eels, anyone?

Certain dishes exist in legend only—the foods people really don't eat, the ones that Brits who don't work in animal farming aren't even aware of anymore, the really out-there foodstuffs, like muggety pie.

Muggety pie is just a pie made from entrails; that's all it is. It's a tripe pie, and it used to be popular in the West Country, especially Gloucestershire and Cornwall. And if there are no entrails, there's an alternative recipe that involves the umbilical cords of lambs and/or calves. To the unsqueamish dairy farmer, this dish is a thrifty use of all available protein and one that suddenly makes haggis look like a T-bone from God's own herd.

Another good place to find offal is between two slices of bread. There's pâté, which Brits have only just decided to abandon calling *meat paste* and feeding almost exclusively to children in their packed school lunches, and then there's tongue—most commonly pork or beef, chicken tongue being quite hard to slice. Confusingly, *tongue sandwich* is also a slang term for a particularly passionate snog, so you should always check what you are being offered before you open your mouth.

WHAT TO SAY: "I have never eaten that. Can I try some?"

WHAT NOT TO SAY: "They make it from *what*?! That's gross!"

Apologizing Needlessly ■

With so many enormously confident British people in the world, it's a shock to think that their international reputation remains that of a wet and eager-to-please race, just because they have the grace and good manners to try to make amends if they have made a social gaffe of some kind.

Being quick to apologize is a fine quality, especially if no offense was intended in the first place. It's a mark of a strong character, but only when used sparingly and from the heart. The trouble is, that is not how Brits like to say sorry. They like to apologize before every statement of personal need, whether it's a trip to the bathroom or taking their turn in a revolving door. They'll apologize for falling asleep, apologize for waking up, apologize for being hungry, apologize for being full.

And this is driven by awkwardness and panic, because if they don't do it, there's a chance a complete stranger might think the worse of them—on even the most spurious of grounds—and that would simply never do. Should that person find needless apologies annoying too, well, things are only going to escalate.

Here are just some of the many situations for which British people will find the need to say sorry:

When forced to brush past a man on a train who is sitting with his legs far apart, as if his genitals are swollen and potentially explosive.

When boiling the kettle in a shared kitchen and finding out there isn't enough water for the person who has only just walked into the room to make tea.

Having been smacked in the face by the arm of a tall man who has suddenly pointed at something across the street.

Having to interrupt a stranger's day to tell her she has dropped her phone on the floor.

Just before hanging up after having been cold-called at home, during an important family meal, by a company selling an unwanted product or service.

Having been barged into by someone who is (a) drunk and (b) flailing his arms around and (c) walking backward.

When confronting a stranger who has suddenly appeared in the garden.

When walking down a narrow corridor and noticing someone at the other end, waiting to let them pass. The apology comes after a brief period of walking with comically exaggerated effort and pretend speed, as if to prove no dawdling is taking place.

When waiting patiently at the end of a narrow corridor for the person already walking down it, especially when this has caused the other person to pretend to speed up.

When arriving at a reserved airplane, theater, or train seat, only to find someone already sitting in it.

When seeing a doctor about a hugely painful or debilitating condition.

When arriving last for a meeting or social gathering, even if it has not yet started.

When crying while talking to a friend about an upsetting situation.

When listening to a friend tearfully talk about an upsetting situation.

When paying for a small, inexpensive item with a twenty-pound note. Especially before 10:00 A.M.

When telling the stranger who has just asked them for a light that they do not smoke.

When walking into an inanimate object, such as a postbox (see: Phone Boxes).

When a conversation has finished, to the mutual enjoyment and benefit of both participants, followed some hours later by a slowly rising sense of horror at one throwaway comment that clearly was not offensive at all in context, and yet could still be taken completely the wrong way, necessitating a slightly panicked text message to, apologize for the comment and then, apologize for the apology.

Note: None of this means that Brits go out of their way to avoid doing things for which they should be genuinely sorry. Far from it.

WHAT TO SAY: "That's perfectly all right. Good day to you."

WHAT NOT TO SAY: "No, it was all my fault. If anything, I should be the one to apologize."

Pubs, Inns, Bars, and Taverns ■

Your friendly local (assuming you are from around here).

Whether they go there to play darts or catch up with mates, whether it's a stop-off on the way home from work or a night out after a hard week, the British have placed pubs at the center of their cultural existence. It's not a coincidence that all British soaps have a prominent pub where the characters meet. In *Coronation Street* it's the Rovers Return, in *Emmerdale* it's the Woolpack, in *EastEnders* it's the Queen Victoria, and in *Hollyoaks* it's the Dog in the Pond.

A good pub will serve a multiplicity of purposes and yet often look as if it is doing nothing more than providing a respite from the rain and the rushing about outside. Pubs, even pubs in the center of major cities, are community hubs, places for large groups of people to exchange local news, keep up with their neighbors, and celebrate their significant events—whether that's a birth, a sporting event, a wedding, or a wake. Lots of tiny villages in remote areas will be able to keep a pub going, sometimes even two, far longer than they can keep a shop. And that's not necessarily because of the inherent drinkiness of British culture (although it certainly isn't because of the inherent sobrietude of British culture either); a good pub is a place where time stops. It's a place to hatch plans, a place to gather forces, a place to be among people, and also a place to observe people.

The classic British pub is slightly dark and feels like a living room with aspirations to entertain. It's not the sort of place where you want to spend too long examining the carpet—if there is one—and the toilets are not for loitering in. If you've seen the drinking establishments in the movies *Withnail & I* and *An American Werewolf in London*, those places are definitely pubs. A pub is a very different place from a bar. A bar is like a pub for young people; it's a place to become drunk at speed, not nurse a half and read the paper. It will have sharply worded slogans on the wall, and mirrors in strange places, and maybe ceiling fans and chrome trimmings. The beer may be bottled or in jugs, but it won't be stacked up in casks, and there won't be name tankards for regular customers to use. There will, however, be s⸍ lots and lots (and lots) of shots. Because of this, the British rep⸍ for binge drinking feels a bit more like a bar thing than a p⸍

On the other hand, the British reputation for figh⸍ parks or managing seven out of ten in a pub crawl and⸍ down in a skip is all pub.

Where were we? Oh, yes, interior décor. A⸍ refurbished one—is saggier than a bar. It'⸍ armchair and most often decked out in ⸍ on the beer taps and mirrors behind ⸍ more plentiful), but it's a less zingy ⸍

those pewter tankards hanging over the stacked glasses can go back generations within the same family. Pubs don't strain so hard for your attention while you're talking to your friends or sitting quietly with your pint. Their natural resting atmosphere is more muted, although clearly plenty of singing and shouting take place, given time. People go to pubs to play games—darts, dominoes, snooker, and various table-top amusements like shove ha'penny and skittles—or make music; play the gambling machines (perfectly legal in all pubs and motorway service stations); sell dodgy electrical goods, cheap cigarettes, and fake designer clothes from the boot of their car; or just talk. They don't go to watch telly (unless there's a really important football match on).

Then there are inns and taverns. An inn is, for all practical purposes, a pub that can provide food and lodging overnight. Now that most pubs also serve food, the differentiation between the two is getting harder to spot. Taverns are indistinguishable from pubs, apart from certain legal statutes that no longer affect the patrons. And it's not uncommon to see places called the Tavern Inn, to add further confusion to affairs. If you see a sign outside saying "Free House," that doesn't mean the drinks are being given away or that you get a free house; it's a term used to describe a pub that is unaffiliated to one brewery and is therefore able to sell a range of ales (see: Real Ale).

Before smoking was banned in 2007, all pubs had a particular smell: a warm and slightly damp fug of hops and grown-ups and fag-ash and sour aftershave that could have been bottled and sold as the very essence of a British boozer (a term which refers to the pub, not someone drinking inside). It's the kind of smell that takes grown-ups ck to being children, waiting on a bench in the garden for two hours a bottle of Coke, a waxy straw, and a packet of crisps.

w, with the smoke cleared and all the sharp edges restored to pubs seem somehow a little colder, even during gasping sum- a roaring fire in the hearth. And of course every pub now ang of furtive smokers just outside. So you get an early smell on the way in, and then you walk through it and skipping ghost of childhood.

Naturally this is going to recede as a problem over time, and it is certainly not worth reinstating smoking—with the attendant health risks—just so people can retain a whiff of the old days. Not that this will stop smokers campaigning for the right to spark up indoors again, but it's hard to see how to keep everyone happy. It's a smell, after all. The people who nostalgically want it aren't the ones who are risking their lives making it, and the people who are making it can't get the benefit of it in the first place, due to all the smoking. And that's before we seek the opinions of the people who neither want it nor make it. So no matter how kindly smokers may offer to throw themselves on their lighters for the common good, that scent is best left where it is, in the past, unless the pub is particularly old and grotty and you've sat down too quickly on the upholstery.

WHAT TO SAY: "A pint of the usual, please, Brian."

WHAT NOT TO SAY: "Do you do cocktails?"

The Shipping Forecast ■

'm writing this on a very special day in British broadcasting history. Today is May 30, 2014; the day one of the cornerstones of British life suffered a little wobble. It's the only day in ninety years that there hasn't been a shipping forecast on BBC Radio 4. There has been a technical fault, nothing disastrous in one sense, but still an unsettling shaking of the schedule.

This might seem like a melodramatic response to what is surely a minor hiccup in broadcasting, but the shipping forecast occupies a particularly resonant position in the audio landscape of British life. It has been broadcast four times a day—12:48 A.M., 5:20 A.M., 12:01 P.M., and 5:54 P.M.—since 1924, with the same calming litany of weather conditions in the offshore areas immediately around the British Isles, incomprehensible to most people, but still utterly bewitching.

And it's not just a matter of people deriving pleasure from something designed to be a valuable service. BBC Radio 4 is the sole British radio station that would continue to broadcast in the event of a nuclear strike. The shipping forecast is therefore the most trusted broadcast from the most trusted broadcaster in the entire nation, and the fun part of this is that most people listening still have very little idea of what is actually being said.

To illustrate this point, this is an extract from a recent forecast.

Just imagine it being read slowly and clearly in a stern but not unfriendly voice, as if it were a modernist poem by Dylan Thomas.

"North Utsire, South Utsire: Northerly or northwesterly five or six, occasionally seven for a time. Moderate. Fair. Good.

"West Forties, Cromarty: Variable four, becoming southerly four or five later. Slight. Fog patches. Moderate, occasionally very poor.

"Forth, Tyne, Southwest Dogger: Southwesterly four or five, becoming variable four. Slight. Fair. Moderate or good."

It has a certain something, doesn't it? The endless mild adjectives suggesting either clear waters or potential trouble ahead; the evocative names like Dogger and Cromarty; the sense that this is important information, that those numbers probably mean something that could be the difference between life and death for those traversing the dark seas. Whether you personally know the science behind each word or not is immaterial, and that's the emotive heart of the thing. It's like being at Bletchley Park during the war and hearing coded naval messages without the key, and letting the mind wander as to where they will be received and what sort of condition the ships will be in when they finally arrive.

As such, the 12:48 forecast in particular has taken the form of a late-night lullaby for Radio 4 listeners; one that evokes the long seafaring history of an island nation, but delivered with the poetic grace of a magical incantation.

That's why Damon Albarn of Blur, when stuck on his first long and painful American tour, playing empty halls and drunkenly bickering with his bandmates, would tune in to the shipping forecast just to feel the security and pull of home once again. He later translated that dislocated feeling (and a good portion of the magical words from the shipping forecast itself) into "This Is a Low," a song that delivers much of the forecast's fathomless magic, floating upon deep and stormy musical waters.

And should any other significant events pop up at the same time as the shipping forecast—England winning the Ashes in 2011, for example (see: Cricket)—the expectation is that they will just have to wait. The last, winning ball actually went unheard by listeners, but the shipping forecast continued, as it always does.

That's what makes the events of this morning so uncommon, to the extent that there have been newspaper stories about the missing transmission. Granted, the fuss is nowhere near as big as that surrounding the 1995 plan to move that midnight bulletin by twelve minutes. That was a colossal hoo-ha that involved petitions, scathing newspaper editorials, and eventually questions being asked in Parliament. In fact, the only similar breach of service in Radio 4's history occurred in 2010, when a forecast was read out that was already twenty-four hours old.

And people noticed. That's the point.

The best description of the peculiar charms in this very British institution came courtesy of a 2012 BBC News interview with Zeb Soanes, one of a team of people who read the shipping forecast every day. He described it as "vital information first and poetry incidentally."

That's not to suggest that it is not poetry, you'll notice, just that it is not trying to be.

WHAT TO SAY: "Cromarty, Biscay, Lundy, and Fisher sounds like a '70s folk-rock act."

WHAT NOT TO SAY: "Dude, that stuff's all on the Internet now, isn't it?"

It may seem like a deliberately glib way to crowbar an old song into a new conversation, but the British honestly really do like to be beside the seaside. Oh, they do like to be beside the sea. And this is because they live on a tall, thin island with sharp edges at every extreme. The sea is never too far away, even at the very middle of the widest part of central England, and there are coastal resorts—from the cheap and cheerful to the quiet and refined—within easy reach of everyone. And so for most British people, arranging to be beside the seaside (beside the sea) has never involved much more than a short train, coach, or car journey. Consequently a series of common holiday traditions and customs have grown up around the British seaside that perhaps would not exist in coastal regions of other parts of the world.

For example, if you're on a beach—any beach—you'll probably appreciate a shop that sells ice cream and cold drinks, inflatable items of the sort you could take into the water, and some play tools for the children: buckets, spades, and some of those plastic sand-shaping devices that look like little jelly molds. Maybe some knickknacks made from seashells, arranged into the shape of a heart you can hang on the wall, and some cheap flip-flops and expensive sun cream and spare swimming costumes and sunglasses. Or, at a push, a decorative vial of sand.

That's the sensible stuff. Quite why anyone would want a long pink stick of mint-flavored candy on a hot day—it's called rock, although it's not the same as rock candy, being more like a thick, porous candy cane—is anyone's guess. It does have the name of the resort running all the way through it, which is a remarkable feat and guarantees sales for people wanting decent (and cheap) homecoming gifts for friends and relatives. But that's not the real reason why sticks of rock have become such a seaside staple.

The real reason, I suspect, lies in that other grand old British seaside custom, making lewd and suggestive comments. In among the "Kiss Me Quick, Squeeze Me Slow" hats and the "Keep Calm and Kiss Me Quick" T-shirts will be a rack of suspiciously old-fashioned postcards showing red-faced men, rotund matrons, and buxom young ladies wearing next to nothing. There's the newlyweds arriving at a guest house on a cold and rainy night, being greeted by a friendly lady who says to the wife, "Do come in, you must be dying to get something hot inside you, my dear," or the young woman watching a strutting Scottish man on a street corner and whispering to her friend, "They say that's the reason he wears an extra-long kilt," or the red-faced colonel who meets a bikini-clad and buxom young mother with a young boy hanging off each hand and says, "You've got a couple of nice handfuls."

Nudist camps feature heavily in seaside postcards too, not least because of the ripe possibility for saucy misunderstandings about things being too small, too big, unsatisfying, hot and spicy, big and fruity, all that stuff. The redheaded man who bends over to light the stove for a cup of tea while his wife clutches a hand to her head and exclaims, "Ginger nuts! I knew I'd forgotten something!"

And that's the old-fashioned stuff. For more modern sexy holiday keepsakes, there are postcards showing mouse and cat faces drawn in make-up upon naked breasts, that kind of thing. Oh, and sweets in the shape of genitals. These are the items British folk traditionally send back home to make people think they're having a proper knees-up, the kind of randy, boozy, hoorah holiday that would make anyone jealous, despite it being apparent to everyone involved that they've spent their time glued to a slot machine (not a euphemism, oddly) in Clee-thorpes and it's been raining, again.

The curious thing about these postcards is they're looked upon with utter affection, as a harmless and charming relic of a sillier time. There's a collector's market for them; books are devoted to them. Long after the demise of the Punch and Judy tents, the donkey rides, the tuppenny waterfalls, and the deck chair attendants, you'll still be able to find a postcard with a caption like "Just married, it sticks out a mile." And the phallic stick of rock fits into this overengorged and giggly mentality like, well, a throbbing prong in a moist crevice.

One old postcard—drawn by Donald McGill, the Rembrandt of seaside sauce—shows a man holding a colossal stick at groin level, pointing upward at the reader's eyes with the wrapping peeled back around the tip, with the caption "A stick of rock, cock?" It's actually not quite as rude as it appears, as *cock* used to be a fairly harmless term of endearment between people (as opposed to nowadays, when it's a fairly harmless term of endearment for a penis).

Still it's hard to imagine many families taking a postcard like that and pinning it to the notice board in their kitchen, even now. They'd probably be too busy sending homemade smartphone pictures of a penis dressed up like a stick of rock.

That's one in the eye for so-called progress.

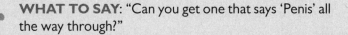

WHAT TO SAY: "Can you get one that says 'Penis' all the way through?"

WHAT NOT TO SAY: "I bought you a hat. It says, 'Kiss Me Quick—I'll Alert the Authorities in a Speedy and Appropriate Fashion.'"

Speaking English When Abroad ■

Call it a hangover from the days of empire, but as a rule the British do not enjoy learning other languages. Or rather, they do learn other languages, but they do not enjoy putting this knowledge to use, as it makes them feel flustered. Any mistake—a missed inflection or badly chosen sentence construction—would be a huge source of embarrassment and an admission of personal weakness.

But the Brits do love to travel the world, absorbing different cultures and traditions. They bring back exotic spices and recipes, musical instruments and incantations, new habits and flaky red skin. And in order to do so, they will probably have spent a good deal of their time making apologetic faces at local shop owners and asking to buy things in increasing ripples of loud, clear, and slightly tetchy English.

British tourists like to feel as if they belong everywhere they go. This is why so many holiday destinations boast English-themed pubs and cafés that serve a decent fry-up, but it is also why many British people avoid those places and head straight for the unwelcomingly local end of town. "We are not a hated nation," they reason, "so we have no reason to fear walking around in broad daylight, waving smartphones in front of our faces and not looking where we're going."

Whether they are correct in this assumption is a matter for further debate, but they do tend to approach all transactions—whether with market traders or rickshaw drivers—with the same brittle air of entitlement, and awkward mock-humility.

It's all in the body language; there's a touch of the bow to the shoulders, a meekness to the eyes, that effectively says, "I'm sorry, I know you must think I'm not from around here, and that must be incredibly frustrating, especially as I'm now about to demonstrate that I don't know any words in your language whatsoever, but if you could see beyond this situation, you would realize that I'm actually not like those dreadful German and American tourists over there. I'm nice! I have empathy! So if you could possibly see your way clear to providing us with TWO. TICKETS. TO. THE. PARTHENON. GRASS-EE-ASS. That would be most obliging. Sorry again."

Of course, if this approach should prove to be unsuccessful, exasperation quickly replaces submissiveness, and eventually it becomes clear that the reason for the breakdown in international relations is entirely the fault of the idiot who has willfully chosen to speak a foreign language in their homeland.

Some Brits find all of the above to be something of a chore and will let all pretense at humility drop, launching into a loud and simple "FIVE-O PINT-OS OF LAGER, POR FAVOR," said with unreserved confidence whether in Spain or Turkmenistan.

Note: The curious thing about this situation is that Britain is an island that can boast at least three distinct and recognized native languages that are not English: Welsh, Cornish, and Scottish Gaelic. It's probably fair to say that it's the English who are the best at repeating themselves at increasing gradients of volume and temper because, as a nation, they've had the most practice.

WHAT TO SAY: "Hello, do you speak English? English? ENGLISH?"

WHAT NOT TO SAY: "Hang on, I'll just look this up in the guidebook."

Sarcasm ■

A sense of humor is like a fine martini: the dryer it is, the better. That means it's not necessary to guffaw if you have made a joke. It's not even desirable. It's not necessary even to smile. In fact, if you can manage to arrange your face in such a way that it's hard to spot that you're even joking at all—no raised eyebrows, no cute eye rolling, and definitely no winking—that's the very best way to interact socially at all times. The fine art of sarcasm keeps everyone on their toes, trying to work out whether that sharp thing you said was meant sincerely or not, trying to work out if you're really the kind of person who enjoys making others feel uncomfortable or just having a dark laugh, and sometimes being unable to speak from all those sharp intakes of breath. What could be more enjoyable?

And you don't even have to be trying to get a laugh in order to use sarcasm. It's a friend to the parent whose child is having an attack of the tantrums—"Still crying? Do let me know when you get dehydrated, there's a poppet." It's a sword of justice for the teacher whose most troublesome pupil has once again failed to hand his homework in—"I can only imagine that today's excuse will have taken longer to invent than the essay would have taken to write, and as such, you get an A." And the handyman whose shelves have just fallen off the wall will find more expression and catharsis in a muttered and bitter "Oh, great" than in fifty swearwords. Even the really good ones.

It's also a wonderful shield to keep prying eyes away from your real feelings. That's the Chandler Bing model of irony and, let's face it, if *Friends* had been made in Britain, he'd have been the hero. Not that the Brits are short of their own heroes of sarcasm. There's the withering scorn of John Cleese, the fathomless cynicism of Rowan Atkinson's Edmund Blackadder, and the sharp barbs thrown around by pretty much everyone in *Absolutely Fabulous*. The banter on *Top Gear* treads a fine line between sarcasm and the genuine opinions of the three presenters at times, and that can be fun to try to work out. It's like a word search for sincerity.

As if to counterbalance this, the deadpan comic Stewart Lee had an astonishing routine in which he said, with a stone face, that he hates *Top Gear* to such an extent that he wishes Richard Hammond had died in the car crash that genuinely almost killed him. Taken out of context, that's a horrific thought, but because his audience was able to filter out the sarcasm from the sincere point being made—which was that there is a culture of saying a shocking thing and then, when challenged, shrugging and saying it was just a joke, "like on *Top Gear*"— it became a thrilling highlight of his stage act. Although he did have to stop midact and explain this, to avoid a nasty confrontation with the press, which tends to take irony at face value.

Sarcasm can even be comforting. Let's imagine you are friends with someone who has just had to have a beloved pet put down. Your friend is terribly, terribly upset, and you have gone round to try to console him on his loss. You may go in with something warm and loving, like a hug and a comment on how sorry you are, how it clearly hurts a lot right now, but in time your friend will come to see that the pet is no longer in pain and this will eventually be of some comfort. That's one way of approaching the situation, and it will probably work just fine.

The other way would be to go in with a sympathetic look on your face, do the hugs and everything else, and then, when you judge the moment to be just right, say you are delighted that the stupid thing has gone, it was secretly stealing your friend's money for booze and had actually been living a double life with another family two blocks away. And it never pooed in *their* garden.

It may seem a bold approach in a vulnerable moment, but, let's be honest, in a situation like this it almost doesn't matter what you say, so long as your friend knows he can talk about his feelings if he wants to. And one school of thought suggests that going in there and presuming to offer your feelings on the situation, no matter how well intended, could actually be selfish and annoying. All I'm saying is that having a dry sense of humor is not always the same thing as being emotionally cold. Far from it.

Not that there has to be a deep wound to soothe either. Sometimes sarcasm is a good way of saying a thing that no one would expect, because to say the expected thing would be boring. In a bus queue, your eyes meet another person's, and you ask, "Been waiting long?" The other could reply with helpful honesty, but there's more fun to be had saying, "Twelve years. I'm actually on my way to school." The trick is not to get in a huff, assuming the other person is being rude, and to come back with something snappy like, "You'd better have the right lunch money—we've gone metric now."

And yes, the day the news came out that the U.S. Secret Service was seeking to develop sarcasm-detecting software for Twitter definitely felt like a victory for British sensibilities.

WHAT TO SAY WHEN SOMEONE SAYS, "SARCASM IS THE LOWEST FORM OF WIT": "'. . . And the highest form of intelligence.' Isn't Oscar Wilde marvelous?"

WHAT NOT TO SAY WHEN SOMEONE SAYS, "SARCASM IS THE LOWEST FORM OF WIT": "I'm so impressed you have bothered to learn that quote. It's a mark of supreme diligence and scholarship on your part and you should be applauded."

Many British people view libraries in much the same way they view
colliery brass bands, male voice choirs, child labor laws, or the
two-day weekend: as a crowning glory of the labor movement. Public
libraries are, by their caring, sharing nature, not a victory for capital-
ism. They're from the same utopian mind-set that gave Britain the
Workers' Educational Association, free museums, and universal suffrage, and the true believers take them very seriously indeed.

People who can afford to maintain their own libraries may not see
the need for them. Anyone who attended private schools with beautifully stocked shelves may not even realize what treasures they were
being allowed access to, and how exclusive that access was. But the
public library is a place to access books—lots and lots of books—in a
way that takes all negative consequence out of the equation (provided
they are returned in good time). And the memories of being taken to
the library to choose and fetch books as children tend to linger long
and fondly in the mind.

A public library is a place where an education can happen from a
standing start. Ask the writer Caitlin Moran, who was home-schooled
and took herself to the local library in Wolverhampton every day,
having decided to read every book in each section in a methodical
fashion, starting with the books about the paranormal. She still wears
a Lily Munster streak in her hair to this day, and that's the point. A

library is a place where self-made men and self-made women can get to work with the self-glue and the self-paint in putting together their self-assembly kits, using the words of geniuses as their instructions. It's a place where trashy novels and high-minded literature flap their fly-leaves seductively in the faces of people with normal, unremarkable lives and invite them to jump aboard for a wild ride. Or read about the inner workings of the internal combustion engine.

It's a community resource that comes from the community, in order to elevate the community, and libraries know it too. That's why you'll find inscriptions on the outer walls saying inspirational things such as "Knowledge is power," as is carved above the door of the public library in Pillgwenlly, Newport. Far more than just a building with books you can borrow, a library is also a place where local history is stored, where maps and ledgers are freely accessible, along with reference books about the law and council legislation and a children's section with *The Gruffalo* and *Room on the Broom* and *Charlie and Lola* and all the adventures of Asterix and Tintin. They are a means by which people of meager resources—people of *any* resources—can feast on the riches of culture and community whenever they wish (providing all of the really popular books haven't already been taken out).

They're also quite stuffy places, often governed by strict policies of quiet reading and no talking: the kinds of places that breed mischief. Many's the rebellious teen who has brightened a librarian's day by de-facing library books before handing them back with a smile (see: Drawing Willies on Things). Playwright Joe Orton and his lover Kenneth Halliwell would entertain themselves in the 1960s by sneaking books out of libraries and replacing the dust jackets with homemade ones, complete with a fresh (and scandalous) blurb about the author and the odd naked man for good measure. When caught, they both spent six months in jail. Did I mention the Brits take libraries very seriously?

How seriously? This seriously:

When recent government cuts threatened hundreds of libraries with closure, amid claims that the Internet was providing some of the valuable services that used to be their sole preserve, tempers began to fray very quickly, particularly among authors and poets, the people whose work was being effectively distributed for free by those self-same libraries. Writers like J. K. Rowling, Michael Rosen, Salman Rushdie, Jacqueline Wilson, and Philip Pullman took great lengths to speak out against library closures and encourage local people to use their library cards more, because they remembered their own lightbulb moments with books and wanted to be able to hand those down to future generations.

Which does bear some comparison with actors campaigning against the closure of torrent websites because that's where they first grew to love movies, except it's totally different because libraries are great. So there.

WHAT TO SAY: "The first thing we did when we moved into the area was get library cards."

WHAT NOT TO SAY: "I just read stuff on my Kindle anyway, so . . ."

Here's a little game you can play if you ever visit the UK. Take a walk down any high street, any thoroughfare with shops on either side, and see how long it takes you to spot a business that has used a pun in its name. If you're stuck, try looking on the backs of commercial vans as they scoot down the road. It won't take long.

That's because the British love nothing more than a good pun, unless it's a really bad one. Comedy purists such as John Cleese may look down their noses at humble wordplay as a source of big laughs—his three laws of comedy are, famously "no puns, no puns, no puns"—but that's his prerogative: he wrote *Fawlty Towers*. For the rest of us, the best we can hope for is to find a sentence, popular saying, or well-known name and twist it so it says something else in a comic fashion.

Anyone who can do it is in good company too. British tabloids depend on bad puns for their headlines, and on their headlines for their sales, which should be ample proof of the pun's enduring appeal. Here are just a few examples:

Kim Jong Il launches nuclear tests: "How Do You Solve a Problem Like Korea?"

Bank bosses apologize for global financial crisis: "Scumbag Millionaires"

The UK is due to receive a chilling Siberian storm: "From Russia with Gloves"

George Michael falls from his car on a motorway: "Scrape Me Up before You Go Slow"

Dorset police are recruiting: "May You Be with the Force"

Inverness football team Caledonian Thistle (nicknamed Caley Thistle) beat Glasgow Celtic: "Super Caley Go Ballistic, Celtic Are Atrocious"

But to really experience the full glory of the British love of wordplay in action, it's back to the high street, where it's important for businesses to grab the attention of passing strangers and force them to remember who they are.

A good place to start is with hairdressers, who have been at this pun lark a while longer than everyone else—in fact, you could even say (wait for it) that they've had (drumroll) a head start (*tish!*).

As well as the classics like Curl Up & Dye, A Cut Above, and Short & Curlies, there are specifically British-themed barber's and hairstylist's with names like British Hairways, Choppy Toff's (*toff* being a gently pejorative term for a snooty member of the upper classes), and Jack the Clipper.

You'll find pop culture references too—Jabba the Cutt, Fatboy Trims, Barber Blacksheep, Shearlocks, Alley Barbers—and names that don't even really work as puns unless you are local. In Edinburgh there is a hairdresser's called Nut Hoose, a name that only makes sense if you know that *nut* is Scottish slang for "head," and *hoose* is a phonetic spelling of "house."

And this has spilled out into other areas of beautification and engussifying, although somehow once you're advertising a business in which your customers have their skin rubbed by strangers, some of the well-meant gags can become a little creepy. Facial Attraction, anyone?

I once saw a tanning shop that gloried under the name U-Rang-A-Tan, presumably without stopping to think that any kind of visual link between their prospective customers and a wrinkled orange ape might undermine what the business owners hope to achieve. There again, I've remembered it for over ten years, so maybe they're cleverer than I thought.

Then there are the food establishments such as Codrophenia, Abra-kebabra, Baguetti Junction, A Fish Called Rhondda, and Breakfast at Timothy's, or the Chinese takeaway in London that also does fish 'n' chips: Wok 'n' Roe.

Or how about the cake shop Much Ado About Muffins? Or the pet-minding service Hairy Pop-Ins, the secondhand shop Junk and Disorderly, the self-explanatory World of Woolcraft, Florist Gump, or Pilates of the Caribbean? Then there's the removal service Jean-Claude Van Man, garden specialists Floral & Hardy and Back to the Fuschia, double-glazing suppliers Pane in the Glass, removal service Toad Haul, the cleaning service Spruce Springclean, and a personal favorite, the drainage services company Suck-Cess.

And that's before we even think about the amount of hours wasted on Twitter every single day with hashtag pun games like #PunkRockCooking or #StarWarsSongs, which are in themselves just digital versions of the same conversations people have in the pub (see: Banter).

The modern world can be a scary, confusing place, but as long as there are people who are prepared to while away the hours trying to make #RoaldDalek a thing, we'll all sleep a lot sounder in our beds.

WHAT TO SAY: "Hang on, I've got one . . . a bathroom fitter called Cistern Sledge!"

WHAT NOT TO SAY: "Of course really it should be Shearlock Combs."

The Bumps ■

This is included more as a panic prevention measure than anything else. The practice of giving people the bumps is no longer as widespread as it once was, but that doesn't mean it no longer exists, and should you find yourself in a position where you're visiting British friends and you, or a member of your family, are suddenly given the bumps, you'll want to know what is going on, how it is all going to play out, and whether you'll need to call for an ambulance at the end of it all.

This is because, in the initial stages, at least, there is not much to differentiate being given the bumps and being attacked by a gang of close friends and family and having your arms and legs ripped off. Luckily it's a tradition that principally affects children, not least because it's harder and scarier to give the bumps to a grown-up, and kids are rarely strong enough to cause lasting damage anyway.

The good news is that for 364 days of the year (and 365 on leap years), you are safe from the bumps. There's only one day of the year in which there is even a mild threat, and that day is your birthday.

That's the one time, amid rousing choruses of "Happy Birthday" and cake and presents and hearty slaps on the back, that Brits of a certain age and experience suddenly recall the nagging fear from childhood that everyone at their birthday party will suddenly give them the bumps, and it casts quite the dark shadow, I can tell you.

Here's how the bumps works: at the apex of a birthday party, once the party tea is finished and there are the crushed remains of biscuits, crisps, and various other treats all over the floor, everyone gathers around the birthday boy or girl to sing "Happy Birthday" and watch them blow out the candles. Just after the traditional universal round of applause some bright spark will yell, "Let's give him the bumps!" and a circle will form.

The lucky recipient will then be laid on his back, and his hands and feet will be seized as if he's about to be pulled apart by wild horses. Then he is hoisted upward. Ideally the hoisters will achieve something approximating shoulder height, or the next few minutes won't just be scary, they'll be painful too.

To describe the physical movement in the bumps is not the easiest, but if you imagine one of those parachute games young children play, where they're wafting a parachute up and down, and then take the parachute out and replace it with a person, that's basically it. The bumpee is hurled upward once for every year he has been alive. Which means he will also fall downward the same amount of times. This is why it's important not to have started too close to the ground.

There again, it is equally important not to perform the bumps too vigorously upward, or underneath any hanging light fittings. We're celebrating a birthday here, not attempting to impale a close friend on the back of a chair or break a rib on the ceiling.

So, having been thrown a numerically appropriate number of times, the person is lowered to the ground, sobbing with relief that the ordeal is over. But is it? No. With a cry of "And one for luck," there's a final bump to administer, and that's the one everyone puts the big heave into. That's the one that will pull shoulder muscles and sprain ankles.

After that, it's back to the party.

Note: Teenagers have their own rules. It's not unheard-of for the bumps to recede once the birthdays start to hit double figures, only to return with a vengeance when underage alcohol starts to enter the equation. British teens can legally drink at eighteen, so birthday parties can get pretty messy, and that only gets worse if you start throwing people around like human pizza dough.

> **WHAT TO SAY**: "Oh, you *guys*!"
>
> **WHAT NOT TO SAY**: "What are you doing to my daughter? Put her down this instant!"

Portable Food ■

The mighty Cornish pasty (sans carrots).

A restless nation will always want to eat on the run, and this creates opportunities for utilitarian cuisine. The kind of meal you can throw down your neck in between finishing doing a thing and starting something else, without having to pause to wash up any plastic tubs or spend the day with a fork in your pocket.

To this end, all manner of meals have been encased in pastry, nature's own Tupperware, and sold for the express delight of busy Brits on the move. There's the sausage roll—a meeting point between a

Danish pastry and a hot dog—the steak slice, the steak and kidney pie, the Bedfordshire clanger, pork pie, game pie, homity pie, cheese straws . . . just grab your dinner, jam it in your pocket, and hit the road.

Some pies are runny inside and served hot. Others—like the classic pork pie—have a filling that's encased in meat jelly and tend to be served cold. There are pies you can buy only at football matches, pies that you eat with your hands, and pies that come served with mashed potatoes and a dollop of hot green parsley sauce called liquor (the great London meal known simply as pie and mash).

Speaking of football, there's a popular pie-related chant aimed at slightly rotund players on the opposing team, fat referees, or podgy linesmen. It is set to the tune of "Knees Up, Mother Brown" and goes:

> *Who ate all the pies, who ate all the pies?*
> *You fat bastard, you fat bastard!*
> *You ate all the pies.*

Because the very worst thing you could be, in a pastry-loving nation, is a pie glutton.

In Scotland, taking things up a notch, the humble boiled egg (surely a fairly portable food already) has been given an upgrade by encasing it in sausage meat, coating the ensuing ball in bread crumbs, and deep-frying it. That's no pool ball in your packed lunch, that's a Scotch egg, and sometimes the sausage meat is replaced with black pudding (blood pudding) or even haggis.

Then there's the Cornish pasty. Essentially a peppery beef stew in an edible pastry flask, the pasty is shaped like a capital D, with a folded-over crust around the curve. This is so that Cornish tin miners, who used to wind up with a lot of arsenic on their fingers, could eat most of their lunch and discard the crust somewhere deep underground. Local legend claimed that the crusts were being thrown as offerings to the spirits of the mine, called knockers.

In neighboring Devon, there's some argument as to the correct ingredients of the pasty. Devonians put carrots in theirs; the Cornish do not. This may seem a trifling distinction but as there's a lot of mythology at stake—including a fondly recounted tale that the pasty once had a second chamber for mashed fruit at one end, making it even more of an all-purpose pastry lunchbox—tempers often become frayed when debating who has the more correct traditional recipe, although no one does the fruit thing anymore. And possibly they never did.

Not that the people who eat pasties from motorway service stations or high street bakers are buying into the myths and legends of ancient Cornwall. They just really, really like pies.

WHAT TO SAY: "Fancy a picnic lunch? I'll bring the sausage rolls; you bring the Tizer."

WHAT NOT TO SAY: "Is there anywhere I can microwave my pasty?"

Let's deal with the big cultural differences first. To the untrained eye, the UK and the United States differ sharply on the kinds of sports they traditionally enjoy watching, whether on TV or in the flesh. There is even a debate over what to call two of them, with both countries having a game they call football, only one of which involves kicking a ball with the foot as a prerequisite of play. For the purposes of this discussion, let's agree that the game the Brits call football is football and not soccer; otherwise we have effectively surrendered the field before the referee's first whistle.

No sport carries the same degree of obsession in Britain as football does. Football players are national heroes, ambassadors for the country, and an inspiration to British youth, even the really badly behaved ones. From its relatively humble origins as a working-class expression of community rivalry, football has grown into a colossal industry, albeit one that still largely depends on the romantic idea of like-minded people—players and fans alike—uniting together against a common foe. It's just that, for the biggest teams, it's no longer simply a case of local players being cheered on by local supporters.

The emotional investment in football begins at a very early age, possibly with the gift of a tiny T-shirt in the colors of your dad's favorite team, or later on, a family kickabout in the back garden or the park or any relatively flat stretch of grass. At this point it doesn't really matter if the heaving pile of elbowing, jostling humanity is all boys or all girls, all kids or all grown-ups; as long as there is a ball in play and the capability to fashion goalposts out of whatever portable items are at hand—jumpers, bags, prams, you name it—there will be football.

You have to pick a professional team to support fairly quickly too, especially if you are from a household that did not see fit to bequeath a firm preference from birth. This doesn't need to be a complicated decision. It's not unlike having a favorite book, movie, or song; the answer to the question isn't what causes the stress—it's the fear of backing the wrong horse. So, for most people there are two ways to pick a team: the old-fashioned way and the most common way:

The old-fashioned method is to find out which football club is nearest to your home and support them. There is no need to do any more than this at present. No requirement to attend matches, learn the player sheet, or even follow the scores on a Saturday, all you need to know is who your team is. However, unless you happen to live near one of the Premier League teams, there's a temptation to bolster up your champion credibility by supporting a club that has a chance of winning trophies. That's the most common way to choose: go for the guys at the top of the Premier League.

Once you've cleared that hurdle, you have to decide what kind of football supporter you are going to be. It's perfectly acceptable to support a team without going to a single match, thanks to the glory of TV coverage and the freely available merchandise that the clubs create to bolster their business (and I'm using the word *freely* entirely incorrectly here). At this level of support, the difference between British and American sports fans is negligible. You wear the T-shirt of your favorite player and gather together with friends to watch the team perform, and there will probably be beer.

If you do go to matches, there are hugely complicated traditions around the sort of food you can expect to buy while there. They sell pies; they sell pickled things; and they sell unorthodox hot drinks like Bovril to keep body temperatures up amid freezing sleet. One of your first jobs as a new supporter is to find out what the old hands like to eat, and then decide whether to join them, or grab a burger on the way in. As a constantly evolving cultural event, football carries a lot of outdated cultural jetsam in its wake, but it's not crucial to engage with all of it.

For example, one thing I'm trying hard not to say is that football is a primarily male concern, because empirically it is not, certainly not from the perspective of the supporters. It's probably fair to say that the British assume that men like football, and certainly women's football has very little public profile compared to the men's game, but there are far too many female fans to make any generalizations stick anymore. Nor should anyone try. Walking out of the supermarket in an England shirt singing a song about Three Lions and carrying a slab of beer as if it's a stag you killed with your bare hands is a treat for everyone, not just the boys.

That said, it is also possible for the myth of the Football Dad to cast a shadow over the relationship between a father and a son when neither party is remotely interested in "the beautiful game." It arrives as a kind of social expectation, one of the things other dads are doing with their kids. Just as new mums worry about breastfeeding, new dads worry about making their children into social pariahs if they don't get the ball out and commence keepy-uppies at the first opportunity. Or at the very least put a game on the TV once in a while; otherwise it could count as a form of neglect.

If the child comes home from school and mentions a footballer his friend likes, should the dad then rush out and buy the kit, or shrug and cue up the latest Disney or Pixar epic? There are no correct answers in a situation like this.

Of course, when a major tournament rolls around, it's a chance for everyone to go to town. A World Cup, the FA Cup final—these are occasions for even the most timid of sporting souls to throw themselves in headfirst. Football is not a complicated game—aside from a rolling argument about the finer points of the offside rule, a slightly fiddly affair that has become a cliché even to mention—so it's not hard to work out what is going on, and as everyone can tell good play from bad, your attempts at punditry will probably be just as insightful and effective as anyone else's.

A World Cup is also an opportunity for Brits to express patriotism in an overt manner. This isn't something that they tend to do exhaustively, not least because there are different flags to rally around and paint on your face: the red cross of St. George for England, the white X against deep blue of St. Andrew for Scotland, and the fantastic red dragon of St. David for Wales. Northern Ireland and Cornwall also have their own flags—and political reasons for using them—and the Union Jack is also brought out at more unified events like the Olympics (see: Putting Union Jacks on Things).

Getting the right flag out at the right time is a thorny issue, best avoided unless you have insider knowledge. As in a lot of countries, the line between patriotism and jingoism is a hard one to spot and an even harder one to agree on, so it's best just to pick a side, settle back, and enjoy the game.

WHAT TO SAY: *"Come on!* My nan could've scored from there!"

WHAT NOT TO SAY: "Y'know what this game needs? Cheerleaders."

Cross-Dressing ■

I used to think the much-trumpeted British love of putting men in women's clothes was an exaggeration. We've all seen *Mrs. Doubtfire* and *Tootsie*; we've all been to bachelor parties or frat gatherings where boys dress as girls. It's a fancy dress staple: put on a big T-shirt, grab a couple of balloons, try not to get too much lipstick in your beard, everyone's happy.

But there really is a long and noble tradition of cross-dressing in British culture, and it's one that runs largely parallel to the history of British transsexuality. Not so parallel that the two things didn't ever intersect, of course, but there are two different histories of men dressing in women's clothing and women dressed as men. This is the one that took place entirely under stage lighting.

To begin at a beginning: in the Elizabethan theater of Shakespeare, no matter what the play dictated, men played all the female characters. This was simply because women were not permitted to debase themselves in such a lewd and bawdy form of entertainment. The Elizabethan court may have held masques in which prominent ladies were permitted to play-act a little, but for public consumption, particularly when the most popular plays would have contained a fair amount of base humor, it was considered to be beyond the pale.

This kind of gender stringency is bound to leave a mark on a society, and it's tempting to conclude that the reason so many of

Shakespeare's comedies concern men dressed as women and women dressed as men is that everyone in the audience would already have been in on the gag that the woman dressed as a man is actually a man, and so's the man dressed as a woman.

Crucially, after this period came a time of strong puritan rule, in which all theater was banned, again because it was considered to be a debasement of fine Christian morals. And it's probably not too fanciful to suggest that this constant association between acting and moral depravity has permanently left the British theater audience a little too giggly in the face of any thrillingly broken—or just plain bent—rules. There are faint echoes of this in every Shakespeare audience to this day. One or two members of the audience still treat jokes whose rebellious sting has been dulled by the passing years as if they are freshly minted sex bullets of bawdy hilarity (see: The Theater), and that's probably because of years of conditioning at school, in which Shakespeare is treated with the same sense of reverence as the King James Bible.

To summarize: The British theater tradition is one of naughtiness, ribaldry, and men dressing as women. Small wonder these three things continue to delight audiences to this day.

After theatrical life returned during the reign of Charles II, a new hybrid form of theatrical entertainment arrived that took aspects of staging, songs, and dancing from court masques and added new characters coming out of the Italian commedia dell'arte—most notably those of the harlequinade: Harlequin; his lover, Columbine; her father, Pantaloon; and his servants Clown and Pierrot—and the suggestive humor, action sequences, and magic reality of mummers' plays.

Pantomimes gathered their own internal logic slowly. After a period of fiddling about with classical Greek themes, they settled on European folk tales, delivered with great silliness and charm: *Cinderella, Mother Goose, Snow White*, and so on. During the Victorian era a kind of Shakespearean reverse became customary, and eventually traditional; the lead female role would be played by an actress, and so would that of the lead male—or principal boy. These are the most serious parts in the production; they provide the love story that will resolve everything at the end. The biggest comedy role in a pantomime belongs to the dame, a formidable matron (or matrons, in the case of Cinderella's sisters) with preposterous makeup and a gaudy, clashing costume. The dame is presented as a maternal force, a woman past the first budding flush of youth, the kind of woman who owns more comfortable underwear (bloomers, mostly) than lingerie, but thinks of herself as a rare and precious flower. She's Mother Goose or Widow Twankey or the Nanny in *Babes in the Wood*. And she's always, always played by a man. Just as the shrewish scolds in Monty Python are played by men and the attractive women are played by Carol Cleveland.

This is really where the international reputation the Brits have for howling at a man in a dress comes from. Pantomimes are an eccentric institution, but as they're linked to Christmas and general winter merriment, and they retain that mixture of cartoon violence (for the kids) and bawdy wit (for the mums and dads), they remain hugely popular as live entertainment. They're also an echo of the days of the music hall, when cross-dressing comics like Vesta Tilley (a male impersonator) would entertain working-class audiences with sly innuendos, pratfalls, and patriotic songs. All of which found its way into the humor of performers such as Benny Hill. He had the vulgarity, the sly bawdiness, and the slapstick familiar to anyone who's seen a panto.

British popular culture seems happy to accept cross-dressing provided it follows that unthreatening pantomime brief. Several entertainers made their name performing in drag, either dolled up to the nines, like Danny La Rue; glittery and frumpy like Dame Edna Everage (the alter ego of Australian comedian Barry Humphries); or hard-bitten and tarty, like Paul O'Grady's Lily Savage. Lily—by far the most waspish character, and the least family-friendly of any of them—even wound up presenting prime-time game shows like *Blankety Blank*.

The most popular comedy TV show of recent years—in terms of audience size, if not critical appreciation—is *Mrs. Brown's Boys*, in which Brendan O'Carroll plays another woman of a certain age who acts in an unladylike, undignified fashion and wears bloomers. O'Carroll may be Irish, but it's a BBC production and has proven to be so popular there was even a spin-off movie.

Meanwhile, the stand-up comedian Eddie Izzard had a less welcoming time of it, despite being one of the most original comic talents Britain has produced, because he genuinely is a transvestite, not a man pretending to be a woman for laughs. So while it is undoubtedly true that the Brits love a cross-dresser, it has more to do with the gigglesome naughtiness than it is proof that they are a nation of fey intellectuals who only come out of their shells in drag.

WHAT TO SAY (WHEN SOMEONE IN A PANTOMIME SAYS, "OH, YES, HE IS"): "Oh, no, he isn't!"

WHAT NOT TO SAY: "Whoa! Is that chick a dude? I'm so outta here."

Movie #1: *The Great Escape* ■

If ever there was a film that illustrated the nature of the special relationship between the UK and United States it's *The Great Escape*. It's a film that makes free with national stereotypes in a time of war. There's a dour Scot who enjoys a drink, a starchy Englishman with a duty to serve, a few officious German officers with no sense of humor, and a great big Hollywood star who can't even be a prisoner of war without getting all rule-breaking maverick about it.

In fact, the more times I've watched *The Great Escape*, the more ludicrous Steve McQueen's antics become. While everyone else in the movie is playing the frustrations and camaraderie of the wartime internees with admirable restraint, quietly digging their tunnels and preparing to make a run for it, McQueen struts and preens, waving his American clothes and his American attitude—and, most baffling of all, his American baseball and catcher's mitt—in the faces of his captors, and not getting taken out behind the latrines and shot even once.

Even when he's been caught trying to escape and taken to the cooler to spend some time in isolation, someone lobs him that ball and glove and he is somehow allowed to play with them defiantly while the guards openly fail to mask their irritation at the noise. That not one of them considers just taking the sports equipment off the prisoner and putting it in the trash serves as a partial explanation as to why they also fail to spot the massive tunnels the prisoners are digging under the camp either until it's too late to do anything about it. The Germans in the movies may be officious, but they're not very bright.

McQueen's not even the only American actor in the camp. James Garner is there; so is James Coburn; and they're not arsing about like he is. They don't seem to require any special sporting supplies and appear fairly keen to blend in with their surroundings, especially once they've managed to escape. Steve merely pinches a motorbike, drives it around until he is spotted, then starts trying to jump over the border into Switzerland in broad daylight. Only his own poor skills as a stunt rider let him down in the end, and he's returned to the cooler with that bloody glove and ball, while pretty much all the other escapees that the Germans managed to apprehend are just taken to a field and gunned down.

Now, the important thing to bear in mind about all this is that the reason I, and millions like me, can pull details like this out of my head is that I've seen *The Great Escape* many, many times. It's a film that rewards repeat viewings, with an abundance of terrific individual performances that tell an important story with appropriate levels of jeopardy and black humor.

Brits adore *The Great Escape*. They love the central theme of the movie, which is all about an oddball collection of men with unique skills coming together to overcome a common foe, a bit like *The A-Team* but bigger and far less daft. They love that it is loosely based on a real escape, from Stalag Luft III in what is now Żagań, Poland, although only a few of the characters are recognizable from actual people and certainly no one escaped on a motorbike. And they love the idea that you can't keep British people down, that native cunning, compassion for your fellow man, and a bone-deep disregard for authority is all one requires in any situation, no matter how desperate.

And they love the theme tune too. Being a nation that still wears the winning of World War II with a sense of personal triumph, the Brits still love nothing more than to take to the football stadiums of the world, especially when England is playing a game against Germany, and sing the jaunty theme music to the film. They may even carry drums and trumpets in order to play it, but they don't have to be there. The melody is whistled in the film—the tune is pitched somewhere between "It's a Long Way to Tipperary" and a military cadence—and whistled in real life too.

In a sense, it's a film in which a lot of people fail to get what they want, and pay a high price for even trying, but that's something that suits the British self-image too. What happens to those men, even though it has been dramatized out of its original context, is far closer to Shakespeare's "We few, we happy few, we band of brothers" than anything that happens to the cocky guy with the ball and glove.

WHAT TO SAY: "Damn it! Don't say 'thank you,' Mac!"

WHAT NOT TO SAY: "Surely the dirt from the tunnels would have made their exercise yard a foot taller by the time they finished."

Cocking a Snook ∎

You can't go around telling everyone that you live in a rigid, class-bound society in which reserve and manners are prized above all things and not expect a little kickback from time to time. That's just human nature. The great thing about British culture is that everyone, from street drunk to lord of the manor, is aware of this tension, and what's more, they know exactly what to do to relieve it.

In a totalitarian society where decorum takes second place to authority, a thumbed nose is a dangerous thing, risking the safety of both thumb and nose. But if you can structure things in such a way that it is possible to demonstrate leadership by proving you can take a joke, this can act as a social safety valve. So all figures of authority will be tested at some point using the ritual of cocking a snook, otherwise known as taking the piss, and they had better be able to deal with it or risk an open mutiny. In fact, all potential Captain Blighs should take note: if you can handle being ribbed, you're all right, and if you also get a round in, you're practically a local hero. That's your real Bounty, right there.

A ripe raspberry in the face of those in authority shows the influence of the Shakespearean fool in action: a person of low status speaking truth to power in a colorful, entertaining way. Most stand-up comedians use this very principle, even when mocking their own audience. And the most potent snook-cocking gesture is the V sign, a ripe two-fingered salute with the palm facing the giver (always the other way around from Ringo Starr, please; we're not spreading peace and love here), as delivered to perfection by yobbish kids telling their elders and betters to eff off.

An unruly youth in action.

It's a step to one side from the downright provocative—and therefore drearily obvious—single digit, and it calls to mind cheeky young whippersnappers from the Artful Dodger to Johnny Rotten and is used by people in all walks of life, in varying degrees of seriousness. It could be the comedian Rik Mayall playing the would-be street poet and anarchist Rik in TV's *The Young Ones* (and getting his Vs all arse-about-face) or the moment in June 2014 when Baroness Trumpington (a real person) flicked the Vs at Lord King (a real lord) in the House of Lords (not a real house). A most regally cocked snook indeed.

Call it a hangover from the feudal system, call it a continuation of the constant ribbing among the gang of mates at the building site or the pub, each with a nickname he violently detests (see: Banter), call it the spirit of Hogarth reborn or the spirit of punk undead, but there is nothing the Brits love like cutting someone lofty down to size. Victoria and David Beckham sitting on thrones at their wedding? Do me a favor. Michael Jackson floating a statue of himself down the Thames? Give it a rest.

When David Blaine came to London in 2003, his plan was to spend forty-four days suspended in a fish tank on a string. It was a feat of endurance that would have been impressive had it not been so palpably unnecessary and yet desperate to appear important. Never has there been a more literal illustration of the phrase "getting above his station"—London Bridge, if you're wondering—than this particular stunt, and Blaine had already blotted his copybook by appearing in a notorious British TV interview in which he said and did almost nothing, save for showing an eye drawn on the palm of one hand. Consequently, while he starved himself for the benefit of the world's media, British wags were attaching burgers and sausages to remote-controlled aircraft, to torment him. They also pelted his Perspex box with eggs and fish and chips and used it as target practice for golf balls.

When presented with a similarly messianic Michael Jackson pretending to heal the sick and cure the lame as part of his performance at the 1996 Brit Awards, Jarvis Cocker of the band Pulp climbed onstage, waggled his bum, and flicked the Vs a bit and was promptly carted off by the police (and quietly released the next day because interrupting pop stars is not illegal). He remains a national hero to this day.

Some impudences are more serious in intent, but still essentially playful in delivery. When Margaret Thatcher died in 2013, some Brits, who weren't fans, rushed to download the song "Ding-Dong! The Witch Is Dead" from *The Wizard of Oz* to try to get it to number one in the charts, undercutting the seriousness and reverence with which the news had been announced. This rank insubordination caused an angry counterreaction from her admirers, not least those who had been trying to be solemn in the first place. It was quite a to-do.

Even Rik Mayall didn't manage to escape a similar dig in the ribs when he died a year later, although as an arch-snook-cocker his was more of a salute than an attack. Rather than creating a solemn send-off, some bright spark put up a blue commemorative plaque in Hammersmith, where the opening credits of his slapstick TV show *Bottom* had been filmed, featuring a prominent scene of argy-bargy with his comic partner Adrian Edmondson.

It read: "Rik Mayall—1958–2014—punched his friend in the balls near this spot."

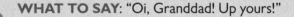

WHAT TO SAY: "Oi, Granddad! Up yours!"

WHAT NOT TO SAY: "I say, do you mind? Get out of my way, you frightful oik."

Dancing ■

There's no stratum of British society in which dancing does not have its place. Whether it's the full *Swan Lake* at the English National Ballet or kids at a birthday party doing the Pizza Hut song while playing musical bumps, dancing is integral to all forms of social conduct: more so than sports, more so than any other branch of the arts. The British love of cutting a rug goes back generations.

There are the morris men, traditional dancers who dress in white and wear bells on their shins and perform time-strengthened choreography that may be as much as five hundred years old. Their dances might occasionally seem out of step with flint-eyed popular culture but the tradition has lasted (and it continues to thrive) for so long that even the origin of the name isn't clear. Some say it's derived from "Moorish" dancing—which sounds plausible but also carries the faint echo of someone squealing, "Hey! Look at me! I'm all *foreign!*" while dancing about—and there is certainly a whiff of exotic logic to proceedings. There is even some blackening of faces in a few of the older traditions—albeit without any explicitly racial context, damning or otherwise—but, as with anything that old, the true intentions behind these traditions have long since vanished, leaving centuries of eager conjecture behind.

There's a lot of history, far too much to do justice to in one hit, especially with the different regional varieties and traditions involved, including bells and sticks and a pig's bladder and swords and a fool and a beast and solo dances and even a competitive dance to win the favor of a "maiden" (sometimes a man dressed as a woman, sometimes not). Viewed from the outside, it's all a delightful muddle, but one that has clearly been meticulously organized.

Over the years, the morris men have had to clear a space next to the break-dancers, street dancers, free-runners, and parkour enthusiasts, not to mention those buskers who paint themselves silver and pretend to be statues. Taking your moves out onto the streets has never been more popular, except you're far more likely to see genuine street dancers at a properly organized competition or flashmob than popping the caterpillar on an unfolded cardboard box in the shopping precinct. As with all aspects of hip-hop culture, the Brits are well represented with b-boys and b-girls, and specialist crews battle for supremacy with other crews from all over the world. There are beginners' street-dance and breakdancing sessions all over the country, and kids' movies are riddled with wisecracking urchins who can bust a move in order to settle an argument.

This isn't a recent development; the relationship between Brits and black pop culture has been one of worship and curation for decades. The 1960s mods may be remembered as devotees of the Who, but it was the sweet grooves of Motown, Jamaican ska, and soul that really oiled their Vespas, and they would habitually load up on pills and dance all night to the latest releases from Detroit, Kingston, and Memphis. A few years later, this utter devotion to '60s soul would create its own dance scene in the clubs of northern England, Scotland, and Wales; a scene of such mythical potency the music itself was corralled in its name. Northern soul was, on the face of it, just a bunch of people getting together to have a bop to some old records, but it carried rules and expectations and one-upmanship and a kind of enviably fierce passion—there were badges with a clenched fist on them, and the slogan "Keep the Faith," for example. You took certain shoes to dance in, the floor would be covered in talcum powder to facilitate spins and slides, and the dancers would embark on a display of competitive peacocking of legendary proportion.

This set the template for every dance culture since—be it disco, hip-hop, electro, house, acid house, techno, UK garage, or beyond—there are experts, there are hedonists, and there are weekend ravers, and everyone gets together to sweat their cares away until dawn. Other, older forms of dancing have had their moments of extreme popularity, like Brazilian samba dancing, which has livened up many a wet parade through the streets of provincial towns. Then there are Irish ceilidhs, Latin American salsa nights, and fitness dances like Zumba. And that's before we even mention *Strictly Come Dancing*.

For the past handful of years the autumn television schedules have seen a showbiz standoff between ITV's *The X Factor* (singing, some dancing) and the BBC's *Strictly Come Dancing* (dancing, obviously). The latter is not only the UK's version of *Dancing with the Stars*, it's the sequel to the long-running ballroom show *Come Dancing*, which was relaunched and renamed in tribute to the Baz Luhrmann film *Strictly Ballroom*.

These relatively archaic references are almost entirely lost in popular culture, and now the name makes absolutely no sense, especially when you consider the British love of both innuendo and pedantry—*Strictly Famous People Dancing* would at least be accurate—but it is an astonishingly popular show, so no one appears to have been put off. And as proof of its enduring influence, enrollment for ballroom dancing classes has increased dramatically since the show began in 2004.

Not that this endless carnival of dance-floor excellence would stop British dads from putting a tie around the head—sweatband style—and doing that embarrassing dance to old ska records at your cousin's wedding, but that's dads for you.

WHAT TO SAY TO A DJ: "Of course, I was into this tune before it was cool."

WHAT NOT TO SAY TO A DJ: "Haven't you got any proper music?"

The NHS ■

To put it bluntly, the only reason there is a National Health Service is because of the Second World War. With families giving up their husbands and sons and homes, sending their children off to live with strangers in the countryside, and pulling together to try to fend off the unpleasant attentions of the German army, there was no possibility that society would simply go back to the way it was once the fighting had ceased. Everyone played a part in the war effort, and in the immediate aftermath, everyone would continue to play a part in pulling Britain back together.

That's the only applicable lens through which to view the NHS. It's not a hallmark of a socialist state; it's the reward for a country that made a supreme effort to unite—from all sides of the political spectrum—in order to prevent invasion and then had to keep pulling together once the threat had gone, because too many previously closed doors had been blown open. Sometimes literally.

That's not to say it was welcomed with open arms when it started or that it continues to operate free from criticism now. There will always be British people who are vehemently opposed to the idea of a national health service, who point out that it is one of the largest employers of people in the whole world, who maintain that nationalized industries breed inefficiency in a way that would never be acceptable to privatized firms handling the same workload, and who complain that the service is abused by people who won't take care of themselves and should not be funded by hardworking taxpayers.

Moaning about the NHS is definitely a thing Brits like, but that's basic human nature when presented with something that appears to be too good to be true: "Universal health care with no financial obligation? Ranked number one in the world* and funded by the state? But . . . but . . . I didn't get you anything except these meager taxes and National Insurance contributions. I feel a fool."

Or to put it another way, they moan about the NHS in the same way people moan about overbearing parents or a needy best friend. The love remains unstated because it's the most obvious, least interesting thing to comment upon. But if the NHS is threatened, that's when the rows break out. Those arguments about employment and efficiency became pretty heated, especially when it started to look like private firms had secured NHS contracts to do, in effect, a worse job for the same money. Public money. And the last few years have seen the heat go up a notch, as the media narrative got stuck on austerity and then went looking for spongers to attack. That's individual spongers from a poor background, you understand, not those private firms.

There again, Danny Boyle's opening ceremony for the 2012 Olympics in London featured a section devoted to the NHS, placing it alongside beloved children's characters and the best of British pop music as institutions the country is proud of. And that ceremony was the single biggest catalyst for the Brits to take off their skeptical spectacles and get unreservedly excited about themselves, and therefore about the Olympics as an event, after months of moaning about traffic gridlock, bus lanes, and ticket allocation. Had the inclusion of the NHS sounded as a wrong note, this would not have happened.

So, yes, there are people who treat it like a particularly frustrating safety harness on the roller coaster of life, people who have lost loved ones or been treated shabbily by NHS staff at the point of greatest

---

* According to a 2014 report by the Commonwealth Fund.

vulnerability, and people who have become enraged by having to wait hours in Accident and Emergency to be seen by medical staff who simply have to keep the conveyor belt moving as fast as is humanly possible. But these criticisms, no matter how forcefully stated or righteously felt, can't compete with the positives.

By which I mean this: find me a British person who hates the NHS after his or her partner's life has just been saved; after she has just given birth to her first child, or her third; after he has just been told a beloved relative has come out of a coma or woken from a life-changing operation. Find me someone who set off for the day in normal shape, had an accident, and came home a month later in an entirely different condition—having spent that time being carried aloft by the dedication and diligence of doctors and nurses who are clearly doing the best they can under extraordinarily trying circumstances—and still complains of gross inefficiency and socialist handouts.

I'm not saying those people don't exist. I'm saying they're the ones you may have to wait longest to get a thank-you card from after Christmas.

WHAT TO SAY: "Oh, hello, are you a nurse? Can I buy you a drink?"

WHAT NOT TO SAY: "I don't see the need for it, as I can afford private health care."

Dunking Biscuits ■

A digestive biscuit preparing to be immersed.

Note: As we are discussing a foodstuff that must, in order to be at its most orally appealing, be moist *and* stiff, we're probably not going to be able to get through this without some of the sentences containing a hint of innuendo. It's a shame to drag things down to the level of the gutter, but with dunking biscuits—as with other, less innocent pursuits—it's not so much about what you put in, or how you put it in, it's about what happens when you take it out, and what kind of mess it leaves behind.

If you had to find the perfect biscuit to suit the British taste buds, it would be somewhere between the moist and crumbly chocolate chip cookie, as favored by American children with their milk of an evening, and the bone-dry, gasping-for-moisture Italian biscotto.

Ideally what they like best is the kind of biscuit you could eat on its own, but which is improved by a brief dip in something hot and wet. Some biscuits really suit a dunk in a cup of tea, others work best with coffee or even hot chocolate, and some don't work at all. There's even a tiny subset of biscuits that don't appear to be changed whatsoever by the experience of being dunked. These may require more of an overnight soak, and as such should be avoided unless eaten dry.

The Garibaldi, for example, is not a great biscuit for dunking. It's a thin, glazed cracker that does not expand or even noticeably soften in liquid. A HobNob, on the other hand, could have been scientifically designed (note: it was definitely scientifically designed) to work best when plunged into a hot beverage. Without having had the chance to suck up a decent finger of tea, a HobNob is just a flattened flapjack (granola bar). Moistened, it becomes, well, like a wet and crumbly flapjack with tea in it. Dunking a biscuit is not alchemy, after all.

Rich tea biscuits are also designed for dunking, but will only suit one dip, and a brief one at that. Allow a maximum of one second for your dipping, and make sure you don't put more biscuit in the tea than you are prepared to put in your mouth in one go. Leave it too long, and you'll wind up fishing damp gunk out of your mug with a teaspoon, and if you bite off only a portion of the wet part, the rest will just flop onto your lapel.

Digestives occupy a happy middle ground between the two. They're structurally far stronger than rich tea biscuits, being made with bran rather than just flour. They can take a longer plunge than rich teas too, and probably won't collapse unless placed under extreme strain (i.e., held horizontally for a while). And there are no oaty bits in a digestive, so people with dentures—or anyone who'd pick smooth peanut butter over crunchy—can enjoy them too.

To add a further frisson of excitement to an already fairly charged and slightly soggy situation*, all the biscuits discussed above (apart from the Garibaldi) are also available with one side coated in chocolate, and sometimes with caramel too. This changes everything. Suddenly the rich tea acts as if it has been given a spine, the digestive loses all pretense of being a healthy option, and the HobNob attains an almost impossibly regal air. Dunk these biscuits, and you've got an entirely different, almost decadent taste sensation to reckon with.

Of course, some biscuits already have an extra sweet layer. Custard creams and bourbons are, like Oreos, double biscuits held together with a butter-cream-type center. This gives them an idiosyncratic reaction to the hot liquid, with the outer biscuits becoming soft but the center remaining quite firm. Naturally, people have their own way of eating these biscuits, whether it's taking a layer off at a time or just jamming the whole thing in at one go. The Oreo twist, lick, and dip approach, as seen on TV commercials, doesn't seem to be that popular, though.

And then there are Jaffa cakes. While being the same size and shape as a biscuit, and fulfilling the same function as a biscuit, a Jaffa cake is not a biscuit; it is a small cake. This has been proven in court. Thanks to a differentiation in the taxation rates between cakes and biscuits, we now know that the difference between cakes and biscuits of the same size is that cakes go hard when stale and biscuits go soft. Jaffa cakes—being composed of a sponge base, with orange-flavored jelly on top, capped with a layer of chocolate—go hard when stale, and mushy when dipped in a hot drink. A dipped Jaffa is therefore not for everyone.

In more recent years, there's been a fresh innovation. The Australians developed the Tim Tam Explosion, in which they bite the opposing corners off a Tim Tam biscuit (basically a large chocolate-covered bourbon) and use it like a straw to suck up hot tea or coffee, before

---

* This is not a reference to the disgusting and possibly apocryphal British public school (meaning private school) game soggy biscuit. You do not want to know what the rules of soggy biscuit are, or what happens when it is played. And you definitely do not want to have to clean up afterward.

jamming the whole thing into their gobs and letting everything melt into everything else. To do this in Britain you'll need a biscuit called a Penguin, but it still works.

Curiously, while Dunkin' Donuts outlets have begun to make their way across the British Isles, the one thing Brits aren't commonly known to dunk is doughnuts. Maybe it's because we were raised with different expectations: the idea of a hard, dry thing becoming a soft, wet thing is perfectly acceptable, while a soft, moist thing becoming a floppy, drippy thing is just gross.

WHAT TO SAY: "Has anyone ever tried two rich teas with jam in the middle?"

WHAT NOT TO SAY: "What is this, a HobNob or a coaster?"

Never mind that this TV show is an international success, that there are people all over the world who know exactly what a Dalek is, what a TARDIS does, and why a sonic screwdriver is more than just an exciting innovation in the field of futuristic DIY, the British would love *Doctor Who* even if it were a purely parochial concern.

There are many reasons for this, some based in childhood nostalgia, some entirely to do with the quality of the ideas in the show. But when the opening ceremony of the London 2012 Olympics left *Doctor Who* out of its celebration of British achievements and attitudes—a last-minute change, by all accounts, fittingly cut for reasons of time and space—there was a sense of outrage, that an old friend had been somehow left out in the cold.

To anyone unfamiliar with the setup of the show, this next bit is going to be a little baffling. There's this guy, and he's an alien. But he's a very British sort of alien. He is, in fact, more British than the British people he takes with him on his travels, and you know this because he most often dresses like an Edwardian dandy with a serious frock coat addiction. He's the archetypal British eccentric, a boffin, an inventor, and because he is a figure of authority and one of the good guys (mostly), his name is the Doctor.

Note: His first name is not The and his surname is not Doctor. He is just the Doctor.

The Doctor is one of an alien (but still somehow British) race called the Time Lords, and they invented an astonishing machine that is bigger on the inside than on the outside. It's called a TARDIS, an acronym that stands for Time and Relative Dimension in Space. You won't ever need to know why this is the case; it just is. As the name suggests—but does not explain—TARDISes can travel in space and time, and they have a circuit that disguises them so they fit into their immediate surroundings.

Being something of a maverick, the Doctor stole a TARDIS and ran away from the stuffy old British Time Lords, defying their policy of nonintervention in alien worlds by repeatedly arriving in the middle of conflicts, taking sides, and then making sure his side won. He ended up living in London in 1963, and his TARDIS changed to look like one of the old police telephone boxes from the early years of the twentieth century that were already being phased out of use (see: Phone Boxes). Then the doohickey that allowed the TARDIS to blend in with its background broke and it got stuck like that.

Rather than spend ages trying to fix it, the Doctor just headed off, traveling everywhere and everywhen, taking some people with him and leaving others behind. Along the way he has met despotic snot monsters that live in malevolent dustbins (that's the Daleks), deeply unpleasant cyborgs with silver headphones on (the Cybermen), and a race of short, bald clone men with a communal Napoleon complex (the Sontarans).

It has also transpired that Time Lords can regenerate, a neat trick that allows them to entirely replace their physical form with another, should they be about to die. The replacing of one Doctor with another does dramatically alter his personality, but he's still essentially the same excitable professor with sparkly eyes.

This means the show can survive the departure and replacement of its entire cast, which it has done many times over the last fifty years, and still cover the same basic ground without abandoning any of its fundamental qualities—simply put, it's a horror show for all the family, dressed as a science fiction show that sometimes tries to be educational. People may have their preferences as to which era of *Doctor Who* they prefer, but fifty televisual years after first arriving on British screens, the Doctor is still to be found biffing around in time and space, still arriving in the middle of unsettling situations and fixing them, and still traveling in a futuristic machine that looks like a relic from the olden days.

He therefore represents the Victorian ideal of the Englishman abroad: a man with a missionary zeal to make the universe a better place using science and moral certainty, with impeccable manners and some very peculiar habits, who will outlive everyone he ever meets because he was lucky enough to have been born into a very special race.

Oh, and naturally he's partial to cricket.

Note: It's also important to mention the theme music to *Doctor Who*. Written by Ron Grainer and recorded by Delia Derbyshire for the BBC's experimental music laboratory the BBC Radiophonic Workshop, the original *Doctor Who* theme is a pioneering piece of electronic music, the first that most British people of a certain age will have ever been aware of, and by some distance the most popular. It's no coincidence that the generation that grew up with *Doctor Who* became the first wave of synthpop pioneers in the late 1970s and early '80s. The current show has rerecorded the theme using an orchestra, making it sound more thrilling but, ironically, less alien.

WHAT TO SAY: "Who is better: Donna Noble or Amy Pond?"

WHAT NOT TO SAY: "So why can't he go back in time to before the aliens attack and just trip them up or something?"

Arguing over What to Call Meals ■

This might get a little repetitive, so bear with me.

The good news is, breakfast is a given. Wherever you are in the British Isles, the first meal you have after you wake up, irrespective of the time of day, whether you've worked a night shift or happen to be a student or are recovering from a bout of stomach flu that kept you up all night and left you cautiously considering a cream cracker at dawn, is called *breakfast*.

Then there's the meal people eat at around midday. Depending on where you are from—in class and location—that is called either *lunch* or *dinner*. Should you be tempted to eat a cooked meal in the interim period between breakfast and lunch, whether because breakfast was just a hurried sip of tea on your way out the door or because you just really like to eat food as often as possible, that meal will only ever be called *brunch*. There are no midmorning meal appointments where everyone settles down to enjoy a nice relaxing *brinner*. That doesn't happen.

There is another term at play, however. If the midmorning meal is more like a snack—a muffin, say, or an enormous sandwich that doesn't come with crisps or a chocolate bar—then you can officially call it *elevenses*. Elevenses is the light nibble British people partake of to get them from breakfast to the midday meal without making unseemly noises from the midriff area. It is to the middle of the morning what an afternoon tea is to four o'clock (see: Tea).

Oh, and in West Cornwall there's the term *croust* (or *crowst*), which also refers to a midmorning snack, although possibly closer to the beginning of the morning than the end. But we're getting a little ahead of ourselves here. Let's go back to naming the three principal meals. Depending on your choice of name for the midday meal, the evening meal will be called *dinner* or *tea*. Or possibly *supper*, unless *supper* is the light meal you eat at nine or ten o'clock because you had an early *tea* (or *dinner*).

So, to recap, you've got either *breakfast, lunch*, and *dinner* or you've got *breakfast, dinner*, and *tea*. Or possibly *breakfast, lunch*, and *tea*, the latter of which is served at dinnertime, with *supper* some hours later. Should you be concerned about offending a gracious host, a decent rule of thumb is that people who live north of Birmingham, or are working class, tend to eat breakfast, dinner, and tea, and people who live in the south, or are generally well-to-do, tend to eat breakfast, lunch, and dinner. This is by no means definitive but it gives you a fighting chance.

If you're unsure of where you are and what the correct nomenclature may be, just refer to any meal that is not your first meal of the day as *dinner*. That's the safest bet.

WHAT TO SAY: "Now, who would like a spot of tea with their tea?"

WHAT NOT TO SAY: "What time is elevenses?"

Tea ■

Tea isn't merely a drink. It's a way of life. It's the panacea that fixes all curses and cures all wounds. It's the first thing Brits turn to in the morning and the last thing they prepare at night. Tea is a balm for the soul, a rallying spot for friends, a punctuation point for the day, and, let's not forget, a nice hot beverage that you can serve with milk and/or sugar.

Tea is the closest to a commonly agreed thing that Brits like, so much so that a British person who does not like tea—and it saddens me to have to reveal that such people do genuinely exist—creates consternation and concern whenever he or she comes to visit. Somehow the offer of a glass of water, a fruit juice, or a can of Vimto feels like cheap hospitality, leaving the host or hostess to worry, and maybe even ask, "Are you sure I can't get you a cup of tea?" as if it needs to be made clear that normal protocol for the greeting of guests has been observed even if the kettle remains unboiled.

And that's another thing: kettles. British travelers in foreign lands—especially foreign lands where the people worship other hot beverages over the mighty cuppa—find the lack of a kettle in their hotel room disturbing. Why would you not want a kettle? What kind of barbarous society neglects to provide tea-making facilities, even if its citizens don't happen to drink tea themselves? Running the coffee machine just for the hot water feels dirty, somehow, but needs must. Tea must be brewed, or the cogs that keep the world spinning will remain unoiled.

Of course, while there's broad agreement that tea itself is a wonderful thing, the process of making and drinking it is one that provokes hot debate. Some people are fiercely loyal not just to a particular blend—and by this I mean Darjeeling, Earl Grey, that kind of thing—but to a brand of tea bags. They'll tell anyone who will listen that it has to be Yorkshire Tea, or PG Tips, or it's just not tea at all. It's like Coke versus Pepsi, but played out in fine bone china cups and saucers.

Actually even the bone china is negotiable, according to taste. The extent to which Brits can be particular about tea is truly striking. So much so that some simply will not allow anyone else to make it for them. It's too important a matter to trust to amateur hands. Some prefer mugs—a big steaming mug of Rosie Lee (tea), that's the only way to do it. And you need to leave the bag in until the water goes dark amber. That is, unless you prefer to use a teapot warmed with hot water before you put the bag in. Or don't use a bag at all and go for leaves and a strainer. Oh, and you have to put the milk in after the tea has been poured. Or before, I forget which. And actually the real tea connoisseurs don't put any milk in. Or sugar. But maybe a lemon? There again, some people heap three sugars in and like their tea really weak, so it's important to check before you serve.

And this is before we delve into the many interpretations of the word *tea*. There's the drink, of course, and the meal (see: Arguing over What to Call Meals), which may or may not be served accompanied by a cupful of the drink of the same name and derives from the term *high tea*, a working person's evening meal, to be taken as soon as they get home from their labors.

But then there's *afternoon tea*, which is the one with the cakes on a stand, the china pot, the finger sandwiches, the fancy saucers, and the expectation of immaculate manners. That's the one that really should be called *high tea*, but because customs don't always develop in a sensible order with names that take into account other customs that already exist, it isn't.

Now that high tea is called just *tea*, the term *high tea*—if it is used at all—refers to a version of dinner (or tea) that involves light food-stuffs, salads, and crudités and dips as well as properly cooked items like pork pies, bubble and squeak (fried leftovers, essentially), crumpets, muffins—more commonly known as *English muffins* elsewhere in the world, although the Brits do call blueberry muffins *muffins* too—and cheese and pickles. The term *pickles* tends to refer to preserves like chutney,* rather than pickled onions or pickled cucumbers, which have their own name: gherkin. This is also the affectionate nickname of the London office building that is shaped like a pickled cucumber.

Then there are *cream teas*, which are a less formal kind of after-noon tea—unthinkable without a pot of actual tea—in which a plain scone is sliced in half, and each half is treated to a dollop of clotted cream and a dollop of jam, usually strawberry. If you put the cream on first, you are following a firm tradition of the county of Devon, where cream teas are very popular, particularly for tourists. If you put the jam on first, you are following a firm tradition of the county of Corn-wall, where cream teas are also very popular, particularly for tourists. Cornwall and Devon are very much the bickering siblings of the West Country, leaving neighboring Somerset and Dorset looking on, ap-palled at the lack of decorum.

Oh, and it may help you to know that there are even disagreements as to how to pronounce the word *scone*—"skon" as in "gone" and "skown" as in "bone." Generally speaking, the "skon" people think that the "skown" people have given themselves unnecessary airs and graces and are aspiring to be posh. And the "skown" people think the "skon" people are common and should really look things up in the dictionary before opening their mouths. The fact that both sides are bickering over the correct pronunciation of a small cake is proof that everyone

---

* Has there ever been a more English word than *chutney*? It's almost disappointing to discover that it's a name for a vinegary mush of spiced, preserved vegetables, and not, for example, an affectionate nickname given to the now-disgraced Earl of Lichmond-on-the-Blather by a beloved nanny. Part of the appeal is that it's an Indian word, coming to Britain during the days of English colonial rule and sticking delightfully to the tongue like itself on an en-Stiltoned cracker.

involved in the argument is posh, and the correct pronunciation is, of course, "scone."

WHAT TO SAY: "Put the kettle on, will you? I'm spitting feathers here."

WHAT NOT TO SAY: "Actually, I pronounce it 'skonny.'"

Comedy ■

It feels faintly idiotic to try to corral the history of British comedy into one small chapter. It's a topic that deserves not so much its own book as its own library. And as discussed in other chapters (not least Sarcasm, Cocking a Snook, and National Treasures), humor is one of the most commonly used arrows in the British quiver of social interaction. It might be important to be earnest, but it is vital to be funny.

There are definite strands to British comedy too. There are the family entertainers and natural clowns who came out of the music hall era: Morecambe and Wise, Tommy Cooper, Frankie Howerd. All of whom could hold an audience in raptures just by being present in a room and raising an eyebrow. It's a similar power that Eddie Izzard has now, as he emits a gleeful "erm . . ." and pretends to write footnotes on his hand. The heirs to this tradition—Michael McIntyre, Peter Kay, Lee Evans—have the chance to stand on some enormous stages in order to lark about because stand-up comedy is big business in Britain right now (and, as always, a thriving cottage industry, too).

Then there are the strategists and revolutionaries. Spike Milligan taking radio comedy by the scruff of the neck and turning it inside out with *The Goon Show*. The *Monty Python* team taking his lead and creating a sketch show in which the ideas often crash into one another or wander off, dazed. *The Fast Show* going one step further: a sketch show with no set-ups and no opening lines, just repeated catchphrases in constantly new and inventive contexts.

Over in the satire corner we begin with *Beyond the Fringe*—Peter Cook, Dudley Moore, Alan Bennett, and Jonathan Miller mocking the British establishment so charmingly and thoroughly they even got to take their very British show to New York and it still worked. *Yes Minister* (and later *Yes, Prime Minister*) repeated that trick, being hugely beloved of the people in political office it was created to lampoon. Fast-forward fifty years and we find Armando Iannucci, having filleted British politics and the media with *The Day Today*, *The Thick of It*, and *In the Loop* now repeating *Beyond the Fringe*'s transatlantic journey with *Veep*.

And then there are the sitcoms, the true ensemble performances like *Dad's Army*, *Green Wing*, *The Vicar of Dibley*, *The Good Life*, and *Only Fools and Horses* and the shows that exist as cages to house comic monstrosities like Basil Fawlty, Tony Hancock, Old Man Steptoe, Alan Partridge, and Patsy and Edina in *Absolutely Fabulous*. Some shows are blessed with both, like *The Young Ones*—or *Blackadder*, in which the only constant over three series of historical shenanigans is Rowan Atkinson's weary sigh at having to deal with all of these idiots yet again.

Some comic talents defy categorization, having built a unique world around themselves. Victoria Wood's skill at delivering the four Ss—sketches, sitcoms, songs, and stand-up—is unrivaled; and her tone of voice, even when delivered through the mouths of long-time collaborators Julie Walters or Celia Imrie, is unmistakable. Alan Bennett has the same quality and has even written himself into his own plays—*The Lady in the Van*—without it appearing jarring or egotistical.

You'd think that would be enough to be going on with, but audiences are so entranced by dazzling sparks of comedic wit that now there's a glut of TV panel shows—in effective, staged parlor games in which comics can show off within a predetermined format—just to keep comedians delivering jokes. So many, in fact, that surely some stand-up comedians make the bulk of their earnings from sitting behind a desk on TV, ready to disrupt proceedings with a sharp quip.

It doesn't even matter what the theme of the show is. It can be a quiz, like *Never Mind the Buzzcocks* or *Have I Got News for You*; it can be a confessional, like *Would I Lie to You?* or *Room 101*; it can provide a framework for comics to joust and parry with their improvisatory (or otherwise) one-liners, like *Mock the Week*; or it can be a tour of the host's twisted comic imagination with special guests taking the funny flak, like *Shooting Stars* or *Celebrity Juice*.

Some of the best panel shows are on the radio, possibly because this enhances the idea that everyone is sitting around a big table with you, the listener, at the head. There's *Just a Minute* (people talking about stuff without deviation, repetition, hesitation, or repetition), *The News Quiz* (satire), and best of all, *I'm Sorry I Haven't a Clue*. This claims to be "the antidote to panel shows," largely by dispensing with the idea that any kind of formal tournament is taking place whatsoever.

There are also the educational panel shows, such as Radio 4's science discussion *The Infinite Monkey Cage* and BBC TV's *QI*, which often just trots out facts of astonishment with little in the way of comedic editorial, because the truth is quite funny enough, thank you. Actually, part of the fun with that show is watching the panelists—insubordinate Herberts all—try to undermine Stephen Fry's professorial authority. An eternally entertaining comic impulse that goes back as far as comedy itself.

WHAT TO SAY: Any line from any show that takes your fancy. They're all gold.

WHAT NOT TO SAY: "*Fawlty Towers* is all very well and good, but it's no *Big Bang Theory*, is it?"

To get the full measure of a community and what it values, a decent place to start is the booking diary of the local village hall or community center. If you see bookings for youth groups, for weight clubs, for orienteering societies, and for musical ensembles to rehearse, a picture starts to form. Maybe there's a decent-sized population of immigrant families who need somewhere to teach their children about the old country, with food and music and dressing-up. Maybe there's a child's birthday party and the kids need somewhere to play pass the parcel or musical chairs without destroying a living room in the process.

You'll find meetings organized by local politicians, exercise classes for the elderly, bingo nights, karate, and ballroom dancing; everything from brass bands to am-dram. Some village halls even become places of worship for families whose religion is not represented by local churches. Visiting priests come from far afield just to conduct the right kind of ceremonies.

But two organizations in particular have prospered in community halls all over the British Isles over the last one hundred years, to the extent that in some cases they've ended up building their own venues that still often resemble village halls: the Scouts and the Women's Institutes.

The Scouts continue in much the same vein as they always have.

They start young, with Rainbow Guides and Beaver Cubs, and then work up through Brownies and Cubs to Guides and Scouts. There's still a uniform—although the girls are not expected to wear Guide dresses anymore—and the vows and practices are still the same as ever. An oath of allegiance is sworn to God and the reigning monarch, and there's a huge emphasis on games, learning skills, badges, and camping. This is how a nation, terrified of the prospect of feral youths running in packs, took matters in hand in the Victorian era, and this is the way it continues to do so now. Of course the kinds of youths who tend to run in packs would not be seen dead in a Scout uniform of any description, but that's not to decry the movement as a whole.

The Women's Institute may appear to be similarly buried by its own history, but it is a far more reactive organization than it seems. To look back over the history of the WI (as it is commonly known) in Britain is to view an alternative history of the twentieth century. Although the original aim of the organization—started in Llanfairpwllgwyngyll, Wales, in 1915—was to encourage women to take an active role in food production during the First World War, as well as other steps to improve the local community, the WI very quickly became involved in the issues of the day, not least the campaign for women's suffrage, and began educational programs that continue to this day. So it promotes that same inspiring mix of self-betterment and community involvement that feeds the Scouting movement (see also: Libraries). This is clearly not something anyone wants to crow about, because that would be unseemly, so certain affectionate myths are commonly bandied about, such as that the WI is all about home baking and Jerusalem—to the extent that when Jennifer Saunders and Abigail Wilson wrote their comedy about a fictitious women's organization of a similar bent to the WI, they called it *Jam & Jerusalem*.

In truth a lot of crafting is involved, whether it's baking or bunting or pickling, but that's come back into vogue in recent years in any case. Plus, as any doughnut would demand to know, what's wrong with jam? And as for "Jerusalem," William Blake's mystical lyric describes a spark of the divine landing on British soil and a struggle for the people touched by that spark to make a better world in the midst of industrial wastelands. It's a perfect metaphor for groups like the WI (and the Scouts), while being opaque enough to sustain the affections of people from any point on the political compass.

You can see the same combination of aspiration and affectionate rib-digging in the movie *Calendar Girls*, which is based on the true story of members of the Rylstone Women's Institute creating a tastefully nude calendar to raise money for leukemia research. Members may find themselves willingly falling in line with the organization's traditions on a regular basis, but that doesn't mean they're above the odd raised eyebrow (and voice) here and there when the red tape gets a bit too sticky.

To this day, women go to the WI partly to see what it is about, with a skeptical smirk at the wholesome do-goodery, and before you can say "plum jelly" they're in for the long haul. A branch in Liverpool was even created to welcome women with a particular affection for alternative culture—metal, goth, burlesque, and the like. They are called the Iron Maidens, a name that deserves not just a round of applause but that devil-horns hand signal in the air too.

Their jam is probably Marmite.

WHAT TO SAY: "Who wants to learn how to make s'mores?"

WHAT NOT TO SAY: "So this William Blake guy asks a bunch of unanswerable spiritual questions and then talks passionately about getting up and doing something? That's like every stoner I knew in college."

The Archers ■

Imagine you're in a pitch meeting for a brand-new serial drama, one you hope will keep going for sixty-five years or even longer. Sitting around a conference table are some of the finest creative minds in the media, each having been told to work up a locality to start from. All soaps are set in a community in which things happen, and they have to keep happening at just the right velocity to keep people tuning in over and over again. They will require cliff-hangers and intense story lines that play out over several weeks, with sudden twists and turns that no one would have seen coming—acts of betrayal piled upon last-minute changes of heart resting atop the smoking remains of a crashed airplane in the middle of a churchful of wedding guests, just after the bride has run off with a robot replica of the best man's mum.

A half hour in, every idea has been savagely torn apart by a shadowy figure sitting at the head of the table. His caustic cigar smoke provides some cover for shame-watered eyes, as the group watch their dreams of making *Space Camp 2000* or *Wild West Prairie Veterinarians* lie scorched and crumpled on the tabletop.

Then one enterprising soul—the last to speak—pipes up: "Sir," he begins in a faltering tone, "sir, what if we made a soap opera . . ."

"Continuing drama," rasps the voice from the top end. "We never say 'soap opera.'"

"Y-yes, sir, that's what I meant, sir. I mean to say, what if we made a continuing drama about a small rural village in England? We could make it an everyday drama about farming folk . . ."

"Yeah, yeah, yeah, and they all end up kissing in the hay. I've heard it all before."

"No, sir! That is to say, yes, there will be some kissing, of course. But it's not going to be just an excuse to get beautiful people to flirt. And here's why: first, we're going to make the story lines actually focus on the genuine working lives of farming folk . . ."

"Genuine working li—"

"And *then* we're going to put everything on the radio—a wholesome and respected station like BBC Radio Four—so that no one can even see their faces. We'll have stories about actual farming problems, with genuinely good advice for any farmers listening in, because that'll be really useful when we start broadcasting just after the Second World War. But it won't just be agricultural; we'll keep abreast of the changing times, of course, and over the course of sixty-five years (and more) we'll have to explore all manner of dark story lines, but it won't feel tokenistic and it won't be rushed just to fit within the repetitive format."

"Son, are you telling me—"

"And the best thing of all, sir, is that we won't bother with all of those endless extreme cliff-hangers. In fact, most of the time the episodes will just end on the most mundane of climaxes imaginable. None of this Flash Gordon stuff; we just get to the end of the scene at the end of the episode and then—*bam!*—we're gone."

"But why will anyone want to tune in the next day?"

"Because they will come to see these people as an extended part of the family; because listening will become part of their routine, part of the fabric of their existence; because we will make sure nothing happens that smacks of sensationalism or artifice. These will be ordinary people doing ordinary things. They won't be artificially witty or suffer unlikely miscarriages of justice just to keep the ratings up. Their tragedies and celebrations will be exactly the same as those of the people tuning in. No matter what happens, what peaks and troughs the people of . . . of . . . Ambridge!—no matter what they have to put up with, they will endure, life will continue.

"And we'll put an incredibly chirpy theme song at the beginning of every episode to welcome listeners, and they'll be reassured to hear it, and eventually it will resound back down their lives to when they were tiny children and they won't be able to remember a time when they didn't know what it meant. Even people who don't listen to the show will find the theme tune reassuring. It will become an alternative national anthem for people who are far from home and in need of comfort."

"People will really do that?"

"If we get the tune just right they will. In fact, if we get the tone of this thing just so, I bet you we can get some listeners to refuse to admit it is even a drama being made at all. We'll make them feel so welcome that they'll deliberately avoid finding out the names of the actors and actresses—we'll have lots and lots and lots of characters so that it'll be hard to learn them all in any case, and we'll strongly resist any behind-the-scenes extra footage or documentaries about the making of the show. We will make this community so vivid and real, fans will feel they are sticking their heads into a comfortable world. Bad things will happen, there will be jeopardy and unpleasantness, but nothing so explosive that it lowers the tone."

"Hmm. And what if you haven't grown up with it? What then?"

"Well, that's the point. It's not as if you need to carry a lot of unspoken backstory in your mind the first time you listen. It will be just like overhearing a conversation in a café or on a bus . . ."

"A *what*, now?"

"I'm sorry, sir, I don't know what I was thinking. I meant to say, like overhearing a conversation at the Ritz . . . It won't take any time at all to catch up because even the big events will be interspersed with little ones. We'll have light and shade, tragedy and comedy, intelligence and stupidity, and a really, really good theme tune."

"And what will we call it?"

"Sir, we will call it *The Archers* and it won't even be about bows and arrows and no one will mind. Not one bit."

And then there's a long, long pause while the man at the other end of the table entirely forgets to take a drag on his cigar.

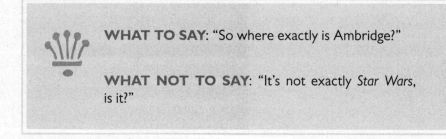

WHAT TO SAY: "So where exactly is Ambridge?"

WHAT NOT TO SAY: "It's not exactly *Star Wars*, is it?"

Emotional Reserve and Decorum ■

No nation prides themselves on an essential void in their national character as much as the British—by which I largely mean middle-to-upper-class people from the south and east of England. They'll watch as people from other nations engage in heated debates in the street, open up to strangers about an intimate medical procedure, or celebrate a happy event by shooting bullets into the sky and smile a quiet smile to themselves. It's the same quiet smile that greets a sudden burst of "Happy Birthday" in a restaurant or someone else's child crying because he let go of his balloon.

"Look at those people," the quiet smile says, "having emotions in public. What strange beasts they are. What must it be like? Alas, I shall never know." And the person will make a show of reading the menu or briskly walk on by, studiously avoiding eye contact and pretending to be invisible. Just being on the outskirts of a scene is enough to cause outbreaks of nervousness and fluttery eye panic, and that's because there is no greater social crime in British eyes—and this time I do mean British—than making a fuss.

Making a fuss is what happens in political debate when a representative of a particular point of view—be that the denial of climate change, the eradication of bigotry, or the suggestion that the moon landings were fake—over-eggs the passion in his or her argument.

Spirit is fine, zeal is positively welcomed, but if the face begins to purple and the voice becomes loud and grating, well, it's all a bit much.

The way to avoid this is to be firm but understated. Show that your arguments were created after examining evidence and testing it thoroughly and you'll be more likely to gain sympathy. This is why Church of England vicars are ingratiating rather than impassioned. Their demeanor suggests that they're secure in the knowledge that God is already looking down upon the parish with fond eyes and listening ears, so there's no point in waving their hands and shouting about it.

Mind you, in all the talk about British reserve and the stiff upper lip and all that stuff, one question very rarely gets addressed: what purpose does it serve to present an equable face at all times?

Some groups of people have had really good historical reasons to keep their feelings to themselves. Romany Travelers across Europe, with their status as outsiders confirmed wherever they went, long ago learned to absent themselves from the cares of the local communities, keeping their feelings and passions private so as not to bring trouble on themselves. And the same applies to any group for whom the balance of power leans in the other direction. Forelock tugging is an act of self-preservation, after all.

So what psychological trick are the English upper and middle classes trying to pull off, acting humble when we know they have, in their time, been among the most arrogant, most furious, most influenced by pettiness and spite, and most generally beastly of peoples that the world has ever seen? Is it conscience? Is it a way of proving to themselves and the world that they deserve to have conquered everything and everywhere because, having done so, they had the good grace not to crow about it?

No. That would involve a level of self-awareness that no conquering nation can afford to carry with it. The more likely truth is that the romantic regionalism of British life left a mark on the builders of empire. Conquering a foreign nation and seizing its assets is all very well, but the heart will always yearn for the rolling hills of the Home

Counties, with village greens and cricket pitches and endless cucumber sandwiches. However, duty must be obeyed and obligations must be met. One day there will be cucumber sandwiches again, and until then, emotions are firmly off the menu.

Take away that empire and you're left with just a bunch of guys who are still being taught not to blub, even when something really stings. Break bones, break hearts, break ranks; it is all the same. Fuss is happening, and that tends to trigger an immediate escape pod in British sympathies. After all, a breach of decorum will lead to another breach of decorum and, if left unchecked, society as we know it could easily disappear in a spluttery puff.

In this sense, being British is a lot like throwing pebbles in a pond, except you really don't want to have to throw them, you feel guilty about all the ripples messing up the shore, and actually you'd feel a lot better about it if you could be sure no one was there to see it when it happened.

WHAT TO SAY: As little as possible.

WHAT NOT TO SAY: "Oh, my God, are you okay? You seem a little, I dunno, not okay? And I can usually tell because I'm a very empathic person. All my friends tell me I'm the person they turn to when they have problems because I'm an excellent listener and I can always come up with ideas to help them get through it. In fact . . ."

Go on, give it a try.

Marmite is perhaps the most contentious item in this entire book, or at least that's what its marketing department would have everyone believe. The company has been running commercials for years claiming that people either love or hate its product, a breakfast spread that looks like boot polish and tastes like burned meat, and since then Brits have taken to labeling all manner of things that polarize opinion as "a bit Marmite."

It's all very confusing for the casual observer who just wants to know what this bizarre substance is, and why anyone would want to put it on their toast in the morning.

Problem is, the more you know about what Marmite is (and its associated international cousins Vegemite, Promite, and Bovril), the less likely anyone is to try it. Generally, the way to make a yeast extract is to add salt to a yeast suspension, and then heat it and strain the husks out. Brewers do this kind of thing all the time, and that's how Marmite was originally discovered, as an unwanted leftover from the beer industry, typically called *top fermentation* or *beer scum*.

You're licking your lips already, aren't you?

Somehow, back in the late 1800s, the German scientist Justus von Leibig decided that the meaty, umami flavor of this unwanted stuff—once it had been boiled and reduced to a brown, gooey paste—would go marvelously on a cracker, and then, incredibly, other people agreed. Lots of people.

So many, in fact, that by 1907 there were two separate Marmite factories in England, both being supplied with plentiful amounts of scum by local brewers. And astonishingly, given that it is effectively an industrial by-product, it's rather healthy too. Despite being quite high in salt, it's got folic acid and the vitamin B complex; Marmite was even used to treat beriberi during the First World War.

Sales have continued to thrive as each subsequent generation of Brits succumbs to the pungent flavor. There are Marmite-flavored crisps, Marmite rice cakes, Marmite recipes (particularly good in a thick-cut white bread sandwich with very strong cheddar); you can spoon it into hot water for an instant hot beverage; there's even a Marmite-flavored snack called Twiglets, which do look remarkably like actual twigs. Tasty for the mouth *and* the eye!

And as Marmite is difficult to get hold of in other parts of the world, the homesick expatriate Brit (assuming he or she is a "lover" and not a "hater") tends to associate it with home in a very specific way. You may find British shops, or delicatessens that sell British goods, proudly sporting the odd jar here or there, and you can be fairly sure it won't be the locals who snap them up.

Even at home, the Brits have given Marmite a central spot in their own cultural mythology. There are special edition Marmite recipes, in which edible gold flecks appear in the murk or there's a faint tang of champagne or Guinness. Marmite XO is a version that has been allowed to mature for extra depth of flavor, like a cheese. There's even Marmite toothpaste.

The packaging has attained similarly iconic status. The familiar dark glass oval jar with the yellow lid has been seized upon for all manner of marketing opportunities. You can buy anything from T-shirts to teapots. During the Queen's Golden Jubilee of 2012, a special jar was made up in the colors of the union flag, upon which the logo was changed so that it read "Ma'amite."

The only comparable condiment in international cooking is probably soy sauce, but that takes a more central role in Chinese cuisine and, besides, it's less scummy in origin.

So, while the marketing department members may continue to high-five one another at the prospect of Brits continuing to compare controversial things to Marmite, in fact it's closer to the truth to say that people either love it or have to find a way to ignore it. Or they don't really mind it. It's only a spread, after all.

WHAT TO SAY: "How much should I put on one slice of toast?"

WHAT NOT TO SAY: "So is this stuff medicine or what?"

One of the most important lessons anyone can learn about British culture is that it is vital to know your place. Knowing your place will save you a lot of heartache when the temperature drops in the room you are in, and you're not sure what you may or may not have done or said. Knowing your place will prevent you from finding out, via a third party, that you have grievously offended someone with the way you held your spoon or the fact that you spoke before you were spoken to, offered an opinion on a topic you are not considered to be in any way qualified to speak on, or sipped your tea/beer/whiskey wrongly, in the wrong place, at the wrong moment.

But don't be afraid! So long as you obey all the unwritten rules without ever demeaning yourself by asking what they may be, and never put a foot wrong or draw attention to yourself, you'll be just fine.

For those lucky enough to have been born in Britain, finding your place is usually fairly straightforward. There are people who are more working-class, salt-of-the-earth, and rough-diamondy than you, and people who are hoitier, toitier, snootier, and posherer than you. The trick is to find the people who exist at roughly the same level of la-di-da as you do, and join in with whatever they're doing. So if your immediate peers are into fishing, then fish. If they're a notch above fishing and prefer squash, play squash, but do not be tempted to try fishing. The fishing people will feel patronized and uncomfortable having a member of the hoi polloi waving their (doubtless) gold-encrusted rod around and braying in such a loud and piercing voice it'll scare off all the fish. It will be horrendously awkward, like watching a Member of Parliament trying to disco dance.

By the same token, if you're a fisher and you're tempted to try squash, do not do it. It'll be like *My Fair Lady* in the squash club bar, all eyes on the guttersnipe who wandered in off the streets with oikish clothes and rough manners. You'll feel harassed; they'll be clutching their valuables and muttering.

The Brits are obsessed with class and have developed exceptionally complicated measurements to determine exactly who belongs in which strata. It's to do with money, and social status and education and employment, and money, and accents and where you were born and how you choose to live, and money. That's basically it. People from a working-class background have the street smarts (or hedgerow smarts, if they're from rural areas), and the upper classes have all the resources, but they don't tend to interact outside of the scripts for *Downton Abbey*. It's the middle classes who worry about this stuff more than anyone, and it's their voice that rings loudest through British media.

A recent British TV hit bears this out. *My Big Fat Gypsy Wedding* was originally intended to be a one-off documentary, a look at the money and preparation that goes into ornate and lavish weddings organized by the Irish Traveler community in Britain. The bride and groom are still teenagers, and their taste tends to be flash and gaudy, as if Liberace were directing *The Dolly Parton Story*. Dresses are often so big and cumbersome they're impossible to walk in—leaving huge bruises on the brides—and the unmarried girls tend to wear extremely bright and revealing outfits to the reception. At every stage, the camera takes an anthropological view, like Sir David Attenborough stalking a wildebeest, inviting the audience to confirm or confound their own prejudices about a community on the (huge, ruffled, and sparkly) outskirts of society, one that has always been largely mistrusted or looked down upon. It was a massive hit. So was the series that followed, because few things drive TV audiences as strongly as gazing in horror at the poor taste of people from the lower orders (see: Reality TV).

Then there's the slang around class. The word *chav* is particularly troublesome. Coined in the early 2000s to mean an antisocial young man from a humble background with expensive taste, the stereotype is of a street tough with a Burberry cap and a heavy chain, wearing expensive sports gear and looking for trouble. Probably from the Romany word *chavi*, meaning child, it's a word coined in fear and distrust and has come to be used to describe any person or behavior seen as beneath the standards of the person talking. So it's always used as a slur, even when not addressed directly to someone's face:

"Oh, James, take that stupid hat off your head. You look like such a chav."

"Screw the diet, I'm having KFC tonight, like a proper chav."

"Come on, Delia, we're leaving. This place is crawling with chavs."

It's an uncomfortable situation, but a hard one to tackle head-on because the one thing people hate more than a snob is a do-gooder. So it's probably best to let everyone fight their own corner and be prepared to serve tea once all the shouting has died down.

WHAT TO SAY: It doesn't matter; it won't help.

WHAT NOT TO SAY: Nothing. People will think you are stuck up.

Taking Dogs into Pubs ■

Brits love dogs. And the ones who don't love dogs love cats. And the ones who don't love dogs or cats are probably mystified by 90 percent of the Internet and can therefore be effectively discounted from this discussion. Oh, and almost everyone likes a pub.

If only there were a way to bring all these things together at once.

Well, there is. People in British communities love to take their dogs to the pub, and this is treated as a perfectly normal occurrence in a way that would not be the case if they chose to take the same dog to the cinema or optician's or around the supermarket (although it's worth checking with the pub before you take the cast of *101 Dalmatians* out for a cheeky pint). The reasons for doing so are many and various: in the snug are the people who've nipped out to take the dog for a walk and stopped for a swift half before eventually wandering back home; then there are the shepherd and collie over by the bar, having a welcome drink at the end of a long day's work; and sitting at a small table, quietly minding their own business, are the solitary companions that refuse to be parted for as much as a minute. On the floor is a saucer with a lick of ale in it and some soggy crisps.

Some pubs are situated at one end of a well-established dog-exercising route and would lose passing trade if they banned canine visitors, so they'll lay out little bowls of water at the door to make sure every dog feels welcome. Often these will be the kinds of pubs with time-worn wooden benches and horse brasses around an open fireplace. They'll have low ceilings and a chalkboard menu with a selection of real ales and another, smaller chalkboard menu with suggestions for meals. They're homely places, essentially a large open-plan cottage into which lots of people squeeze, particularly at the weekend (see: Pubs, Inns, Bars, and Taverns).

There's probably another dog already there: a slow, tubby old Labrador or a calm, friendly border collie. Not the kind of dog that would snap at heels or jump up and knock drinks over, and definitely not the kind of dog that would attack a timid pooch, even one hiding under a bench, overcome by all the noise and smells and whining loudly. That's your dog, and it's embarrassing, given how cool the pub dog and everyone else's dogs are being. If it happens to you, the correct response is to make angry shushing noises to the dog, as if you're in charge, and to blush and say sorry to the room in that strange, strangulated voice that requires an exaggerated facial mime of saying the word and uses no consonants at all (see: Apologizing Needlessly). That's because, in a pub that allows dogs, the dog owners feel under scrutiny as responsible owners if their dog does not behave.

Incredibly, some dog-friendly pubs also have cats, and often these animals have been so well conditioned by years of having strangers and strange animals in their territory that they also remain cool and unflappable, sometimes under extreme provocation from uncool visitors (like your dog). Granted, that's what cats are like all the time anyway, but the demeanor of a pub cat is slightly different. It's as if they've signed a binding contract to be languid and unbothered by all the noise and nonsense, to put up with the indignity of a thousand wet dog noses in their intimate areas and the try-hard growls of immature bullmastiffs, so long as no one—seriously, *no one*—brings his or her cat to the pub.

WHAT TO SAY: "Oh, what a lovely dog. Do you mind if I stroke her?"

WHAT NOT TO SAY: "Excuse me, sir! Why is your dog eating my starter?"

Who knows what magical devices may be being constructed within those four wooden walls?

Gardening is a passion common to people from every part of the British Isles and across every social division. From cress on wet tissue paper in old eggshells to tiny window boxes to little green back-yards, from home-grown veg in allotments to the Chelsea Flower Show and the opulent rolling lawns, tennis courts, and stables of Surrey, the tending of a well-kept garden brings out the amateur horticulture expert in a surprising number of Brits.

And nestling comfortably amid all that garden splendor, in a quiet and unobserved corner, the humble shed. Where else is a person going to keep the lawn mower, the strimmer, and all the shearing tools required to prune privet hedges into exciting shapes? One cannot expect to leave deck chairs and fair-weather garden furniture outside all year round—where else could it go? How should one store a half-empty tin of creosote if not in a wooden hut that was once coated with the contents of the other half of the tin?

But the appeal of the shed isn't restricted solely to gardeners, and this bit isn't really about gardening. It's about men, and in particular men who feel the need to potter. It doesn't really matter what form the pottering takes; it can be making model aircraft or laying out train sets or painstakingly painting model soldiers or varnishing an old guitar until you can see your too-old-to-rock, too-young-to-die face in it. It could even be pottery or potting plants or smoking pot. Or—if you have a moment for some gratuitous wordplay—playing snooker on a miniature table (potting), putting shrimp in a ramekin (also potting), making baby toilets (pottying), or just sinking into a state of decrepitude (going to pot).

Where was I? Oh, yes, so in order to enact all of these hobbies, or simply to garner some apparently essential time away from the bosom of the family without actually going out, British men retreat to the shed.* There they can keep pigeons or read history textbooks or brew, drink, and recover from homemade ale without undue interference from anyone else. And being essentially just a wooden building in a garden, the shed is perfect for just such a purpose. Roald Dahl wrote books in his shed, Nick Drake wrote a song about a man in a shed, and Dylan Thomas wrote all of *Under Milk Wood* in a shed, although his overlooked the sea, so it is hardly typical.

Some men deck theirs out like a pub, with optics on the wall, a little radio hanging from a nail, and enough seating for a couple of

---

* British women who retreat to the shed also exist, of course, but they're slightly rarer.

mates. Others install recording equipment and egg-box sound insulation, as if their shed is an only marginally more modest Abbey Road. There may be an easel and some oil paints, or a latex goblin mask for a weekend's LARPing. Radio hams love a shed. So do actual hams, if the home meat-smokers are to be believed. Jon Earl, from Clevedon in Somerset, used his shed as an acoustic gig venue, racking up hundreds of very, very cramped performances from visiting folk acts. It's a space in which anything that can be conceived can be achieved. But mostly just conceived, because the dream is always more enticing than the reality. To that end, some sheds have simply one comfortable chair and a little fridge, or just the chair and no fridge. And some crazy fools just use the shed to keep their garden tools in.

If the Brits like to think of themselves as lionhearted—and they do—it's partly the bravery thing, but also because the males have a need to wander away from the rest of the pride and have a quiet sit-down somewhere shady from time to time.

WHAT TO SAY: "My shed is also a fully working dental surgery."

WHAT NOT TO SAY: "And where does your wife put her hobbies?"

Sport, as any cultural critic will happily confirm, is a metaphor. Most commonly it's a metaphor for a conflict of some sort and a useful way to lance the boil of tension between rival communities. But while football is a metaphor for a great big punch-up in a pub car park, and rugby is a metaphor for a great big punch-up in a pub car park while holding an ostrich egg, cricket is a metaphor for a more medieval, chivalrous kind of battle entirely.

It starts with two participants wearing protective armor on either side of a short stretch of field, each facing the other and holding a stick. Once a particular signal is given, the men charge at each other, as if about to start a joust like knights of old, except without the horses. But here's the twist: they're actually on the same team, so they just run to where the other player was just standing and, if conditions are agreeable, they run back again, scoring points as they go. That's one bit.

Then there's the attack from the opposing team. They surround the two knights, as if preparing for a guerrilla attack on their respective castles, which in the game are represented by three wooden stakes in the ground (the stumps) with two little wooden spindles resting on top (the bails). Collectively this tiny structure is called the wicket, and the players have to protect theirs at all costs, or they will be thrown from the ramparts (invited to leave the field of battle and partake in a fine tea).

Taking their cues from siege warfare, the fielding team members just wait nearby, in spots that have all been given significant (but silly) names—gully, point, fine leg, mid-wicket, square leg, and so on—while one of their number bombards the castle of one of the knights with a little red leather ball. This can arrive at great speed or more slowly, spinning around with uncanny accuracy, and it is up to the knight to swat it away using his weapon of choice. Let's call it a bat, and let us therefore call the brave knight waving it around Sir Batsman.

There are six possible things that can happen to our hero while facing an incoming ball. He can swipe and miss; he can swipe and miss and the ball can hit his stumps, destroying his castle; he can swipe and miss and the ball can hit the padding on his leg, and if it is deemed to have prevented contact with the stumps, his castle is said to have been destroyed, even if it is still standing; he can hit the ball over the boundary line at the edge of the field without it touching the floor, which means he is so great he gets six points; he can hit the ball over the boundary line with a bounce or two, which means he gets four points; or he can hit the ball somewhere within the boundary line.

If the latter happens, he and his teammate face a choice: either make a run for the sanctuary of the other person's castle—just like they did in the Crusades—or stay put and hope for the best, risking nothing and gaining nothing. If they run and leave the ramparts undefended, there's a chance there won't be a castle to come home to (depending on how close the ball is). Should that happen, the exposed batsman is out, and a new knight is brought on to take his place, bringing with him a whole new castle.

So those are the basic rules of cricket. But that's not where the chivalry and courtly customs end. Cricket is a social event. It's just a far more refined affair than certain other sports, with their beer and burgers and shouting. Certainly a village green cricket match—the most often eulogized vision of English pastoral life—is closer to a formal garden party than a rowdy gathering in a sports bar. And to be really eloquent in the ways of cricket, one must have studied *Wisden*, the cricketer's almanack (their spelling). Wikipedia is no alternative.

And this respect for the customs of the sport, as well as the sport itself, is also reflected in the way cricket is presented on TV. While football and rugby commentators talk about passion and commitment and fire and skill, cricket commentators famously talk about anything agreeable that enters their heads. While still well versed in the statistics and significance of every key event in a match, they will happily discuss the weather and the cake someone sent in, in a manner that is entirely innocent and free of manufactured enthusiasm. And there's a really good reason for this: cricket matches go on for ages, because they're a metaphor for siege warfare. Even the short ones are long, and the long ones are practically infinite. So TV commentators are not there to make the event seem more exciting; they're there to keep you company, to raise morale, and to prevent you from worrying unduly about dwindling supplies.

I have argued with ardent cricket fans about whether the sport they love so well, with its arcane wisdoms, long-standing traditions, and infinite subtleties, should be considered less a sport and more an art form. To which the only sensible answer is no, stop being silly, it's a sport. Granted, it's a hugely ritualized sport in which all the participants wear theatrical costumes, so there is some crossover with interpretive dance. But while interpretive dance can represent any human emotion imaginable, cricket is really only good for two: the thing about fighting, and the thing about being a touchstone for a mythical vision of England's green and pleasant land.

WHAT TO SAY: "I see the captain has taken his position at silly mid-off. Would you like another sandwich?"

WHAT NOT TO SAY (WHILE BOWLING): "Dunna-nunna-nunna-nunna, dunna-nunna-nunna-nunna, *Batsman!*"

The Underdog ■

Winning is boring. Triumph is an airless plateau, a vertiginous and windy peak upon which the winner feels a momentary blast of hot elation and then a freezing stab of ice to the heart when the realization hits that, once you have hit the pinnacle, there is nowhere else to go but down.

That's pretty much what people who are used to not winning would say, at any rate. They might also add that winning isn't everything, that it's the taking part that counts, and that beating other people is a recipe for a polarized society and anyway you can't build character unless you've been kicked around the block a few times. People who are used to not winning have a lot of comforting rationalizations like that. Nonwinners are more interesting, after all.

Whether it's because of a strong sentimental streak, a need for things to be seen to be fair, or because the historical narrative of Britain is that she is always a great nation and a world leader—while the actual narrative of modern politics, sport, and culture suggests a less glorious truth—nothing is guaranteed to ensnare British attention like an underdog.

Let me give you an example. In the 1988 Winter Olympic games, the United Kingdom entered the ski-jumping competition for the first time, sending over a man called Eddie Edwards. By no means a bad skier, Eddie narrowly failed to qualify for the British team in other disciplines, so he took himself to Lake Placid to train as a jumper. Unfortunately he was slightly held back by several facts: he weighed around twenty pounds more than any of his rivals; he had no money for equipment and had to borrow some boots that were so big he wore six pairs of socks to get them to stay on; he had to wear thick glasses, even while jumping, and these were prone to fogging up.

Guess what? Eddie Edwards did not win a medal. In fact, he finished last in both the seventy-meter and the ninety-meter events. What he did do was create a one-man media hurricane around himself that, in the final tally, ended with a nickname ("the Eagle"), a book (*On the Piste*), daily tabloid stories on his struggle, TV interviews all over the world, and even a pop song ("Fly Eddie Fly").

Meanwhile, the Olympic Committee changed the rules of entry after 1988 specifically so that rank outsiders like Eddie could not compete, thus sealing his underdog status forever, and their reputation as big mean meanies. Kicking an underdog? For shame.

Susan Boyle has a similar tale. It's a combination of looking entirely unheroic while doing something quite remarkable—either through natural talent or sheer naïveté—that drives all the attention. The Brits love humility, and they are vaguely suspicious of beauty, so if someone comes along who is less than conventionally attractive (and let's be clear, this simply means less than conventionally attractive for television) and is having a go at something genuinely scary or even slightly nerve-wracking (again, for television), the nation will be united behind him or her. So all it took for Susan Boyle to be an instant hit was to look as if she could not possibly be talented and then to be actually, genuinely talented. That's it. Put that voice in Katherine Jenkins's mouth, and there's no shock, no great reveal; the eyebrows stay down. In a sense the greatest emotive pull in Susan Boyle's perfect moment was the pantomime of surprise on the faces of the *Britain's Got Talent* judges. It felt as if everything was turning downside-left.

This is a common factor (no pun intended) in all TV talent shows. Every year the BBC's *Strictly Come Dancing* fields a celebrity contestant who has to learn how to *paso doble* despite having spent far too many years ordering pasta, doubly. And every year the public continues to vote them back in week after week, happily getting rid of far better dancers, because it annoys the judges. It's like the story of David and Goliath, except there are four Goliaths (one with comically pursed lips) and David is an overweight former politician or TV presenter (see: Reality TV).

Speaking of politics, nothing fires political debate in the TV age like the plucky outsider who has come along to give the two main political parties a symbolic bloody nose. It doesn't matter what the issues are or which portion of the political spectrum the party hails from—although the far right does seem to be very good at playing the underdog card—give yourself the status of political underdog, pose the comment "Yes, but you *would* say that. What if we did things my way for a change?" and you're guaranteed an interview slot on news TV, talking about the needs of ordinary hardworking people.

Of course, once power has shifted from underdog to overdog, the drive to continue support ebbs away. The big winners in music, for example, are routinely castigated for deliberately crafting their work so that it will appeal to the broadest audience possible—that's just cheating—whereas artists that do not sell well are clearly doing it for the art, and again, need the support and encouragement of their fans. When the band Elbow won the Mercury Music Prize in 2008 it signified a huge shift in their national image. Overnight they went from lost gems, rough diamonds with a lot to offer, to national treasures, fully polished and set in a big crown. And as soon as the fans had finished saying that justice had finally been done, other people started to say they were boring and, worse, boring on purpose.

But being the underdog is a perilously hard thing to let go of, once it has let go of you. The music magazine *Q* once ran a feature in which Kate Moss interviewed David Bowie. At one point both international superstars congratulated themselves on their "outsider" status, which may have been true in the beginning of their careers, and may still appear true to them, but, my crikey, it isn't true anymore.

WHAT TO SAY: "Of course, I preferred Eddie the Eagle's early work, before he became commercial."

WHAT NOT TO SAY: "I am the champion, my friend. And I'll keep on fighting till the end."

Cheering the Bad Guy ∎

Ask any British actor working in Hollywood today and he or she will tell you that the real fun in movies is playing the villain or, at a push, the antihero. True heroes have to be tough and principled and square jawed and capable and all those things, but do they really get to do anything interesting beyond saving the day? Nope. They have to play fair, they have to be sympathetic, they have to not die, and while they may get the big snog at the end, their experience is nowhere near as much fun as that of the people who get to put their lives in jeopardy in the first place.

Meanwhile, the baddy has preened and sneered and mocked and glared. He (or she) has had all the darkest lines, often delivered in the most threatening of voices with outrageous affectations of boredom or cold malice. Seeing as the movies are all about fantasy, what could be more fun for an actor from an etiquette-afflicted nation like Britain than to play so delightfully against the rules?

And rather than fretting over the public reaction to them pretending to be evil, British actors really don't mind appearing to be utter sods, chiefly because they understand that their audience—especially a British audience—love an utter sod. It's probably a hangover from pantomimes, where the evil character is openly booed and hissed from the audience whenever they appear, but the Brits particularly like a sod if he or she is clearly the sort to prize intellect over emotion, sharp wit over plain speaking, and dark mischief over do-goodery. Think Alan Rickman in *Die Hard,* or Alan Rickman in *Robin Hood: Prince of Thieves,* or Alan Rickman in the Harry Potter movies. Any time you see Alan Rickman, or any British actor, playing a baddy and looking at the hero's integrity, moral certainty, and principles with piteous disdain—as Tom Hiddleston does when Loki confronts Black Widow in the first *Avengers* movie (complete with a beautifully delivered medieval insult)—you'll have a sense of the mental terrain. Think Cruella de Vil gazing greedily at a puppy and you're there.

It's partly an accent thing too. Scottish accents are great for strong emotions and threats, Welsh accents are great for comedy and sudden nastiness, and the various American accents deliver heroism and anger beautifully, but for true chilled evil, marble slabbed and slippery with malice, you need a posh English accent with lots of sharp consonants. It's custom-made for cracking snide and then purring, "Kill them; kill them all," into a walkie-talkie, while smiling.

And the Brits have created more than their share of magnificent baddies in their time: think Iago in *Othello*; think Richard III or Lady Macbeth. Or how about grumpy old Heathcliff in *Wuthering Heights?* We may know what's causing his ill temper and we may feel some sympathy, but he's still a bad boy through and through. How about Sherlock Holmes's nemesis Moriarty, as delivered in *Sherlock* with petulant black-eyed indifference by Andrew Scott? Delicious rotters all. And that's before you count the genuinely demonic protagonists in *Frankenstein, Dr. Jekyll and Mr. Hyde,* and *Dracula.* Their names are in the title because they're the best characters in the story, just as the best *Star Wars* movie is *The Empire Strikes Back* and the worst is one of the ones with no Darth Vader in them.

Small wonder that British audiences are so thrilled to see Benedict Cumberbatch hiss and bellow his way across the screen in *Star Trek Into Darkness*; Tilda Swinton's impassive frostiness as the White Witch in *The Chronicles of Narnia: The Lion, the Witch and the Wardrobe*; or Anthony Hopkins slurping at Jodie Foster in *The Silence of the Lambs.* Ralph Fiennes excels at playing utterly diabolical swine, whether in *Schindler's*

List or the Harry Potter movies. And Ian McKellen always seems to make antiheroes of his characters, whether they are supposed to be baddies or not.

Even in cartoons, whether it's *The Jungle Book* or *The Lion King*, the actor with the plum job is always the one who gets to deliver slithering evil through the medium of his or her own dark (and yes, plummy) voice. Because even children know that being naughty is more fun than being nice.

WHAT TO SAY: "Boo!" and also "Hiss!"

WHAT NOT TO SAY: "No, Mr. Bond, I expect you to diet."

Desserts with Unappetizing Names ■

To be fair, the Brits just like desserts. To say they only like desserts with unappetizing names is to do a disservice to Angel Delight, the Bakewell tart, the syllabub, flummery, and every other sweet thing that sounds like it was handmade by the Teletubbies using all the yay! machines in their scrumminess factory.

However, pudding is a luxurious item, and one that can stand a little affectionate ribbing. So while it's preposterous to take a perfectly lovely-looking suet sponge with raisins, coat it in thick, sweet custard, and call it spotted dick, it's not because the people who made it wanted to keep it all to themselves; it's an old, old name, possibly derived from the second syllable of the word *pudding*. It's not even a reference to someone called Richard. And do you know what the same pudding is called if it contains plums instead of raisins? Spotted dog.

Mmm! Lovely custardy dog: a perfect end to a Sunday dinner.

The humble jam roly-poly—a kind of jam-filled Swiss roll that could not sound more squidgy and delicious if its proper name ended with a baby's chortle—suffered a similar fate. To keep the roll all together, people would pack it in an old shirtsleeve before boiling it. Thanks to its shape, with perhaps a little bit of jammy seepage at either end, it became known as dead man's arm, or dead man's leg, presumably for people who wear shirtsleeves as spats.

Any sweet pastry that has been filled with currants or raisins in a

A genuine spotted dick & custard.

thick black layer of sweet goodness runs the risk of being referred to as flies' graveyard, or flies' cemetery, because raisins look a bit like dead flies. There are regional variations on this; the squared-off slab version, known as a fruit slice in Scotland, or a currant slice in Northern Ireland, is referred to in the northeast of England as a fly pie.

In fact, the biscuit Brits know as a Garibaldi (see: Dunking Biscuits) has taken this whole fly theme and run with it. Depending on where you are, Garibaldis are known colloquially as fly sandwiches, dead fly biscuits, or squashed fly biscuits. And yet the humble Eccles cake, which resembles a tiny circular pastry pillow packed five-deep with raisins, has escaped with not one disgusting nickname relating to flies or anything else.

It's not even a working-class thing. Eton—one of the most prestigious educational establishments in the world—has a traditional dessert it serves at the annual cricket game against the similarly rarefied Harrow School. It's a beautifully simple affair, a mixture of strawberries, cream, and meringue pieces (although practically any summer fruit will do). Being highly educated, precision-minded young men, the pupils have elected to call this dish Eton mess. Factor in the fact that these are teenagers at an all-male school and, well, maybe you'd rather make your own at home.

One popular spiced tea cake, made in southern parts of England, languishes under the terrifically health-conscious title of lardy cake, lardy bread, or, for reasons probably connected to obesity, lardy Johns. In Yorkshire, a similarly blunt approach to the long-term effect of certain ingredients created the sconelike fat rascal. And while a similar rich-battered little cake in Newcastle would be called a singing hinny, a few miles over the border in Scotland they call them fatty cutties.

Of course, most of the best of these affectionately off-putting names come from the past, and some describe recipes that are rarely put to good use anymore. Encase a whole lemon in suet and boil it for hours, and you've got a Sussex pond pudding (which just makes it sound like a frog spawn sorbet). Add currants and it's closer to a Kentish puddle pudding.

No, hold me back before I eat your helping too.

WHAT TO SAY: "So what's really in this 'breast-milk ice cream'?"

WHAT NOT TO SAY: "Come away from this place, Myron. I can't even repeat what that man just offered to show me . . ."

Movie #2: *The Railway Children* ■

The Railway Children is an uncomplicated story that plays charmingly with a topic dear to the hearts of British culture: class, and the fear of what happens to good people when their social status is lost.

The essential story is the same whether taken from the original book by E. Nesbit or the 1970 movie adaptation by Lionel Jeffries, although the latter is really where the bulk of the affection comes from, not least because of the central performances by Jenny Agutter, Dinah Sheridan, and Bernard Cribbins.

It's the tale of a middle-class Edwardian family by the name of Waterbury, told through the eyes of the three children, Bobbie, Peter, and Phyllis. They have an idyllic life in the London suburbs, with servants and status and as much food as they could ever need. Then Mr. Waterbury—a civil servant in the Foreign Office—is accused of being a spy and arrested. Mrs. Waterbury decides to move the family to rural Yorkshire "to play at being poor for a while."

This naturally unsettles the children, who at first appear to be slightly spoiled and overly accustomed to their little luxuries, so when they all have to up sticks and move to the countryside (after getting a dressing-down from the family's own servants) it's something of a shock. The narrative hooks are by now well in force. Working-class viewers will enjoy the distress of these posh kids having to slum it, and middle- and upper-class viewers will be empathizing with that distress.

Mrs. Waterbury elects to make ends meet not by scrubbing floors but by writing short stories, because that is the class to which she belongs, and at first the family struggles to find enough to eat. Peter resorts to stealing coal from the railway yard, but prim, proper Bobbie forces him to put it back. During the upheaval the three children form an emotional attachment to the railway that runs at the end of a field near their house, waving at the passengers every day and developing a special friendship with a particular Old Gentleman on the 9:15.

They then embark on a series of adventures that effectively knock the sharp edges of privilege off them. Asking the Old Gentleman for a handout may result in the delivery of a handsome hamper of food, but it also delivers a firm rebuke from their mother, who does not approve of charity. This does not stop her from taking in a Russian dissident who has collapsed on the station platform, because she is a kind person. The distinctions, while subtle, are clear. Charity bad; compassion good.

The children take this as their model in becoming morally upstanding and independent citizens themselves. They prevent a train from running into a landslide, the Old Gentleman turns out to have connections that can reunite the Russian with his family, and they save a young lad who has collapsed in the train tunnel while taking part in a "fox and hounds" paper chase (who turns out to be the Old Gentleman's grandson).

Perks, the mostly affable working-class station manager, acts as a form of reality check for the three, as he also gives them a valuable lesson in class conflict when they conspire with the local community to celebrate his birthday with useful and thoughtful gifts. At first he considers their efforts to be a humiliation, an act of charity from a community that looks down their noses at him and his family, but eventually he comes to realize that everyone gave what they wanted to give and he is enormously touched. It's at this point that Bobbie discovers her father has been sentenced to a long spell in prison and won't be coming back.

Except the Old Gentleman has once again worked his magic, and one day the children are surprised to discover that everyone on the 9:15 is waving excitedly at them. Bobbie wanders down to the station and spots a tall man on the platform, obscured by smoke. In a scene that continues to draw wet eyes and red faces from British fathers of all ages, she wails, "Oh, Daddy, my Daddy!" and rushes into his arms.

That's all there is to it. Three privileged kids discover the life-enriching effects of mixing with the lower orders, being good in a crisis, not asking for handouts, and being kind to everyone they meet. It's the same plot as *Cars* or *Doc Hollywood* or any film in which the common good beats down personal entitlement.

But the charm of *The Railway Children* comes from its placement in an era untouched by the ravages of either world war, a supremely confident, and entirely innocent, moment (compared to the horrors that were to follow) when the British were the dominant power in the world and felt like they were doing a good and moral job.

It's also a moment from which most of the dominant clichés of English culture are drawn. There's the love of the countryside, affection for the romance of steam railways, and the strict observance of the rules of etiquette and manners. The cottage the Waterburys live in is not thatched, but it might as well be. So it's almost a set text for romanticized Englishness; and it's a model of class friction. A view that is only exaggerated if you take the slightly sharp view that Bobbie's anguish at the end seems to come as much from the relief of being rescued from their horrific life among the poor folk as from the joy of seeing her father again.

I mean, you can take that view if you want. I'll be over here dabbing my eyes again.

WHAT TO SAY: "So none of those kids thought to get a paper round?"

WHAT NOT TO SAY: "Those girls stopped that train by waving their underwear at it? And this is a movie for kids?"

Innuendo ■

Rather than embark on a lengthy history of the British love of talking about sex without talking about sex—taking in pantomimes (see: Cross Dressing), seaside postcards (see: Saucy Seaside Postcards), dirty songs, music hall comedians and an entire film franchise (the *Carry On* comedies)—let's imagine I'm putting up a tent and I'm telling you how it's all going. This will hopefully not only shed some light on things, it may even reveal all, and when I say all I mean *everything*.

I could start by pointing out that I've laid a sheet down and I'm running my hands along my pole, up and down, gently checking that everything is firm and smooth, until it is fully erect. Then, having had a gentle feel about to make sure I'm in the right area, I carefully stick it right up between the flaps, so the spike goes into the little hole. It's a tight fit and a little bit fiddly to get the angle just right, but it's very satisfying once it's done.

I brace my pole with a little wiggle—we don't want to go off half-cocked—then get to work doing the same thing in the other hole, so both ends have been firmly buttressed, leaving me free to devote my attention to the other areas. For a while, you'll find me beavering away, facedown and working around the outskirts with a collection of devices I keep in a little bag. I'll start by manually driving my prong through the undergrowth, and once I am satisfied that it has gained a decent purchase, I'll commence hammering away until it is time to roll over and change position.

An aside: I find if there are too many people around while I'm getting it up, I tend to get a bit tense and stiffen. It only takes a bent peg or an unexpected leak for things to become a little heated and that's when the vulgar language starts to fly. There again, it's less fun on your own, so it's best to ask just one close friend (or two, if you're sure you can trust them to cooperate) for a hand with the fiddly bits.

Anyway, once all the pounding is done, the material should be straining on all sides. It's at this point I start to pull on the first guy I can lay my hands on, untangling and then stretching the dangling hawser until it is practically rigid, and then I whack my spike in, holding on tight all the while. There are a few guys located all around the tent and if they're not kept nice and stiff, the whole thing will go limp and collapse after even the most gentle blow. I've also got to be a bit careful that I don't accidentally knock the guy off the head of my spike, otherwise I'll have to take hold again, slip my finger in the hole, and pull until I can feel the strain, then slip the guy's end over the top with my fingers.

When all the guys have been pulled and tethered, I gently tug at the zip, being careful not to catch it on anything on the way down, and, having carefully removed all obstacles and ensured there are no barriers to entry, stick my head all the way in. I may have taken the precaution of pulling a hood up for protection first, particularly if it's really wet, and I'll enter tentatively at first, but with growing confidence, until I'm all the way inside.

That's when the inflatables come out. I spread them on the floor, put the nozzle in the correct flange, and start pumping and pumping for all I am worth. This can be tiring work, and I'll be red faced and sweaty before too long. With each thrust, my hands roam up the back, across the top, and down to the bottom, squeezing and stroking, until I am finally happy at how firm everything feels. When I have pumped until I just can't pump anymore—it's quite a workout—I pull the nozzle out, jam in a plug, and then I can just throw myself facedown on the rug, panting and spent.

Conclusion: If you meet any Brits and they mention how much they enjoy innuendo, make sure you give them one.

 WHAT TO SAY: "Would anyone like to nibble on my juicy pear?"

WHAT NOT TO SAY: "Pear as in fruit, obviously. Grow up."

Y ou may think you are attached to your dog; you may have feelings
toward your cat that border on obsessive; but trust me, no one is
as soppy about animals as the British. Or at least, if they are, their soppiness won't be as sharply juxtaposed with the unsoppy way they treat
humans.

In fact, legislation preventing cruelty to animals arrived on the
British statute books long before legislation preventing cruelty to either children or vulnerable adults. This is partly for stout business
reasons—animals were transport, livelihood, and food—although
sentimentality does come into play too. Even now, British TV plays
heartrending commercials every day for dog rescue charities or cat
sanctuaries, plus public awareness movies about leaving dogs in a hot
car without cracking a window, and the narrative is always the same:
How could humans treat us this way? What have we ever done?

Brits adore animals. They knit things for their pets; they embark
on public crusades to protect not just endangered species but individ-
ually disadvantaged creatures. They build special bridges and cross-
ings for bats, hedgehogs, and frogs and create legislation that protects
certain animals from being disturbed once they've made a nest in an
attic space or loft. Rather than making *Lady and the Tramp*, with its
unforgiving dog pound and cruel dogcatchers, they write *101 Dalmatians*, in which the baddy is a cold stepmothery baggage who wants a

puppy-hair coat. And they make heartwarming TV shows based in Battersea Dogs and Cats Home, which is that same unforgiving dog pound, only far, far nicer.

British children's literature is riddled with anthropomorphized animals that speak and interact, either in an animal re-creation of human communities—*The Wind in the Willows*, for example, or the tales of Beatrix Potter, starring Peter Rabbit, Squirrel Nutkin, and Jemima Puddle-Duck—or in a rationalized version of feral nature, as you'd find in *The Jungle Book*. Then there are the narrator animals that exist in trying times: the horses in *Black Beauty* and *War Horse*.

George Orwell knew exactly what he was doing when he chose a farmyard as his metaphor when satirizing totalitarianism in *Animal Farm*. It's almost as if an affection for our four-, two-, and sometimes no-legged friends replaces the kind of demonstrable, uncluttered public outpourings of warmth and kindness that other nations reserve for, y'know, people. Because animals can't be guilty of anything malicious, in the way that humans apply the term, it's harder to be tricked or hoodwinked and therefore defenses can come down more fully. A cat may throw up on your pillow, but he will never defraud you of your life savings.

Take the singer Morrissey, who epitomizes so many of what are typically considered to be the great English virtues. He's bookish, soft-spoken, poetic, and misty-eyed about the past. But two topics are guaranteed to get his (presumably very well-treated) goat: one is the royal family, of which he is not a fan, and the other is cruelty to animals. In the latter case he's so committed to the cause that he refuses to play in venues where meat is sold, or cooked for the crew, or at festivals where burger vans are visible from the stage. His feelings on international issues of animal mistreatment such as whaling, vivisection, seal clubbing, and factory farming are heated and venomous, to the point of wishing similar treatment for whalers, vivisectionists, seal clubbers, and factory farmers. And while he can be something of a single-issue bore on this topic, his views are entirely in keeping with the passionate rhetoric of the British animal lover.

Calls for fund-rasing or direct action against vivisection, foxhunting, badger culling, and the like, frequently emphasize the cruelty to the animals. The pro-foxhunting/badger-culling lobby claim that this misty-eyed view of country affairs is a wrongheaded interference and often state the opposing case with equal vehemence. This pitting of tradition against sentimentality is a recipe for a colossal dustup. But foxhunting and badger culling are not the only animal-related public scandals in British society. In 2013, the news was dominated with stories of frozen meals, in particular beef lasagne, having been contaminated with horse meat in European processing plants. That's because, despite the long list of things they definitely will put in their mouths (see: Offal), the British don't eat horses. They love them too much.

Every summer, during the long parliamentary recess that means hot political news stories tend to be fairly thin on the ground, one of the tabloid papers finds and publicizes an animal that has been treated poorly, most commonly in a country with laxer animal protection laws and a cavalier approach to pet ownership. Take the 2010 campaign *The Sun* ran to save a Russian donkey by the name of Anapka, who was being regularly hoisted into the sky in a paragliding PR stunt. Or indeed the 1987 campaign, run in full elbow-jostling competition between *The Sun* and the *Daily Star*, to rescue another donkey, this one called Blackie.

Some of the more right-wing papers have tried to capitalize on this trend by running provocative stories about restaurants and cafés that served halal meat, implying that any adherence to traditional Muslim forms of slaughter (for commercial reasons) was the thin end of a wedge, the fat end of which was Britain becoming an Islamic nation. Naturally the stories spent a lot of time discussing the method of execution in tones of mock outrage, and these are the stories that sell their papers.

They may be overheated examples, but they're driven by a hard commercial truth: the British love animals and they will set the dogs on anyone who dares to claim otherwise.

WHAT TO SAY: "If you want to be in a dependent relationship with someone far needier than you, get a dog. If you want to be the dog, get a cat."

WHAT NOT TO SAY: "I'm sorry, you can't let him sit there. I have allergies."

The British Christmas ■

Note the qualifier there. This isn't about the universal joy of Christmas, as observed in all participating cultures in exactly the same way all over the world. No, while the Brits are as sentimentally attached to the idea of a season of goodwill—and end-of-year blowout, the birthday of Jesus Christ, and a big pile of presents under a sparkly tree—as anyone, they do things their own way, maintaining their own traditions and looking rather blankly at yours.

They have even invented their own extra day to add to the festivities: Boxing Day, the day after Christmas Day. It was originally a day put aside for the servants of well-to-do households to see their own families, and for St. Stephen's Day offerings to be left at the local church, but these days it is simply a day for recovering from the excesses of Christmas Day. Some families leave the opening of presents until Boxing Day, but this is very rare and must result in early-onset stress ulcers for the children involved.

Boxing Day is also the first day of the sales, so shops can get rid of all the stock they brought in especially for Christmas. So while some Brits will blearily rise at noon on Boxing Day and try as hard as they can to focus on the kettle, others will have been up since 4:00 A.M., queuing to grab a bargain cashmere cardigan or fancy jacket. But that's all in the post-Christmas lull. There's a wealth of festive tradition to wade through before we even get to Boxing Day. Here are ten things it would not be a British Christmas without:

Mince pies

For the uninitiated, these are not made from actual minced meat, but sweet mincemeat—a black jam made of dried fruit, citrus peels, and sugar (see: Desserts with Unappetizing Names). Brits talk fondly of the first mince pie of the season (which can begin anytime from late September on, depending on how quickly the supermarkets can clear their summer stock from the shelves); then comes the excitement of the first mince pie on Christmas morning, accompanied by a glass of Buck's Fizz; and the regret with which the very last one is eaten before it is time to turn over a new leaf on January 1. After that, it's back to the Eccles cakes and fly pie.

Hoping for Snow

Opinions vary sharply on snow depending on whether you're in the north or the south of the UK. Southerners tend to wish for a white Christmas, and news stories and special weather reports will be crossing fingers and scanning the sky for the peculiar bruising that snow clouds carry. Northerners, particularly those in Scotland, tend to accept the months of sleet and snowdrifts with weary resignation, as if to say, "Yes, a white Christmas is very nice, but a white *always* is just annoying." And because it doesn't happen very often, people living on the south coast, particularly down in the far west, tend to find the experience of actual snow, even for Christmas, to be deeply unsettling (pun intended).

Pantomime

The season for panto—a British theatrical confection that predates its own association with Christmas—tends to run from the beginning of December right the way through until March (see: Cross-Dressing).

Father Christmas

The British know who Santa Claus is; they just choose to address him by his familial title instead. Okay?

Christmas Crackers

Always a fiddly thing to explain. The Christmas cracker is a shiny, colorful tube, open at either end, with three chambers that are tethered by a cardboard strip that has a tiny gunpowder charge on it.

The central chamber contains a tissue paper crown, a small toy or puzzle, and a piece of paper with a joke on it. At a specified point during Christmas dinner—it could be right at the beginning, in between courses, or at the very end: family traditions vary hugely—everyone picks up a cracker at one end and offers the other end to someone across or around the table. They have a short tug-of-war, and the cracker splits, making the gunpowder bit give off a slight cracking bang. The person left holding the central chamber then has to put the crown on, play with the toy, and read out the joke.

Christmas cracker jokes are famously terrible and based on appalling puns. This kind of thing:

Q: What does Simon Cowell like best about his breakfast?

A: The Eggs Factor

Sometimes the joke paper has a riddle instead. These aren't any better, but that's part of the fun.

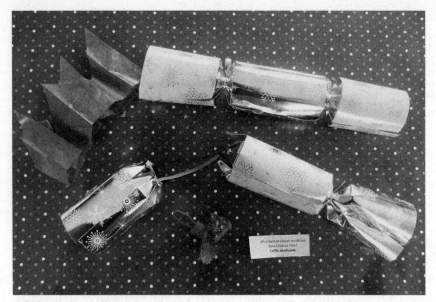

The anatomy of a Christmas cracker.

Christmas Dinner

Turkey is the most popular roast meat for the Christmas dinner, but even if the meat is the same across all British tables (and it's not unheard-of for nonvegetarian families to go for duck, goose, or pork instead) subtle variations are to be found in the other dishes on the table. Goopy white bread sauce, for example; parsnips; or pigs in blankets, which is, for the British, the name given to tiny sausages wrapped in bacon. Christmas dinner is also traditionally the one time of year when people are prepared to consider eating Brussels sprouts.

The table holds no green bean casserole and no candied yams. Some people do roast and serve the vegetable Americans most commonly use to make candied yams, but it's called a sweet potato and it is not something that requires marshmallows.

Christmas Pudding

The word *pudding* doesn't mean the same thing in Britain that it does elsewhere. As well as being a catchall term for dessert, *pudding* refers to a steamed or boiled dish that is cooked in muslin; so you can have steak and kidney pudding, and it won't be anything like a meat blancmange at all. Christmas pudding is a steamed sponge made with citrus zest and dried fruit and booze. It is traditionally served on fire, thanks to a dousing in brandy beforehand, and with coins buried in the mix for good luck. It's important that you know both these facts before tucking in, especially if you wear dentures or an immaculately lacquered beard.

The pudding is served with either brandy butter (sweet butter with brandy in it), brandy cream (cream with brandy in it), or brandy sauce (a white custard; may contain more than trace amounts of brandy).

The Queen's Speech

At 3:00 P.M. on Christmas Day, the queen addresses the nation, as the reigning monarch has done almost every year since 1932. It's usually a summary of the year, pointing out particular highlights and suggesting ways in which we could all be nicer to each other in the year ahead. Time the Christmas dinner correctly and it's also a cue for the grown-ups to commence snoozing in front of the TV, only waking up halfway through the big Christmas Day movie.

Christmas Cake

This is a fruitcake—often drenched in brandy—covered in marzipan and thick white icing. The sort of thing you might have at a wedding, except the bride is a snowman and the groom is a tree.

Christmas Songs

Every year songwriters and pop stars try to add to the small pile of eternally popular British Christmas hits, songs that are fit to hold their elf-hatted heads up alongside such giants as "That One by Mariah Carey," "The One about Chestnuts and Open Fires," and "White Christmas."

The British canon includes "I Wish It Could Be Christmas Every Day" by Wizzard, "Merry Xmas Everybody" by Slade, "Last Christmas" by Wham! and "Happy Xmas (War Is Over)" by John Lennon and Yoko Ono. But the single most popular festive song, the one that reenters the charts every year and blasts from every British shop from October onward, is "Fairytale of New York" by the Pogues and Kirsty MacColl. It's not the most family friendly of choices, containing ripe language from a drunken row between the two protagonists in the song, but it's got all the vinegary chagrin of real Christmas, the air of bitterness and regret that comes after a family row, and a note of optimism when the Christmas pudding is brought in. It's the palate cleanser to go with the season's traditional ton of creamy sweetness; and therefore, despite being written by an Irish man about two down-at-heel New Yorkers, it distills the essence of British festivities perfectly.

WHAT TO SAY: "Happy Christmas!"

WHAT NOT TO SAY: "It's okay if I just heat the Christmas pudding up in the microwave, right?"

James Bond and Sherlock Holmes ■

B ritish fiction's two most famous solvers of cryptic mysteries share a
definite link, one of attitude, morality, and temperament. Crudely
put: they are both sods. Charming sods, delightful sods, but sods
nonetheless.

Holmes is a rotter simply as a side effect of his maniacal need to
instill order on everything. This compulsion not only to notice everything but also to ascribe most likely motive to it and make deductions
based upon those motives drives out all possible human need for admiration, confirmation, or affection. His need to be seen as the best
comes from the scientific observation that everyone else is slower and
less methodical than he is.

Consequently he is brash, arrogant, quick-tempered, and impul-
sive. If his superpower were in his muscles and not his brain, he'd just
be a bully; but because he's a chippy smart-arse who solves murders,
people adore him. That said, he's the kind of man who can really sustain only one true friendship because groups of friends would not put
up with him dominating the room in the way that he does. Holmes's
one acquiescence to vanity is to befriend Dr. Watson, whose diaries tell
the story of Sherlock's life and work. So he's not quite a lone wolf, but
he's certainly a packless alpha male (dragging a biographical blood-
hound in tow).

Bond is slightly different, but not by much. No less of a sociopath and with no less of a cruel streak, he expects the company of women as his reward for being the best at what he does. Actually, *company* is perhaps the wrong word; what Bond craves is the *acquisition* of women, and we don't really know whether he is the best or not, but he certainly does not recognize any rivals for the title.

The Bond franchise may have taken great steps to give the women in the films a sense of personal autonomy regarding their utter inability to resist the charms of this known player—mainly by using innuendo-laden names like Pussy Galore, Plenty O'Toole, Xenia Onatopp, or Holly Goodhead. The day the producers of the Bond movies realized their best hope to replace Sean Connery in the lead role was an actor with the actual name Roger Moore must have been a fine day indeed—but his cavalier treatment of his conquests before and after the credits roll merely serves to prove that they have as much individual importance to him as a single bullet in his Walther PPK, or one good martini.

Speaking of which, Bond goes around the world gleefully dispatching henchmen and rotters with a cold disregard for human life and applying the letch fingers to almost every woman he meets—always with a one-liner ready, because a British man without a noticeable sense of humor is no kind of man at all—and yet the one thing he is guaranteed to get snippy about is if someone makes his cocktail wrong. Mr. T could not pity a fool as much as Bond does, should his martini be stirred, not shaken. The Daniel Craig rebooted Bond even got to make a gag out of this, by getting James to snap, "Do I look like I give a damn?" when asked—by a bartender, no less—if he preferred his drink shaken or stirred. But he still got shirty about it. Like a sod.

So what is it about these two imperious swine that has so captured the British fancy? Well, Sherlock Holmes represents British scientific exploration. He's a boffin, a swot, and he was created in an age when British engineering and scientific exploration were the envy of the world. Sherlock is not the toughest guy in the room—although there have been some efforts to change this, most recently in Guy Ritchie's

Sherlock Holmes films, where Robert Downey Jr.'s Holmes is quite the bare-knuckle boxer—but he's the smartest, and he possesses the withering scorn of the Great British Scold too.

It's no coincidence that Holmes has been resurrected so many times recently, now that we're in an era when science is under attack from people who feel that they know what they know, and that this is enough knowledge to be getting on with. By contrast, Holmes is a poster boy for angry facts, an arch refuter of all codswallop, and while the Brits are as susceptible to hokum as anyone else, they often like to think of themselves as rationalists first. With Holmes, the subtext is always "Well, you would believe that, wouldn't you?" which is a very lofty perch from which to view the world.

And then there's Bond. By no means the cleverest person in the room, or the wittiest, he succeeds because he's the most confident, and he has no concern about the consequences of his actions. He was invented during an era of worry for the British. The Second World War had just ended, espionage was the new front line, and the most effective weapon against global superpowers (or decadent supervillains with remote island bases) was sheer nerve and a decent local phrasebook.

Manners, deportment, etiquette, the ability to play a decent hand of poker, and a fairly snotty attitude toward cocktails: Bond is a cad and a rogue, but he's cool and English and he won't stand for any nonsense; he drives mouthwatering cars as if he doesn't care that they're going to get smashed up (see: Cars and *Top Gear*); and he always gets the girl. He can travel the casinos of the world in a tuxedo, being rude and beating off all comers (pause; eyebrow raise to camera). Why wouldn't the Brits love him?

Ian Fleming knew this, because he had been a kind of proto-Bond himself, and he poured all of that experience and concern into a character who would also never, ever admit to being rattled. Bond's appeal is that he remains unsentimental even when everything is falling apart around him. He is an inspirational figure for the ideal of the well-traveled Englishman dismayed at the collapse of empire. And the films are as much a send-up of what Bond sees as the idiocies of the rest of the world as they are super action movies.

Bond and Holmes are not only antiheroes, they carry their own critics along with them, shrugging in exasperation to the audience, as if to say, "*This* guy, eh?" Dr. Watson's loyalty is sorely stretched at times, and yet he remains solid and dependable, while endlessly pointing out his friend's many social flaws. Bond spends a lot more time alone in the field, but when he reports back to base, his is not a hero's welcome. No matter that he has saved the world many times, he'll still feel the sharp edge of the quartermaster's tongue if that Aston Martin got blown up. And M isn't exactly one for the high-fives either.

So the message from Holmes and Bond is partly that being extraordinary doesn't excuse being a sod, even when you've saved the day, but also that being a sod does look like a hell of a lot of fun (see: Cheering the Bad Guy).

WHAT TO SAY: "The game is afoot!"

WHAT NOT TO SAY: "Mr. Bond, I'd like you to meet my new assistant, Jenny Talworts."

Anyone Who Gets a Round In ■

In sitcoms it's always the way the restaurant bill is divided up that causes the most interpersonal stress between friends. Some people want to split things evenly; others want to pay for only the food and drinks they personally consumed. There's no right answer, glowering happens, and everyone ends the night feeling slightly tense and tetchy with one another.

It's much the same in pubs, except the British pub is a community hub—whether literally, in rural areas, or socially, in urban ones—so the stakes are far higher and the consequences far greater if mistakes occur. The nature of social drinking is that the people around a pub table immediately become an exclusive gang. You get your circle together, someone offers to get a round in, and that means eventually everyone will, at some point, be expected to return the gesture. Anyone who is willing to get his (or her) round in early will automatically be considered a good sort. It's a sign of not getting above your station, of considering yourself one of the gang, and so it's an easy win for newcomers to an established social group, and, what's more, they'll all have to buy you drinks all night, and that'll make you feel popular. Considering the fact that the British are notoriously slow in offering positive feedback or effusive greetings—in many areas of the UK it is considered more than acceptable to hail anyone, from old friends to new sexual partners, with the catchall grunt "Alright?" to which the expected reply is the similarly expressive "Alright?"—this is not a feeling to be taken for granted.

Some British people still weigh up the relative worth of their fellow humans according to the willingness with which they get the drinks in. They'll offer a warm, but brief, appraisal that concludes, "And he is always quick to get his round in," as if this were on a par with saving his platoon from certain death thanks to a particularly selfless and heroic deed.

And the reverse is also true. The very worst crime of etiquette one can commit in a pub—beyond fighting, perving, spilling drinks, and being a crashing bore—is to fail to buy your round. Woe betide anyone who takes the drinks he's offered, keeps schtum whenever someone asks who's getting the next round in, and then leaves early before it's his chance to offer reciprocity. Woe and raised eyebrows are also on the cards for the person who lingers just outside the pub as everyone walks in, so that he's at the back of the pack when everyone reaches the bar. He may get away with it once—but it will be duly noted; he may get away with it twice—but it will be openly discussed behind his back. The third time, that's when the trouble starts. He'll get a reputation for having short arms and long pockets, for being tighter than Pavarotti's trousers, for being (whisper it) a skinflint.

Being stingy carries such a social stigma that tales of legendary tightwads are handed around in hushed tones. Rod Stewart has been said to be particularly parsimonious—apparently he's the "let's just pay for what we ordered" person who will "forget" money for the tip and the champagne—to the extent that Ronnie Wood, Rod's former colleague in the Faces, famously referred to him as being "as tight as two coats of paint." Being in a band together, the two of them would have had the "are we doing rounds?" conversation, and Rod must have disappointed Ronnie with his answer.

The "are we doing rounds?" conversation is the miser's safe escape from the social minefield of pub protocol. It's a way of establishing that no one is going to be indebted to anyone else tonight, because you already know you can't fulfill your end of the bargain. The best thing about the "are we doing rounds?" conversation is it takes place at the very beginning of the evening, when it's still acceptable to opt out and when everyone is pleased to see each other and excited about the night ahead. In marked contrast to the "are we dividing this equally or just paying for what we had?" restaurant conversation, it's possible to get "are we doing rounds?" sorted very quickly, with the designated driver and the concerned parent with an early start being given a free pass because soft drinks are so much cheaper. Small groups of mutually supportive round-getters can form quickly, with everyone else getting their own drinks (or even forming a fruit juice subgroup that gets its own rounds more slowly and with far less expense), and the night can continue unsullied by petty bickering.

Mind you, the canny drinker with an eye for social sport can still employ a few dodges here and there, especially if he wishes to avoid having to carry a wobbly tray of full glasses across a packed pub, such as the one when you've just arrived at the pub and you slip a twenty-pound note into a friend's hand and get him to get the drinks while you secure a table. But these are just minor points of protocol, the sort of trifling victory no one will be upset about conceding.

And you do still end up getting a round in, so there's no harm done.

WHAT TO SAY: "Who wants a top-up?"

WHAT NOT TO SAY: "Ah, I appear to have mislaid my wallet. Could one of you get me a brandy and I'll get the first round next time?"

Bell Ringing ■

A pervasive myth has long held that the British think of themselves principally in medieval terms. They live in small, isolated, rural villages, inside thatched cottages near a village green where they like to sit out with a picnic hamper, eat pork pies, and drink ginger beer, while the ruffians from a neighboring village are given a firm thrashing at cricket.

Sorry, did I say medieval? I meant hobbity.

In fact, that's chiefly an English (as opposed to British) archetype and, like all good generalizations, it contains just enough evidence to be suggestive of the truth—there are indeed many villages in the UK that have thatched cottages, village greens, and wickerwork—while conveniently ignoring the millions of people whose lives are not, and never have been, anything like that. Some Brits don't even like ginger beer.

But one aspect of the great mythical English village resonates through to even the most urban of environments, and it's all to do with bells.

Out in the British countryside are many, many churches. You've seen *The Vicar of Dibley*, right? Well, it's like that: ancient buildings that have served as a moral fulcrum for generations, possibly with something of a leaky roof problem and very often with a bell tower of some description. Those bells have rung out for significant events in the community: baptisms, marriages, and deaths being the most common. And sometimes they are just rung for the joy of ringing.

The same is true in cities, with bells taking a particularly prominent role in London mythology. The nursery rhyme Oranges and Lemons runs down a list of the bells of various London churches, and some people claim you cannot call yourself a true Cockney unless you were born within the sound of the bells of the church at St. Mary-le-Bow, Cheapside (known as Bow bells).

And bell-ringing societies abound across the country. People from all walks of life (sort of) and all ages (more or less) come together to learn how to create intricate peals and ring the changes. They come to ease the stresses and strains of the working week by yanking on a massive rope and making a terrific row with some mates. And no one can criticize them for that.

So you can hear bells in the country and you can hear them in the towns and cities. But there are two particularly magical times to hear church bells, two moments at which those resonant chimes are at their most appealing.

The first is a Sunday morning in which no one has a hangover, there's nothing pressing that needs doing, and everyone is in a good mood. These are the bells that say, "Congratulations, you are about to embark on a British Sunday. Expect little, ask for less, and you will be duly rewarded."

The second is slightly more subtle, less easy to define in universal terms, and a lot more personal.

The author Dodie Smith coined the phrase "twilight bark" to describe the amount of noise dogs make in reaction to other, faraway dogs when the light starts to fade in the day. It's in *101 Dalmatians* as a device for the dogs to carry messages across a great distance. A peal of church bells at twilight on a fine evening—spring, summer, autumn, and even winter if there's a decent frost and the air is dry—has the same resonant, pregnant quality as the twilight bark. Time may as well not bother counting for a bit; what the bells do is provide an audio map to the place some people call home.

In London or Glasgow or Swansea, that map may also feature the wheezing rasp of heavy traffic, car horns blaring, high-heeled shoes on paving slabs, and the distant rumble of trains. In Shillingford, Praze-An-Beeble, and Bagginswood it may be pockmarked with the lowing of cattle, the sharp caws and hoots of evening birdsong, and the hissing of insects in the long grass, but it's the bells that draw all of those details in. It's the bells that cast the spell of mythical England.

Play a recording of the church bells of home to a lost British traveler and he or she will be back on that warm grass listening to the warm crack of leather on willow before you can say, "But I thought you said you were from Birmingham."

WHAT TO SAY: "Shh! Is that . . . Are those . . . Chorlton-cum-Hardy? Here?!"

WHAT NOT TO SAY: "Of course, most churches use recorded bells these days."

The Royal Family ■

Pulling together a coherent picture of how the British feel about their own royal family is like trying to work out how they feel about the Beatles. The history of the nation is unimaginable without their presence, their victories are embedded in the fabric of cultural life—although in the case of King William I, his victory is embedded in the fabric of the Bayeaux tapestry—and all their follies and quirks have been absorbed into popular myth.

But with the Beatles it's easier to discuss and assess their contribution to British life because they made a palpable thing. They created music that people can still listen to and have an opinion on. Whether you enjoy that music now or not—and enormous amounts of British people still do—is immaterial. It is there for future generations to judge, while reading up on the social revolution that blossomed in their wake and grumpily answering test questions like "The cultural impact of the Beatles was created by the postwar baby boom and has been entirely exaggerated by it. Discuss."

With the royals the contribution is less clear, apart from the Queen's Honors List and the Queen's Speech on Christmas Day (see: The British Christmas). However, that does not mean their actions are of little consequence or interest to British people. The royal family are there to represent the nation, and this does cause heated debate about the extent to which they do that and whether they should continue. There are fans and there are critics, and in between there are people who are interested but not passionate, people who are passionate but not interested, and somewhere, right in the middle, a woman polishing her car in Dudley.

Having had their role restricted from ruling to reigning, the royal family have become, in the greater public imagination at least, a state-funded soap opera. There have been moments of warmth and empathy, moments of flintiness and discord, and one enormous moment of high drama that came to entirely refresh the public's relationship with the modern monarchy.

The period following the death of Princess Diana was a strange time to be British. It came at the end of a long media scrum around her every move, one that was wearying to watch from the outside, so it can only have been exhausting from within. After years of declining affection for the royals—best represented by the strong national debate over the repair bill after a fire damaged Windsor Castle in 1992, the queen's self-confessed "annus horribilis"—public scorn for Prince Charles and his mistress Camilla Parker Bowles, and a tell-all autobiography, a postdivorce Diana had given a recent interview in which she discussed moving away from the royal family, saying, "I'd like to be a queen in people's hearts but I don't see myself being queen of this country."

Imagine if an actress or pop star said something like that now. No matter how beloved a figure they may appear to be in the media, imagine how annoyed some people would be at the hubris in a statement like that. And it arrived when strange stories about Diana were a daily fixture of the news. The trouble with a tiring media scrum is that often it's the person at the center who appears to be creating all the mayhem, not the camera people and reporters and editors—who would claim to be acting out of public demand anyway. Nonetheless, at the moment Diana died, she was not the queen of British hearts. Her death was a huge shock, but it didn't become the iconic national tragedy until slightly later on. It took a short while for emotions to shift from "What has she gone and done *now*?" to "Good-bye, England's rose."

And that transition was created entirely by a congregation that had not been represented until that point. News people believed that the national conversation around Diana was about her being a fallen princess who had let fame go to her head a bit. Her charity work, her public appearances to support causes close to her heart, and her willingness to be visibly among the people less fortunate than herself may have raised cynical eyebrows among small-r republicans, but for a good deal of the population it proved she was a people person and a force for good. Her sudden departure, leaving her two boys behind, prompted that silent cohort into action. They began to lay flowers outside Kensington Palace and Buckingham Palace. Bunch after bunch, wreath after wreath, over a million in total, until it became clear that this was a national wake.

That was the moment at which the conversation around the royal family changed. This heartland support was taken as a cohesive movement, an outpouring of national grief, and the media subtly adjusted their coverage to appear more humbled. Even the queen, who had resisted making a public proclamation about the accident, had to acknowledge that usual protocol was insufficient for the public mood, and addressed the nation. Those small-r republicans with a sense of self-preservation also read the mood and shushed up for a bit.

And that's essentially the way things have stayed. Having been at the center of an international tragedy, the general public view is that the next generation—Princes William and Harry, and also Princesses Eugenie and Beatrice—have suffered enough and deserve every moment of happiness coming their way, and people are more than willing to help them celebrate their successes. William's marriage to Kate Middleton was a way for everyone to reset the clock, take a step back from the stern politics, and wallow in some heartwarming pageantry on a global stage. Plus it was a free bank holiday and a chance for a knees-up, and that's always welcome.

William has now assumed the greater part of his mother's charitable image in the public eye, as well as furnishing the nation with another fairy-tale princess and heirs to his throne, while Harry maintains the fine tradition of royals who get a bit daft when drunk and end up on the front page of the tabloids. The monarchy is in very safe hands.

WHAT TO SAY: "Do you think we could change the national anthem? It's a bit dreary."

WHAT NOT TO SAY: "Queen of hearts? Was there even a job vacancy advertised for that? I'd have gone for it."

Phone Boxes ■

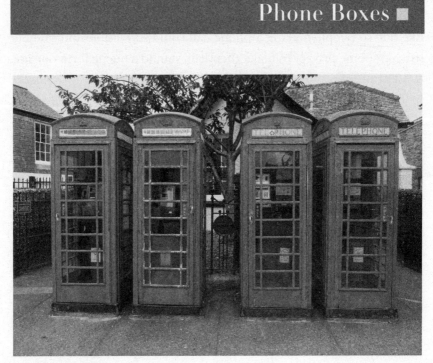

Four K6s, loitering.

It may be a tribute to the many gallons of blood spilled in the centuries-long struggle to forge a nation out of warring bits of kingdoms, or it could be that subconsciously the Brits feel happier among warm colors, the way a daisy bends toward sunlight, but, my crikey, there are a lot of prominent red things on British streets.

Stand on a roadside in London and you'd be forgiven for thinking every object that provides a valuable public service has been painted an identical shade of red, so that Londoners can be on a constant state of alert as to where they are and what dangers may be present. These include: postboxes, double-decker buses, Royal Mail delivery vans, and fire engines, but the most iconic of all are red phone boxes.

The K2 phone box (and later K3, K4—complete with postage stamp machine—K6, and K8), as designed by Sir Giles Gilbert Scott, became a part of British street life at around the same time as the blue police box (see: *Doctor Who*). It's a cast-iron affair, closed to the elements, with six rows of tiny windowpanes on three sides, and it was built like that so people making a phone call could stay visible and safe but still have some privacy to make their call, should a queue form outside.

The redness is mainly the post office's fault. When postboxes were first introduced to British streets, they were a deep, bronzed green color, to subtly blend with the grass and trees, or to remind city dwellers that such things existed. Sadly this thoughtful approach met with a few problems: the postboxes were just too subtle, and people kept walking into them.

This was before smartphones, so no one was texting or tweeting—unless you count the little cartoon birds circling their dazed heads—and in response, the Royal Mail (which operated both the mail and telephone services at the time) elected to paint the postboxes all bright red. Then it did the same thing when the first public phone boxes were built.

Naturally, this kind of crimson public gaiety was stiffly resisted at first, probably with a petition or two from outraged locals demanding they tone it down a bit. But then it wasn't long before London buses decided to get in on the act; and fire engines were always red, because, y'know . . . fire.

Fifty years later, when the K-series of phone boxes were abruptly painted yellow to match the livery of the newly privatized British Telecom, there were louder howls of outrage, which became eye rolls of disgust as the entire design was abruptly phased out. Their replacements were silvery, glassy, and open to the elements from the ankle down—so that no one could shelter in them overnight or leave puddles of unpleasantness behind. Despite having been a firm fixture of

British streets for the last thirty years, they remain uncelebrated as an item of street furniture, probably because they just look like phone boxes. And they are not red.

The K-series, on the other hand, pop up all over the place. There are discontinued phone boxes that serve as tiny book exchanges or libraries in rural areas like Somerset, Cambridgeshire, or Cornwall. There's one in Settle, North Yorkshire, that houses small works of art; there's a K4 in Warrington that still has its tiny stamp dispenser; and the K6 in Glendaruel, Argyllshire, has been converted so that it now houses a defibrillator, for a thrillingly retro lifesaving experience.

Some have been sold to private owners to use as shower cubicles. In Kingston-upon-Thames, twelve old K6s have been arranged to look like a row of toppling dominoes in a sculpture called *Out of Order*, by David Mach; and the street artist Banksy cut one up and reassembled it to look as if it had been attacked—it lay collapsed in a heap on the ground with a pickax sticking out of its back and red paint leaking onto the pavement. And there are still eleven thousand functioning K-series phone boxes from which it is possible to make a phone call, if you know where to look.

Even if you take all the phone boxes out of the equation, you're still left with enough crimson, scarlet, and poppy-hued objects on the streets of London, Inverness, Swansea, and everywhere in between, to maintain a state of constant national public vigilance at all times.

In this respect, being British is not unlike being a mouse, or, if that seems too base a comparison, a thoroughbred (but skittish) horse.

WHAT TO SAY: "Hey, buddy, can you direct me to the . . . oh, it's there."

WHAT NOT TO SAY: "Seriously? People used to walk into the . . . *oof!*"

I t's bubble-popping time! A certain number of people may be interested in reading a book about British culture because they believe the world is going to aitch-ee-double-hockeysticks in a handcart and entertainment media are throwing vacuous nonentities out there as hard and as fast as they can and it's the end of civilization as we know it unless the British—with their tradition of theater and literature and thinking hard about stuff—have the key to making everything okay. Surely they won't have fallen prey to the base demands of reality TV? Surely they've seen through the giddy parade of desperate egos and stuck to watching BBC dramatizations of the lives of prominent scientists, starring Benedict Cumberbatch or Tom Hiddleston? Surely? Please?

Sorry. That hasn't happened. I mean yes, Benedict Cumberbatch has made those dramas, that's still a thing, but the Brits are as dazzled by reality TV as anyone. Heck, they invented some of the most successful brands in the genre, and they're still exploring new ways to put members of the public in front of the camera. One type of these shows has people (and celebrities) trying to be talented for judges—*The X Factor, Fame Academy, Britain's Got Talent, Strictly Come Dancing*, all that lot—and another shows people (and celebrities) living in a place for a while, while TV producers tell them to do things. *Big Brother* being the most notable example, though *I'm a Celebrity . . . Get Me Out of Here* is the real champion. *Big Brother* may encourage people to acts of extreme humiliation, but only *I'm a Celebrity* could put a dismembered kangaroo penis in George Takei's mouth and expect him to eat it.

On other shows, people (and celebrities) have a job to do and require expert help—like house hunting in *Location, Location, Location* and *A Place in the Sun*—and on yet more shows, people (and celebrities) have a specific task to perform that they're actually quite good at, until everything comes apart under the pressure of the cameras and there's a lot of crying—*Come Dine with Me, Masterchef, The Apprentice, The Great British Sewing Bee.* Currently the Brits are in the midst of an annual love affair with *The Great British Bake Off,* because it turns out that while making a cake isn't necessarily all that hard, baking a better cake than the person next to you, to a stopwatch and sometimes without a recipe, is. That the silly Brits find such delight in other people's baking disasters may come as some comfort to the heck-in-a-handcart contingent.

Then there are the augmented reality TV shows, in which young people who already live in a place (and who eventually attain the status of celebrities if the show's a hit) interact with one another in a way that is both scripted and also very much unscripted. There's the well-to-do set in *Made in Chelsea,* the perpetual party people in *Geordie Shore,* and the decent, but slightly odd young folk from *The Only Way Is Essex.* In each case we get a snapshot of a young community starting to figure out what they want from life, amid a lot of drinking and partying and snogging the wrong people.

And the really fun part of all this is that the people (and celebrities) who appear on these shows then get to appear on other shows as celebrity guests. It started when contestants from *Popstars* and *Pop Idol* began to show up in the *I'm a Celebrity* jungle, prompting some wags to suggest that the show would be better titled *I'm Out of Here . . . Get Me a Celebrity* and that the cross-pollination of TV talent is reaching hay fever levels.

Oh, but that's not the end of the tale, not quite. In 2013 Channel 4 developed a stunning reality TV idea that was entirely devoid of jeopardy or skill on the part of the contestants and turned the concept of a show with a panel of judges facing the public completely on its head. The premise of *Gogglebox* is simple: a series of families from a wealth of different backgrounds and circumstances watch TV and pass comments among themselves, and they're filmed doing so. Their reactions to the shows of the week are frequently extreme, hilarious, judgmental, wrong, right, and all points between. And yet it's a TV show about watching TV, one that puts you, the viewer, in the homes of them, the viewers, except you haven't won a TV BAFTA. They have, and guess what? Some reality TV show presenters—like Kirstie Allsopp from *Location, Location, Location*—really don't like it.

I'm not sure where that leaves us in regard to that handcart, mind you. On the road to Hull, perhaps.

WHAT TO SAY: "Pass the Bovril; you're about to see a British *Man v. Food*."

WHAT NOT TO SAY: "I mean, *Who are these people? Who are they?*" etc.

Drawing Willies on Things ■

While the street art of Banksy may fetch millions of dollars and provoke discussion and debate among art buffs the world over, another form of urban beautification predates his earliest stencilings and those of his graffiti forebears; one that is far more influential, more vibrant, more provocative, and a lot more fun.

No one knows who decided to draw the first set of male genitals in the most public space he could find. Possibly it was something that happened shortly after the early adoption of tools, maybe it was shortly after the cognitive breakthrough that allowed humans to understand graphical representations of things, but whatever the moment was, you can bet the descendants of this early enfant terrible of caveman art ended up moving to the British Isles at some point.

What else could explain the volume of penis-related wall art in communities across Britain? There's tons of it, if you know where to look, although if you're expecting brightly colored frescoes depicting, say, a wriggling chorus line of male appendages (maybe on the wall outside a members-only club), or a single huge one just hanging there, all tumescent and glowing with rude health, you'll be sorely disappointed.

What you need to keep an eye out for is a quiet corner, just a blank bit of wall slightly to one side of a main thoroughfare; or possibly the interior doors of a lift in a timeworn shopping center or the cubicle doors of a gents' toilet next to a beach; or even a relatively fresh patch of concrete. Visit enough of these places, and you'll find a crudely drawn cartoon of an erect penis, possibly with attendant testicles and, for the connoisseur, some attempt at depicting pubic hair and maybe a teardrop of something unmentionable coming out of the end.

This may be lovingly rendered in permanent marker or spray paint, or even crudely etched into the paint using a metal stick or some keys—the giant chalk figure carved into the hills of Cerne Abbas in Dorset has an enormous great knobbly club (and an impressive penis too)—but all the details will be there. And I'll wager there isn't a community in the country that doesn't have at least one, somewhere.

Note: Not an actual Banksy.

Now, the important thing to state is that very few Brits actually go out drawing willies on things. It is not a national obsession in the way that talking about the weather (see: Talking about the Weather), queueing (see: Queuing) or complaining about late buses, could be called a national obsession. There are no phallic graffiti clubs, no knob scribblers' society; no one ever talks about the penises or how they got there. But someone clearly must be doing it. And they get about too. Given the sheer area covered and the speed with which new surfaces are attacked, either it's one very strange individual with a helicopter or enough people are doing it to allow one to say, with some confidence, that it is a thing that Brits do. That's statistics for you.

Having said that, Rod Stewart did devote several paragraphs in his autobiography to his habit of drawing penises on things, including the passports of the boy band McFly. His advice for them, should they become concerned about facing a stern customs official, was to "turn it into a tree and say your three-year-old did it," so maybe it's all him. Or San Francisco's Claire Wyckoff, who has taken to using Nike+ to draw willies on the maps in her phone when she's out for a run. Or maybe it's the town planners who designed Edinburgh's Bellenden Gardens (the name is enough of a giveaway, surely) so that it looks suspiciously penisy from above. It might even be the social commentator who spray-painted one onto the bonnet of a brand-new Bugatti Veyron in Seattle in 2014. Whoever it is, they get about.

To round off with an illustration (only not the one you're thinking of): A new cycle path was recently opened near my home. It's a beautiful thing, running through a patch of woodland and encouraging commuters to take their morning and evening journeys away from the potholes and traffic of the main road and along a silky smooth path, enjoying the sights, sounds, and smells of the natural world as they do so.

For a ceremony when the path was opened, local dignitaries came, a ribbon was cut, and the radio station mentioned it in a news bulletin. It was considered a big deal, because it was expensive to build and had not arrived without some problems, but finally this glorious asset to the local community was finished and ready for use.

Within twenty-four hours of that cycle path opening, someone had etched an enormous thirty-foot penis into the tarmac with a muddy stone. The message was clear: this thing is finished when *we* say it is, not before.

WHAT TO SAY: "Look, Marjorie! Some bright spark has defaced the 'Welcome to Ipswich' sign with a . . . well, bless my soul!"

WHAT NOT TO SAY: "Of course, they've got the shading all wrong on the scrotum."

The island of Great Britain, though relatively small, has played gracious host to many immigrant populations over the last ten thousand years or so. Some were welcomed voluntarily; others had to use weapons to make everyone remember their manners. But each successive wave of funny-talking foreigners has left a mark on the dominant accent of the local area, and each of these marks has had centuries to percolate, develop, and solidify.

The opposite is also true. The various Welsh, Scottish, and Cornish accents sound the way they do because they are the result of non-English speakers in those areas having to learn and speak English through the filter of their own indigenous language. This then goes on to affect the way people speak in border areas, with vowels being stretched and consonants sharpened and twisted left and right, depending on which hill or valley one happens to be in at the time.

Other factors are at play too. Accents in rural areas tend to be slower and more ruminative, like the long belch of a thoughtful cow, whereas the postindustrial urban accents are faster, sharper, harder, and full of teeth. People with middle-class or upper-class backgrounds have different accents from people with working-class backgrounds, and this holds true from the Orkneys to the Channel Islands. There are accents derived from music, from fashion, from watching too many cowboy movies, and from being privately educated by Professor Henry Higgins.

The British are very proud of their regional accents and exceptionally defensive if anyone ever gets them wrong, to the extent that they will leap with evident glee upon any actor foolish enough to attempt one and fail. The most notorious examples of this are probably Dick Van Dyke's rubbery Cockney in *Mary Poppins*, and whatever it was Russell Crowe thought he was doing in *Robin Hood*. But if an actor gets it right—as Renée Zellweger does in the Bridget Jones movies, Gwyneth Paltrow does in *Shakespeare in Love*, and the cast of *This Is Spinal Tap* do—it is as if they have been given an actual superpower, or become an honorary Brit. You have never seen any puppy roll over to have his tummy tickled as fast as the Brits welcome a Hollywood star that can do a decent local accent.

That's not to say all Brits can do all British accents; far from it. As with all forms of regionalism, it's fine to mock people from even farther away who just don't get it, but that doesn't mean people in Ipswich can do a perfect Swansea dialect or that the Inverness brogue is easy to replicate if you're from Derry. So when the Scottish David Tennant appeared, playing the Doctor in *Doctor Who* as an Englishman, it was as if he were an entirely different person from the guy with the same face and the Renfrewshire burr.

Conversely—and for reasons that aren't immediately apparent— British actors who can do a decent American accent aren't really considered to be that impressive and may even appear to be pandering to a Hollywood hiring system. This is true even if the movie is set in an American location and the character could not possibly be British. Somehow there's an air of disappointment, as if they have been somewhat sullied.

This may be simply a result of overardent admiration, in a sense. I mean, we've all had a go at it, whether trying to be Elvis, Aretha, or Eminem at karaoke or reciting gags from *Ghostbusters*. The American palette of accents, the logic suggests, are uniform and easy, whereas the British palette of accents are enormously varied and hard to master. It's part of a particular form of British arrogance that says I can do what you do—anyone can do what you do, because it's in my face all the time—but you can't do what I do. I'm special.

And yes, it's every bit as reductive and arrogant a stance to take as that of Johnny Shouts-Too-Much from outside the British Isles yelling, "Alroiught, mayte?" with too many vowels and claiming it as a British accent, whatever that is.

But then, it doesn't really matter where you are, or where you're from, so long as there's an "over there" to be in competition with, always a reason to bunch together with immediate neighbors and poke fun outward.

That's probably a legacy of all those invasions too.

WHAT TO SAY: "How do you say bath: ba-th or bar-th?"

WHAT NOT TO SING: "Eets ah joily oilyday wiv Meeeery."

Science ■

It would be wrong to characterize Britain as a purely secular nation. Probably more people actively believe in something than are openly hostile to the idea of a faith, but these beliefs don't take a particularly central position in the national rhetoric. So if any politicians wish to justify their actions using faith, they are guaranteed a rougher ride than if they attribute their decision to an act of personal conscience or (heaven forbid) public interest. That's not hostility to religious belief, just a healthy skepticism of politicians trying to avoid accountability.

But if it came down to a choice between faith and science, Brits would probably rather follow the facts (and keep Christmas, arguing that, one, it's an act of tradition that predates Christianity anyway and, two, it's too good to throw away on a silly argument).

That's not out of a particular affection for cold-headed logic over hot-headed faith, despite what Christopher Hitchens may have had to say on the subject; it's just that Brits, being back-bedroom tinkerers and model-plane enthusiasts by temperament, tend to be enormously excited by the possibilities of science. The legend of British scientific advancement is that some of the most notable breakthroughs came about by chance—as in the popular myth around Newton and his apple—or through the passionate diligence of talented amateurs.

This makes science appear to be something that anyone with an interest can take up and fiddle with, and still achieve results. Charles

Darwin, for example, was a rather poor student who first trained as a doctor (he didn't like operations) and then studied theology at Cambridge. Naturalism was his hobby, albeit one that he devoted more time to than his proper studies. That his personal struggle between faith and the study of nature has since been replicated on the world stage is just one of the reasons the myth of the talented amateur scientist is so beguiling. He is the personification of the battle between creationism and evolutionism (although that's perhaps not a helpful comparison if you'd rather the latter hadn't won).

And then there's Fleming and his penicillin mold: an accidental discovery that went on to save millions of lives. Or John Harrison beavering away on gears and springs and making accurate timepieces—like the marine chronometer, which allowed sailors to accurately reckon their longitude—just because it was something he wanted to learn how to do. Or young Francis Crick blowing glass in his uncle's shed in order to conduct chemical experiments, before excelling in the fields of physics and then biology; Michael Faraday educating himself by reading books while apprenticed as a bookbinder and then becoming a dominating force in chemistry and the investigation of electromagnetic forces; and Jocelyn Bell Burnell discovering pulsars while still a graduate student. That's British science for you.

And there's something gripping about the personalities of the great theorists, observers, and builders that linger in popular memory too. The Brits love a boffin: Isambard Kingdom Brunel, in his chimney hat, putting a bridge over every gorge; Newton's devoted research into alchemy and the occult; three-year-old James Clerk Maxwell pointing at every object he came across and asking his mother, "What's the go o' that?" and then taking that ardent curiosity into his precocious school days and adult life.

Not to mention Stephen Hawking, whose colossal intellect, strong personality, and sense of humor transcend the limitations of his physical body in a way that inspires admiration but not undue reverence, because as far as the Brits are concerned, he's one of the family. This means he's ripe for a bit of ribbing. Ricky Gervais once quipped that his success had made him pretentious: "Born in Kent and talks with an American accent."

He's the most recognizable scientist in the world, the most prominent theoretical physicist of his age, and—in the popular imagination at least—a man who is leading the charge out of the dark matter and into the visible electromagnetic radiation. He's also known to be self-deprecating, someone who enjoys appearing in TV comedies like *The Big Bang Theory* or larking about with John Oliver. Which means that, despite having more reason for doing so than anyone, he hasn't committed the cardinal British sin of becoming bigheaded.

WHAT TO SAY: "So a boffin is like an adult nerd, yes?"

WHAT NOT TO SAY: "Do you think Hawking can do any sweet jumps on his ride?"

The BBC ■

The NHS and the BBC are often spoken of in the same breath as organizations the British should be proud of, and indeed they are. Both come from what critics would call a nanny state, one that believes in giving people what is good for them rather than what they want, although the BBC was created in the era when this meant strong medicine, rather than free school milk. But both organizations take a lot of flak for having the nerve to exist, while also taking a central and lifelong role in the lives of an overwhelming majority of British people, in a huge variety of different ways.

The BBC is a state broadcaster funded directly by every household with a television. The money doesn't come from general taxation or subscriptions, but from an annual payment called the license fee or the TV license. In return everyone gets ten channels of national TV, ten channels of national radio (some analog only, and the rest digital), plus forty local radio stations and the World Service. And no commercials! Then there's BBC Online, a hugely respected current affairs resource, and the iPlayer, which provides a free catch-up service on all BBC programming. The idea being that whatever the age, social background, gender, sexuality, or political affiliation of the audience, there will always be something to listen to, or watch.

And, by and large, this works wonderfully. While at times sections of BBC output can feel a little like a bowl of oatmeal on steak night—

principally because the target audience is so incredibly broad that you can't hope to please everyone all the time—it has also created some of the most internationally successful programming, by any yardstick you care to mark up, in television and radio history.

To make any list of highlights can only seem like stuffing a random grab bag made of nothing but holes, but hats are all the way off for any of the following: *In the Night Garden*; *Newsnight*; *Only Fools and Horses*; *Panorama*; *Horrible Histories*; *Life on Earth*; *The Day Today*; *Top of the Pops*; *State of Play*; *The Sky at Night*; *Dad's Army*; *Our Friends in the North*; *The Thick of It*; *Kermode and Mayo's Film Review*; *Being Human*; *I, Claudius*; *Stewart Lee's Comedy Vehicle*; *Luther*; *Monty Python's Flying Circus*; and Benedict Cumberbatch and Martin Freeman bickering in *Sherlock*. All of these shows (and those described in detail in other chapters) deserve to be praised to the skies.

And there's another reason why, to the majority of British people, the BBC feels less like an enforced state broadcaster and more like a member of the family. Despite having never fallen prey to the strictures of communism, there is something deep in British culture that seeks to elevate the common good (or more accurately, that believes that British culture seeks to elevate the common good). By which I mean the British Dream, if such a thing exists, is one that spends slightly less time worrying about individual persons getting everything they want, and more time making sure everyone makes the best of their lot in life. It's there in Lord Reith's leadership of the BBC from 1927 onward: the drive to "inform, educate, and entertain" is the backbone of the BBC even now and has become the ruler by which its best endeavors are measured.

It's also there in home improvement shows like *DIY SOS*, in which a team of builders arrive at the home of a family with some fairly serious problems—long-term illness, sudden disability—and renovates everything. Everyone pulls together to help people who have been struggling alone for too long, and naturally there are tears before the credits roll. For all that the Brits enjoy sending Gordon Ramsay and Piers Morgan out around the world to tell people off, these relatively small acts of kindness say just as much about how they wish to view themselves.

As a result, the BBC remains a beloved and trusted institution, to the extent that big news events—and this can be anything from the outbreak of a war to the death of a pop star—must be verified by BBC News before the Brits will believe them to be true. And this continues at a local level too. During any cold snap, listening figures for BBC local radio shoot up as parents check to see if the schools have been closed. Other media outlets may have that information too, but the Beeb—known affectionately as Auntie—is the first place most people will look, and that's because they know they'll always find what they need.

WHAT TO SAY: "Frankly, it's worth the money just for *Wonders of the Solar System*."

WHAT NOT TO SAY: "I need the toilet, but I can probably wait for the next ad break."

Avoiding Confrontation ■

To be honest, I'd rather not talk about this now. It's not really an issue. Everything is perfectly fine and, anyway, whatever my silly old feelings on this topic may be, they are simply not worth lingering over. It'll keep. Let's not get into it now. Seriously, I am very happy with things the way they are; nothing about the act of avoiding confrontation is bothering me and if it were I would be the first to tell you. And you are not to take my silence on this topic as any form of passive-aggressive preemptive strike or anything like that. I shan't be returning home to pen an angry letter to your superiors, and you'd be quite wrongly painting me as an egregious beast to assume I would ever do such a thing.

So what I suggest is that we just put this whole sorry chapter behind us and forget that it ever happened, and in return I'll make sure not to bang on endlessly about you to my friends and family and Facebook as though it was a *bloody nerve* to expect a thoughtful and entertaining discussion of the famous, and possibly overmythologized, talent the British—most specifically those British people who are English and middle class and not from the north—have for tolerating things they should really complain about, in order not to make a scene. That is certainly not the case. At all. It really, really isn't. And if it were, that would make me some kind of weasely hissing prig, and I'm really not. Honestly.

Some people like to be frank about every feeling of need they experience; at the moment they experience it, in a kind of eternally updated verbal blog with no searchable archive. They're hot, they're tired, they're hungry, they're frustrated, they're bored, and they're waiting for the opportunity to tell you these things even while you're talking to someone else about something else. In contrast, the Brits—and again, this is most often a middle-class English sort of a thing—prefer to think of themselves as being too dignified to bother complaining about anything.

Don't be lulled into thinking that this means they don't notice things that are unsatisfactory. That would be a mistake. It's just that, even if a soup is too cold or the bus conductor is too brusque before elevenses, the mind will scroll ahead to the inevitable messy consequences of making a complaint, and those seem every bit as bad as the original problem, so the best thing to do is affect a sour demeanor, purse the lips as tight as a cat's bum, and radiate bad vibes outward. That's the full extent of the confrontation. To admit to having been troubled by something as inconsequential as feelings seems like a weakness and, worse, an unpardonable breach of decorum, and there are many British people who would rather die than make a fuss, even when it is palpable that they are silently furious.

However, some things are simply beyond the pale and require immediate attention. Anyone talking in a cinema, or demonstrably having failed to set their smartphone to mute during a play, can expect to be the recipient of a pretty stinging irate whisper (ZING!). Park inconsiderately, or in the space directly outside someone's house on a busy street, and you can expect to find a very strongly worded note under your wipers when you get back (KAPOW!). Supermarkets that deliver unsatisfactory vegetables? Not just an e-mail, but a tweet too (BOSH!). And to the selfish swine who puts on loud music—fizzily audible even on headphones—while traveling in the quiet carriage of a train, or, worse, receives a phone call without immediately running for the carriage door, you can expect an apocalyptically theatrical tut when you get back to your seat (OOF!).

We don't want anyone to think the Brits are pushovers, after all.

WHAT TO SAY: "I said I don't want to talk about it. It's fine. Really very fine, okay?"

WHAT NOT TO SAY: "I asked for *one* sugar in this tea. Are you trying to give me diabetes? Outside, now!"

Wimbledon ■

Unlike almost every other sporting event, bar the Olympics, Wimbledon could have been designed specifically so that a particular kind of British sporting aficionado can get their fix: the part-time expert.

Part-timers don't necessarily have the wherewithal to devote constant vigilance to the various tennis tournaments of the world and the rankings, seedings, qualifiers, and whatnot. While maintaining a passing interest, they're not really there for the other events, but they do require an annual fix of around a fortnight, just to find out how everyone has been getting along. Wimbledon—the tennis tournament that manages to cram in so many things that are not tennis—fits the bill magnificently.

Lost in the pageantry of the event—the royal patronage, the faint echo of one-to-one combat with blunt weapons (to the death, unless it rains)—the part-timer absorbs a year's worth of tennis information during the first couple of television broadcasts, then very quickly begins parroting key facts about Djokovic or Federer (or, if he's an armchair wag, "Joke-ovitch" and "Federerer") and assessing the potential of any British players who stand a chance of winning.

As far as the British media are concerned, there's a strict hierarchy of interest around five trophies during Wimbledon fortnight. The mixed doubles is at the bottom—but still above the boys' and girls' and wheelchair tennis draws, which are practically invisible, sad to say—with the ladies' doubles and gentlemen's doubles taking fourth and third place respectively. Holding steady at number two is the ladies' singles championship, but the real point of obsessive interest, especially for the part-time expert, is the gentlemen's singles final, and most important, whether there is a British player in it or not.

This quest—another faint echo of a military past, this time of King Arthur's search for the Holy Grail—has come to dominate everything about Wimbledon for the British, which is a shame. It's a hugely charming tennis tournament that has its own character and traditions. All the players have to wear white, for example; even the stroppy ones who claim to have their own sense of style (or sponsors with very colorful logos). People feel honor bound to eat strawberries and cream, and they drink Pimm's and hand bottles of Robinsons barley water to their children as if it were the 1920s all over again.

But rather than relax, kick back, and neck some serious fruit, British people pine for a British (gentleman's singles) champion. Before Andy Murray won in 2013, there hadn't been a British (gentleman's singles) winner at Wimbledon since Fred Perry in 1936, a fact the part-time experts are all too familiar with because it was a constant feature of media reports on the tournament. Not that they got all their facts straight. Some of the ecstatic headlines after Murray's win rushed to proclaim him the first British champion in seventy-seven years, completely overlooking the fact that Virginia Wade won the ladies' singles trophy in 1977. It might seem picky to mention it, but having the energy for this kind of argument is also part of the fun of being a part-time sports fan.

Before Andy, Britain's greatest hope was a photogenic young man called Tim Henman, and his attempts to win—pockmarked with the slightly scolding rallying cry from his fans: "Come on, Tim!"—coincided with the advent of a huge TV screen erected within the grounds of the All England Lawn Tennis and Croquet Club, facing a raised bank of grass that formed a kind of natural amphitheater. Of-

ficially known as Aorangi Terrace, thanks to that area's previous oc-
cupation by the London New Zealand Rugby Club, this was the perfect
place for milling press and media people to rush out and get vox-pops
without disrupting play. As most of these will have begun with the
question "Do you think Tim Henman can win this year?" or, later,
"What is your reaction to Tim Henman's defeat?" the area took on the
talismanic name Henman Hill, and this has stuck.

There have been subsequent attempts to rechristen it Murray
Mound, or even allow some of the women players who have managed
to do well to lend their names to it. These have been stiffly resisted,
partly because renaming a hill is a faintly ridiculous thing to do, but
mostly because Murray won. There's no romance like a doomed romance, no pain like that felt by a nation that pooled all of its faith in
one man, a nation that risked all, and lost. Henman Hill will retain its
name as a tribute to all those dreams that were lost in the heat of battle
(see: The Underdog).

But apart from the media hoo-ha, Wimbledon has a delightfully
egalitarian spirit. Non-ticket-holders can just turn up on the day and
get into Center Court, Court 1, or Court 2 just by joining a colossal
queue (see: Queuing), although they do often stay overnight to be sure
to bag a seat. Also, the local schools traditionally supply the tournament's ball boys and ball girls, who have to pass a fitness test and show
themselves to be generally, y'know, on the ball, but are by no means
hardened sports professionals.

It's a sporting event where the matches are so long and arduous,
they become impressive even to people who don't like sport, which is
what makes being a Wimbledon part-timer so easy. Those players are
out there for hours, on their feet, blamming away with very little to
sustain them apart from a bite of a banana and a sip of barley water.
No strawberries, no cream; and at the end of a five-hour match, they
pack their own bags and walk away. They do the hard work, so you
don't have to.

WHAT TO SAY: "Remember the year it rained and Cliff Richard led the crowd in a singsong?"

WHAT NOT TO SAY (ANYMORE): "Come on, Tim!"

Grade-B Swearwords ■

If you are of a gentle disposition, or prefer to believe that all British people, from St. Ives to Inverness, are possessed of the kind of manners and decorum that would make Betty Crocker feel uncouth and dirty, this bit might be a little hard to take. However, the sad truth of the matter is that the British excel at swearing. And they're proud of it too. Not only are all the best swearwords Anglo-Saxon in origin (something to do with those hard *k*'s and *t*'s and satisfying *f*'s and *s*'s) but there's infinite expression in their delivery and use.

For example, there's a world of difference between dropping a few choice expletives because the wind has caught your umbrella and wrecked it and calling someone an effing idiot because he or she pushed into the queue at the post office. You can use swearwords to add emphasis, to puncture pomposity, and to win the heart of a fair maiden (albeit one with a robust sensibility, who has probably had more than enough of dealing with sodding dragons).

And that's just if you're using the kind of grade-A swearwords people understand all over the world, the ones live broadcasters have late-night fever dreams about, particularly when discussing a fracas in the Kentish countryside. Fortunately other words in circulation provide equally adaptable forms of obscenity, without once troubling the censors at the FCC (although Ofcom would take a dimmer view).

One of the most expressive is *bugger*, a truly delightful word to say, especially now it has shaken off most of its judgmental provenance. Originally derived from an Old French word for "heretic," *bugger* came to be synonymous with *homosexual* (one who commits *buggery*) in the sixteenth century, but took on an alternative meaning, denoting someone who deserves nothing but contempt or pity, in the eighteenth. Since then, the edges have become softened, and to be referred to as a bugger now is almost affectionate, in a gruff kind of way.

To be told to *bugger off*, while still a firm invitation to go away, comes from a similarly warm place. And nothing undercuts the drama of disappointing news like a well-placed, explosive "Bugger it!"

Oddly popular both in the postindustrial north of England and in the resolutely rural West Country, *bugger* is the kind of word that is best left out of polite conversation, but will seal a friendship in trying times.

The same cannot be said for the other British grade-B wondercuss: *wanker.*

Loaded with the same Anglo-Saxon weaponry as other, more famous swears, the W word denotes one act, and one act only, and that is masturbation. To refer to someone as a *wanker* is fighting talk. You're not just suggesting he spends far too long enacting rituals of self-love, you're saying he's not fit to breed.

It is not a word the Brits tend to find charming or affectionate, unless used within a close circle of friends. To draw a parallel with American slang, it's probably slightly above *jerk-off* as an aggressive noun, and way above *jackass*, but slightly below most words that describe sexual organs. To even hint at it, say, by making a well-known hand gesture at a reckless driver in gridlock on a hot day, is to invite hostilities, if not an episode of actual road rage. Having said that, *tosser* and *tosspot* are comparatively mild, despite carrying the same meaning.

Punk fans will already be aware of *bollocks*, which means nonsense, as in "Stop talking bollocks, you lying bugger!" or testicles. Oddly, to refer to something as *the dog's bollocks* is to praise it highly, probably as a swearier alternative to *the bee's knees.*

And below these are a host of even milder expletives that pepper British English like curried quail's eggs in a game pie: *sod* (as in "Sod it!" or "Sod off!") or *git* ("Shut your face, you mardy git!"—also used as *get* in Liverpool) or Ron Weasley's perennial favorite, *bloody hell.*

Just something to bear in mind the next time you hear that tired old line about swearing being a sign of a poor vocabulary.

WHAT TO SAY: "Five pounds for a pint of lager? Do you take me for some kind of wanker?"

WHAT NOT TO SAY: "Good afternoon, Lady Malmsbury. I see some sods have been buggering about on your lawn."

In an era of YouTube plays and constantly updated download figures it's bizarre to think of a time when there was just one weekly marker of musical success that mattered. For people of a certain age, the British Top 40 singles chart—which counts sales alone, not radio play—used to matter like nothing else, to the extent that they can still recall chart statistics that are over thirty years old: the singles that went to number one in the first week of release; the bands or singers that had the longest run of chart toppers; the songs that should have got to number one but were elbowed aside by unworthy novelties; all indelibly etched on the brain.

The national obsession with the chart was fueled by two things: BBC Radio 1's chart rundown on a Sunday night and *Top of the Pops*.

Top of the Pops was at one and the same time the most elitist (you had to be popular to get in the door) and the most egalitarian music TV show ever devised. In theory, anyone could get on and perform. All they had to do was sell enough singles (in the right shops) to get their song into the Top 40. The higher the record, the louder the clamor to get them on *Top of the Pops*; and by the same token, no record sales: no chance. Music shows that were curated by the taste of the production team could not dream of the variety displayed on a weekly basis on *Top of the Pops*. You'd have some nonsense novelty tune rubbing shoulders with the latest pin-drop reverie from a critically adored artiste. Folk would happily meet metal, blues would meet pop, punk would meet hip-hop, and parents all over the country would tut and roll their eyes. It was a revolving snapshot of the week in pop music, devoid of all context because there simply wasn't time to explain what was going on.

Similarly, as an effort to keep up in prestreaming times, pop fans would make their own chart mix tapes by running the Radio 1 chart show through a tape deck and applying nimble fingers to the record and pause buttons. It's somewhat romanticized now as a childhood rite of passage—no doubt similar things were going on all over the world anyway—and it's a cliché even to mention it, but, my golly, it happened a lot. Personal music taste was curated out of capricious sales information. Songs would be rudely shorn of introductions and long fade-outs and jammed together simply because they were nearby neighbors in a list. Now that there are magazines devoted to raking over the past of music in forensic detail, and the ability to find any song whenever you want it, it seems unbelievably irreverent that anyone would do this, and of course that's where the charm of the process lies. It's pop music, not jazz.

Simon Cowell rather spoiled it all, while providing the old charts with their final hurrah. During the early 2000s the drive to create spangled reality TV out of record company machinations revived flagging interest in the process of making singles, at a point when only committed pop fans—by which I mean teenage girls, ick!—were buying them. Everyone else bought albums. With the promotional push of a weekly TV show like *The X Factor* behind them, new singers could get that crucial first-week number-one status that had been the preserve of cultural phenomena like the Beatles, Slade, the Jam, and, latterly, Westlife.

This was a Penn & Teller moment. *The X Factor* and *Pop Idol* suggested that making pop music was like a Find the Lady street hustle: you let viewers in on the trick, point at the card, show the card, and still keep the money. The claim was that talent was being discovered—

and that's true to an extent—within the framing device of TV. In fact, a good percentage of the winners were decent singers with appealing faces but little of the charismatic charge of good pop stars. The one thing very few of them had, apart from divertingly batty sideshow acts like Jedward (if you don't know, don't ask), was any discernible X factor. But they dominated the national conversation around pop music for years, thanks in part to some great pop singles by Will Young, Girls Aloud, and Leona Lewis, among the more usual victory lap mush that the format usually demands.

From 2005 on, download sales were included in the chart tally, and this started to show some strange anomalies that were once again attributable to the influence of TV. Old songs would enter the chart for a hot week, just because they had been featured in *Britain's Got Talent* or *The X Factor* auditions. Adele's "Make You Feel My Love" spent fifty-five weeks biffing around the chart, thanks to a weekly mauling by would-be superstars. The chart doesn't care about any of this stuff, of course, but some of the obsession with pop statistics was starting to wear thin, possibly thanks to distortions of this sort.

Time for one last showdown. The finale of *The X Factor* is always timed for the third week in December, so that the winner would release a single in the week before Christmas, thus ensuring a Christmas number one. This carries a certain prestige, albeit one that people only really started to pay attention to once it was clear someone wanted that prestige all to themselves.

Which brings us to 2009, when an inspired Facebook campaign, started by Jon and Tracy Morter, suggested that "Killing in the Name" by Rage Against the Machine would be a worthy alternative Christmas number one to the winning song from an *X Factor* champion. This caught the public imagination in a big way (see: Cocking a Snook), and so, as a protest against the soulless industry of reality TV pop music, people bought a song they already owned, to get it to the top of a list they didn't really feel that interested in anymore.

And the chart being the chart, it just absorbed this rude invasion, carried on counting, and moved on. Rage Against the Machine appeared on the Christmas *Top of the Pops* (stripped of their curses, naturally), and Joe McElderry, that year's *X Factor* winner, got his number one the following week.

WHAT TO SAY: "I got this tattoo to mark the day 'Vienna' by Ultravox was kept off the top spot by Joe Dolce's 'Shaddap You Face.' Some wounds never heal."

WHAT NOT TO SAY: "Pop songs are for little girls. I prefer real music."

Coronation Street ■

We find ourselves back in the same dingy meeting room as before (see: *The Archers*). It is ten years later; the shadowy man
has recovered his composure and has lit a fresh cigar and once again
the conversation is dominated by the need to find a new continuing
drama. The desk and floor are still littered with the scrunched-up remains of pitch ideas. There's one about a family who take over a country hospital, and another about a community that lives and works in
and around a huge power station. None have been greeted warmly
and once again the atmosphere is tense, and a little damp with feelings.

A voice pipes up from the other end of the table, a voice ripe with
elasticated vowels, betraying his northern roots (you'll have to imagine the vowels, as they would probably die on the page).

"Sir, what if we had a soap opera—"

"Damn it, haven't I told you we don't call them that? Get this guy outta—"

"A serial drama—my apologies—that simply tells the lives of the
working-class residents of a street."

"A street? That's it? That's the worst idea I've ever—"

"Not just any street, sir. This one will be in Manchester. In Salford,
actually."

"What in the blue blazes is a Salford?"

"Ah, Salford is a city, but also a borough of Greater Manchester, sir.
I'm from Salford and I'm here to tell you that the working-class people

of Salford, particularly the working-class women of Salford, have seen more drama than all of the actors of Shakespeare's stage."

"Son, have you put too many sugars in your coffee? What could be more boring than a drama set in a normal street?"

"But that's just the thing, sir. It won't be boring at all. All we need to do is get the dialogue right—and we will—and we'll have a drama that can play calamity and farce at the same time. The Salford wit is one of the sharpest in the world and we'll use it, by golly! We'll create a set of characters who are used to dealing with hard knocks and more than capable of picking themselves back up again. I know these people. I grew up around them: the tough old battle-axes going to war over the garden fence in their hairnets and curlers; the free and easy glamour-pusses trawling the pubs looking for some excitement, anything to raise the spirits after a dreary day; and the stuck-up madams who consider themselves a cut above. And the men! Randy chancers, put-upon husbands, would-be tycoons, and pretentious college puddings . . . we'll take the lot! Our characters won't be able to stop themselves from bickering before we've even got the cameras rolling."

"So it's a show about women arguing over a fence?"

"No, sir! Let's say the whole community lives in a street in a made-up district we'll call . . . Weatherfield. All the houses are redbrick terraces, small and poky, and back-to-back so everyone is in each other's business all the time. Then we'll put a pub at one end of the street—let's call it the Rovers Return—and a shop at the other. That way they'll have to talk to each other in the open and in front of other people."

"Ah! A pub! That's something I can relate to."

"Well, quite so, sir. Actually, that's a big part of the appeal of the show. It won't feel provincial to Manchester because most of our audience know what goes on in a pub. The Rovers will become part of British iconography, a place where beloved characters will live and fall in love and fall out of love and fight and argue and make up and sometimes even die. Most of the time they will just gather and shoot the breeze. And because we'll have got the dialogue right, it'll be like a window into ordinary lives."

"Yes, but who is going to want to watch ordinary lives?"

"Everyone! *Florizel Stre*—no, wait—*Coronation Street* will become the longest-running TV serial drama in history. It will make commercial television a viable success in Britain and become one of the most—if not *the* most—watched TV shows in the country for over fifty-five years. Even the theme music will become iconic. We'll get a mournful little jazz tune with an optimistic flourish at the end and it will become an integral part of British cultural life for decades. There will be reggae versions, polka versions, you name it."

"I'm not even going to ask what 'reggae' is."

"It will all become clear in the fullness of time, sir. The point is, this will be a continuing drama in which ordinary people are finally given the dignity to be the heroes in their own Greek tragedy, while being constantly undercut by vicious asides from the chorus. It's going to be full-blooded, stiff of backbone, and wholly ripe. Our street will be so vibrant it will make these black-and-white television sets look like Technicolor."

"Color TV? Not in my lifetime, sonny . . ."

And with that, there's another long pause, broken only by the gentlest hiss of embers slowly tumbling down a straining shirt.

WHAT TO SAY: "What time is tea? It's just I don't want to miss *Corrie*. Ken Barlow is going to give Deirdre what for."

WHAT NOT TO SAY: "What is this so-called 'ot pot they sell at the pub? Is that even food?"

Movie #3: *Trainspotting* ■

Had *Trainspotting* been made two years earlier, or two years later, it would have been a very different film tonally, and it would probably not have carried the moment in the way that it continues to do to this day. It's a film that still dares the viewer to ask how on earth it ever got made, what can have been going on in popular culture at the time that it would be considered a good idea to make something that heartwarming from such a blood-freezing topic.

It arrived in the middle of Britpop; a moment of intense celebration for British culture. Having spent a good portion of the 1980s working out how to make their own entertainment, thanks to the decline of British industry and spiraling unemployment—especially in the industrial cities in northern England, Scotland and Wales—a generation of British bands and designers and filmmakers suddenly appeared in the mainstream, as if fully formed, with a homegrown aesthetic inspired by their favorite moments of the past. It was a parallel breakthrough to that of Nirvana and alternative culture in America a year or two earlier, one in which a creative, mutually supportive arts scene suddenly became swamped with attention. But the emphasis was different. Never mind slacker ennui in ripped jeans, the Britpoppers dressed smarter, more colorfully, and appeared determined to live out their fantasy of re-creating 1960s Swinging London in the 1990s. It may have taken a certain amount of cocaine confidence to carry this off, but there was no shortage of that.

As a mission statement, it all looks a smidge boastful and empty with the benefit of hindsight, but the great thing about enhanced confidence of this sort is that it creates a sense that things are possible. Things that have been unsaid can be said; artists and performers who would normally struggle to get any kind of attention can find themselves with an actual audience, of a decent size too.

Irvine Welsh was one of the beneficiaries of the times, in this regard. An uninhibited writer, with particular affinity for street-level grot and a good ear for transcribing Scottish slang and idioms, he wrote the book *Trainspotting* as a series of lost stories from heroin addicts in Edinburgh. Lost because, while their tales contain all the horrors associated with the drug in the usual media narrative—health lost, opportunities wasted, lives taken—there's a defiant edge, in which the characters not only describe the reason people take drugs in the first place (spoiler: they really like them), they defend the lifestyle as an open rejection of the kind of naff inspirational guff you find littering up people's Facebook feeds nowadays. The character Mark Renton, who took the lead role when the book made the jump to the screen, opens and closes the movie musing on the 1980s aspirational slogan "Choose Life"—a two-word exhortation for people to *behave*.

Danny Boyle, the film's director, was also the right person for the moment. He had already turned heads with his first movie, the thriller *Shallow Grave*, in which three flatmates' lives are turned upside down by the discovery that their new lodger has died and left a huge sum of money in his room. One of the stars was Ewan McGregor, and he would become Danny's Mark Renton: a skinny reprobate with a big face and a broad, open smile.

In the retelling of these dark tales—crammed with moments of disquiet and disgust—some of the triumphant Britpop atmosphere seeps into the story, like a wonky curtain failing to stop the day invading a room. In fact, the poster for the movie remains an iconic image of the times, endlessly parodied. Renton's gang of rotters are shown as being huge fans of the Lou Reed/Iggy Pop end of the musical spectrum, as is practically mandatory among Scottish music fans of a certain vintage—and there is an astonishing overdose scene that makes great use of Reed's "Perfect Day"—but rather than sinking too heavily into that decadent '70s drug cliché, the movie incorporates the arrival of dance music and a shift in drugs from snoozy old heroin to lively, bright ecstasy.

Underworld's song "Born Slippy .NUXX" appears at the end of the film, just as things are starting to look up for Renton. And while the song was originally intended as a larky approximation of a drunkard's internal monologue, those saturated, forgiving synths—arriving as dawn breaks and Renton finally leaves his past behind—act as a form of musical redemption for all the perfectly horrid horrors that have preceded it. It is a baptism of sound.

Consequently the soundtrack of the movie became as integral to the times as the film itself, and that song in particular became an instant anthem of this superconfident, up-for-it Britain. This was the kind of Britain that could remove a sitting Conservative government from office after nearly twenty years, a Britain in which great things got done by the least likely of people. It wasn't just post-Oasis braggadocio; weirder things were happening too. Just as Nirvana's success opened the doors for unlikely stars like Beck and Eels, in Britain we had Pulp and the Divine Comedy. The entirely left-of-center Gorky's Zygotic Mynci came really close to having actual Top 40 hit singles; British artists were putting animals in fish tanks and messing up their beds and there were superclubs offering a Miami raver lifestyle in freezing northern backstreets. Stuff was going on.

Naturally it couldn't last. A creeping paranoia began to set in during 1997 as the bouncy castle of Britpop began to develop the stone ramparts and deadly earnestness of empire building. Suddenly you couldn't have it all; you couldn't live forever; you were stuck in a bittersweet symphony, chained to an okay computer. Things could only get worse.

For Danny Boyle, though, that same confident sense of possibility amid trying times has gone on to inform his most celebrated achievements to date: not just his films, like *Slumdog Millionaire* or *127 Hours*, but the opening ceremony of the 2012 London Summer Olympic Games, in which he roped in the queen to pretend to skydive into the stadium from a helicopter in the company of James Bond. If you were looking for a better example of great things done by the least likely of people, it might take a long search.

WHAT TO SAY: "Hey, is that Jonny Lee Miller?"

WHAT NOT TO SAY: "So are there no trains in it at all?"

The Great British Fry-Up ■

Just one potential fry-up (L to R: hog's pudding, bacon, fried slice, sausage, egg, mushrooms, tomato, chips and beans).

The anatomy of the fried breakfast—henceforth known as the "full English" or "fry-up"—is one that can be tailored to suit almost any taste. Granted, the two principal players in this particular gastronomic drama are bacon and sausages, but great lengths have been taken to try to re-create their essential qualities so that British vegetarians can join in with everyone else. Vegans will have a tougher time of it, but the marvelous thing about the modular nature of the full English is that, given the right ingredients, cooked in the right way, no one is entirely excluded.

There's a bewildering array of options that vary according to location, personal preference, and the kind of establishment you're sitting in, but the key ingredients in a fry-up tend to be picked from a list that looks something like this:

Fried egg: usually sunny-side up.
Bacon: back, rarely streaky. Thicker is better, and cooked until leathery.
Sausages: probably the least reliable component in terms of quality.
Tomato: cut in half and grilled, griddled, or fried.
Mushrooms: fried.
Baked beans: a staple of the British diet and a reliable garnish for most fried dishes.
Toast: to mop up any leftover juices.

To these, the British menu will often add a few strange terms, suggesting food items that you may not be immediately familiar with:

Black pudding: a thick slice of blood sausage, fried.
Bubble and squeak: potato fritters that may also contain cabbage, onions, or carrots.
A fried slice: fried bread.

Then there are your specialist variations:

Square sausage: sausage meat hammered into a square.
Haggis: sliced (see: Offal).
White pudding: a blood-free alternative to black pudding.
Hog's pudding: a West Country variation of white pudding.
Tattie scones: potato scones—like hash browns, only more so.

And a selection of extra carbohydrates, for the hard-core glutton:

Hash browns: just to bump up the starch.
Chips: for when hash browns just aren't enough.

The important thing to know is that while the fry-up can be enjoyed on any day of the week, at any time—there are cafés that specialist in all-day breakfasts—cramming in that amount of saturated fat in one sitting isn't always advisable, especially if your day job involves sitting quietly at a desk smacking your fingertips on a keypad. Rationing is key, and so a really good fried breakfast, while highly prized, tends to be something that is put aside for special occasions. By which I mean the day of your wedding, the day of someone else's wedding, the weekend, getting to the airport on the first day of a holiday (also requires a pint of beer, no matter what the hour), a meeting with an old friend, a meeting with a new friend, a hangover, a Monday, lunchtime, the day after an upsetting (or inspiring) event, or a trip away from home that requires an overnight stay in a hotel.

This last option is surprisingly powerful. Staying in a hotel is not just an opportunity to order room service—like the rock stars do—or invest in a stout set of earplugs if the couple next door are over-amorous, it's a chance to live a momentary dream of indulgence and luxury. In normal life, no one is going to bother to dig the frying pan out if there's a chance of an extra fifteen minutes of sleep. Toast, or a hurried banana on the way out of the door, will do just fine.

In a hotel, though, someone has already made breakfast. It's there, ready for you. It would be not only wasteful to turn it down, but downright rude (and as we know, the British are nothing if not slaves to decorum). It would be like waking up after leaving a tooth under your pillow, finding that it has magically been replaced with a coin in the night, and then leaving it there because too much money is bad for the soul.

WHAT TO SAY: "It's okay, I'm going to skip lunch anyway. And dinner."

WHAT NOT TO SAY: "Can I get some syrup for my bacon?"

Children's TV ■

As adults, it's often hard to let go of the thrills of childhood, and when those things come dancing into the corner of your living room, it's as if they are extended members of the family. So rather than carrying on a *Brideshead Revisited* relationship with childhood toys, dragging a teddy bear wherever they go, a significant proportion of British adults have an internal hard drive stuffed full of theme tunes and voices, cartoons and friendly adults, taken from the children's programming of their formative years.

But it's not just aimless nostalgia—which would be perfectly fine— some of those shows stand up to repeated viewing even in an era of *Kung Fu Panda, Frozen*, and *Monsters, Inc.*

British children were, and continue to be, extraordinarily well served by their televisions. From the earliest dreamy homemade stop-motion animations of Oliver Postgate—a Roald Dahl–ish spinner of yarns with a voice like a honeyed bassoon who created *Bagpuss, The Clangers, Ivor the Engine*, and *Noggin the Nog*—right up to the BBC's *In the Night Garden*, an even dreamier modern classic for tiny tots, magical things kept pouring into the living room. Spells cast by a *Magic Roundabout*, or terrifying dubbed fairy tales from eastern Europe like *The Singing, Ringing Tree*, continue to resonate in the back of British minds.

And as with every item of minor trivia upon which opinions can be forced, this forms the basis of one very long and often rewarding pub conversation. One that you can always start if you're stuck with people you don't know.

Start with something nice and easy, a breezy reference to *Paddington*, *Camberwick Green*, or *Mr. Benn*, then if it's looking like they might bite, throw in a *Womble* or two—with the deathless bonus fact that *the Wombles* were so popular they had actual hit singles, one of which was promoted on *Top of the Pops* by members of Fairport Convention in Womble costumes—and prepare the final baited hooks to drop in the water. Try a *Danger Mouse*, a *Take Hart*, a *Count Duckula*, maybe something cultish like *Jamie and the Magic Torch*, *Button Moon*, or *Trap Door*. If you're getting really desperate and nothing seems to ignite the conversation, it's time to break out the big gun: *Grange Hill*.

The hard-hitting school soap *Grange Hill* is your fail-safe because it had the lot: an instantly remembered theme tune, characters that everyone remembers (Tucker Jenkins, Gripper Stebson, Roland Browning, Bullet Baxter), and characters that dimly tug at the memory (Miss McCluskey, Ziggy Greaves, Pogo Patterson, Danny Kendall). Then there was the story line in which Zammo McGuire became addicted to heroin. That kicked off a campaign around drug awareness, and another hit single, "Just Say No," sung earnestly by the cast. Brits of a certain age remember the whole affair as if it happened to someone on their (Sesame) street.

Of course, this only works for Brits in their thirties and above. If they're still in their early twenties, the same conversation can be attempted but there's a chance they will flinch a bit. Some of the memories will be a bit too fresh for comfort, and childhood will still feel like something they have escaped, rather than lost. Still, the key reference points will be shows largely based on people who work in public service industries: *Bob the Builder* (who also had a hit single), *Fireman Sam*, *Postman Pat*, *The Story of Tracy Beaker* (lived in a foster home with foster carers), and *Thomas the Tank Engine*.

Dustbinman Nigel was never a thing. Don't even mention it.

WHAT TO SAY: "Have you ever noticed how the names of the Teletubbies correspond with the members of the Who? John Entwistle is Po (faced), Roger Daltrey is Laa-Laa, Keith Moon is certainly Dipsy, and Pete Townshend is Tinky-Winky, swinging his handbag."

WHAT NOT TO SAY: "I never watched TV as a kid. I used to read books, actually."

The kinship between Britain and America is often characterized as a complicated one, an indefinable and slightly sullen cultural exchange that hides under the vague umbrella term "special relationship" and tries hard not to pick faults in either direction (although they definitely could find some if they were forced to). That said, there's evidence of enormous affection on both sides: British kids in baseball caps and hoodies listening to hip-hop and keeping a weather eye out for "the feds" would be lost without American culture, and bookish American teens with Tom Hiddleston tumblrs, Adele's latest in the earbuds, and a stack of Conan Doyles to work through would be similarly cut adrift.

In fact, while the American view of Britain is probably generally fond but largely disinterested (present company excepted), it's very easy to illustrate how most British people see America, using one figure from popular culture: Jermaine Jackson. To be specific, the Brits are Jermaine Jackson looking at Michael Jackson (who, for the purposes of this illustration, is America) at some point during the 1980s and trying to figure out where all his emotions are coming from.

On paper, Jermaine has a lot to offer. He's the older sibling, has talent and charisma, and stands as a reminder of his younger brother's roots and faltering early steps. He shares a lot of common reference points and, while there has been tension in the past, there's a lot of understanding and admiration there too. At one point, he was the leader, the strong, confident voice ready to take over the world. But he has since withdrawn in the face of '80s Michael's scorching charisma, and now his contribution, while worthy, and well loved by people who take the time to learn about such things, is as naught when compared to that of his brother.

Sometimes they work together, and everyone looks at Jermaine again. And sometimes they work apart, and . . . well, it's different.

Jermaine knows this to be true, and he understands why things are the way they are. He is as impressed with Michael as anyone, and he knows that to stand against his exceptionally talented brother's moment of total assurance would be foolish. He has even taken up some of Michael's characteristics, become something of an expert in the things his impish sibling has already abandoned. Almost like a curator.

But that doesn't mean his view is uncritical. Jermaine still feels the pain of being overtaken, knows that his brother's ascent has been at his expense, and not without leaving behind some valuable things along the way. Which would be bad enough (no pun intended) without the sense that troubling things are happening over there at Neverland and someone should really say something. Structural changes are taking place that hint at future problems that could take down the entire family, but while Michael remains the uncontested King of Pop, all Jermaine can do is watch and ponder quietly while still being borne aloft by all the hoopla.

Or to be less metaphorical: Brits love America. They love the food and the music and the TV and the movies and the culture and the weather and the landscape and the optimism and the confidence and the baseball caps and the sneakers (only they call them *trainers*, because they are used when training, not sneaking).

But sometimes they also love saying that America is a bit dumb and easily dazzled. And they can find plenty of evidence for that too.

WHAT TO SAY: "Hi, I'm your new neighbor. Would you like to come over for root beer and snickerdoodles?"

WHAT NOT TO SAY: "Hey, buddy, how do I get to Chel-ten-*ham*?"

Desert Island Discs ▪

When preparing an interview with someone in the public eye, it should be fairly easy to sit down, ask questions about her life, and come away with some plain and honest truths. But if you really want to color in the picture, and find out what that person is really like—the things that motivate her, the way she grieves, her formative influences—you'd be better off asking her about her relationship with music.

That's the simple truth that underpins the format of one of British radio's most successful shows, and one that remains a national favorite over seventy years after it was first devised.

The format for the BBC's *Desert Island Discs* is based in a simple question, first posed in 1941 by the show's creator, Roy Plomley: if you were stuck on a desert island, which eight records would you wish to have with you?

Of course, the answer is nowhere near as simple, and plenty of people have unraveled when having to choose which of their audio darlings to leave behind and which to include. Do you pick songs that were with you during key moments in your life, or do you pick songs that you really like at the moment? Do you try to cover a broad enough sweep of music to represent the full range of your music taste—ask any Brit what kind of music he likes and without fail he will airily say something like, "I like a really eclectic mix of things"—or do you just pick the longest possible songs you can, in the certain knowledge that no one can stand to hear just eight songs over and over again without pining for variety like an unstroked dog pines for attention?

The answers to the question form the backbone of an extended interview, in which Roy (or most recently Kirsty Young) asks a notable figure to tell the story of his or her life, with significant breaks to explain these records and play them. Then at the end, the guest is offered the Bible (or equivalent book of faith), the complete works of Shakespeare, and a third book of the guest's choosing, and one luxury item, on the understanding that it cannot be used to aid in an escape. One final twist of the knife, as the guest is asked to choose his or her one favorite of the eight, and that's the end of the show.

It's a featherweight conceit, one that takes longer to explain than it does to grasp, but the glory of *Desert Island Discs* is that the format creates a bespoke radio show around each of its interviewees. They are placed into a comfortable sonic space in which uncomfortable truths can be relatively painlessly expressed; they feel they are standing on home territory, that everyone else is on their desert island. Consequently each show is its own entity, a different place to visit. And since the BBC unveiled an online archive of over five hundred episodes, it's possible to island hop not just in space, but in time too.

Of course, it's not all about revelations. Sometimes you really do just get to hear what some A-list celebrity or public figure thinks about music, and that can reveal interesting truths about the person's character. Themes start to emerge: politicians pick records that will curry favor with their constituents; serious actors pick serious records that make them seem deep and thoughtful; grumpy TV chefs, for whom taste is all, often pick bland, mulchy, and unseasoned records, because you can't be an expert in everything.

Sometimes there are guests for whom music is clearly nothing but a background noise, but even that has its own psychological fascination. Surely everyone loves music on some level, don't they? And if not, why not?

But the real hook of *Desert Island Discs*, the one British listeners have been wriggling on for decades, is that question. It would not be a stretch to claim that everyone has some idea which records they would choose. It's not uncommon to overhear people, when hearing a beloved song on the radio, exclaiming, "This is one of my desert island discs," proudly, as if opening a golden envelope at the Academy Awards.

And that's because to be on *Desert Island Discs* is a public honor, a rite of passage for anyone with an ambition to be noticed. It's Carnegie Hall, a shot at the White House, the front cover of *Time* magazine; and British listeners treat it with due reverence, always vaguely wondering what they would do if presented with the same dilemma.

WHAT TO SAY: "You can't pick 'Mustang Sally' over 'Nessun dorma'! That's just wrong!"

WHAT NOT TO SAY: "Of course, nowadays you'd have your entire music library on your iPod anyway. Which would have to be solar powered . . ."

Creating New Worlds ■

It's tempting to blame everything that happens in Britain on the weather. We already know Brits enjoy talking about it; they certainly take perverse pleasure in going on long walks in it; and when it closes in, there's little to be done except sit by a hot thing with a cup of hot runny stuff nearby and imagine what other, more welcoming realities must be like.

It's not a simple case of dreaming of a world in which it is possible to go and buy a Sunday newspaper—so called because it is packed with such an acreage of supplements it won't be fully digested in a month of Sundays—and return home without the paper becoming a sodden papier-mâché model of an Arctic roll. Bad weather makes everything seem gray and dreary, and that's what the British makers of worlds seek to escape more than anything else.

So when C. S. Lewis conceived of Narnia, it was as a place of binary extremes: a golden kingdom, glazed in sunshine and scented with the blossom of spring, or a frozen wasteland, a paradise in waiting. At no point does Aslan's kingdom experience sludgy autumnal drizzle or the kind of dreary sogginess that characterizes the British February. In every other respect Narnia is Britain, of course; a medieval Britain with no mud, better toilet facilities, and a lot of mythical creatures, but still recognizably not Italy.

J. R. R. Tolkien's Middle-earth is familiar territory too. The Shire is clearly an affectionate caricature of the eternal myth of British village life, with sun-dappled harvests and lots of drinking, pipe smoking, and tall tales about dragons. Granted, Tolkien's sharp eye could not resist showing the hobbits up for being provincial—they are, in every respect, the little people—but for all that there is adventure and astonishment taking place in the wild lands over yonder, home is where the hobbit heart is, especially if it is not raining.

That's not to say British fantasy writers are obsessed with the myth of the great British (meaning English) countryside. Terry Pratchett rather likes a spot of rain, and his Discworld, while still notably medieval, is muddier, wetter, and murkier than the golden visions of Tolkien or Lewis. But that's because his books are supposed to be funny. Mud is always funnier than sunshine. Douglas Adams had a similar tack in the *Hitchhiker's Guide to the Galaxy* books. By making the character Arthur Dent as English as the children in *The Lion, the Witch and the Wardrobe* and as parochial as Bilbo Baggins—he travels space and time wearing the dressing gown he had put on shortly before the Earth was blown up—and then plopping him onto a spaceship, Adams gets to play with the traditional British values of being a bit starchy, uncool, slow on the uptake, and obsessed with finding a decent cup of tea.

Then there are Wonderland and Neverland, two magical worlds in which all the rules of (respectively) Victorian and Edwardian British society are turned on their heads to prove to children that they have been put there for a very good reason. Alice goes hurtling from rabbit hole to croquet lawn, being grown by cakes and shrunk by potions and threatened with execution by a crazed queen. It's a horrifying ordeal, even for such a bossy girl, and an unbeatable metaphor for children knowing their place and not being in too much of a hurry to grow up. On a similar note, Peter Pan actively refuses to grow up and take responsibility, living on an adventure island and fighting with an eternal father figure who is scared of the passage of time (that crocodile—*clockodile*, more like—with a ticking stomach: a literal consumer of bodies).

Sometimes the fantasy worlds come to provincial Britain, as is the case with H. G. Wells's *War of the Worlds*. We get to see Martian invaders in the suburbs of London. No flying saucer attacks on Big Ben or Buckingham Palace, but a journey on foot through Woking, Leatherhead, Shepperton, Walton: the kind of humdrum areas in which notable things are unlikely to occur. J. K. Rowling used the same trick when she placed Harry Potter in a respectable house in a suburban estate, having been hidden there by the wisest wizard of a secret wizarding society, who realized that no one who knows their *lumos* from their *expelliarmus* would ever want to live in such an uncharming place.

Wells also created *The Time Machine*, in which a professorial character travels to a far future in which the realms of airy intellect and basic instinct have been separated genetically into two races, the Eloi and the Morlocks, because, from his Victorian standpoint, he could not conceive of a world in which people could breed across class boundaries. George Orwell took this one stage further in *Nineteen Eighty-Four* (a dystopian England in which it is always a wet Wednesday), by showing a totalitarian regime in which the working classes— the proles—are 85 percent of the population, but so removed from society, as expressed through the hierarchies of the ruling Inner Party and middle-class Outer Party, that they're not even considered worth keeping under surveillance. As long as they are fed and entertained, and troublemakers are weeded out, no prole need ever have to worry about a trip to Room 101.

There's even a parody of this writerly response to inclement weather in Aldous Huxley's *Brave New World*. In a future dystopia in which natural urges have been both indulged and restricted, the character Helmholtz Watson faces exile and chooses the Falkland Islands over somewhere sunny, as he believes the bad weather would help him focus on writing. As if to prove this point, *Nineteen Eighty-Four*—which Orwell put together some sixteen years after Huxley's *Brave New World* was published—was largely written in a farmhouse on the Scottish island of Jura during a bitter winter, a mild summer, and a relentlessly wet autumn. George Orwell, who had never had the healthiest lungs thanks to his devotion to strong hand-rolled cigarettes, was suffering, first from the tuberculosis that would ultimately take his life a year or so later, and then from the unpleasant aftereffects of a new TB drug. Consequently there's a distinct lack of golden sunshine in that book, or talking lions, for that matter.

WHAT TO SAY: "Fetch the umbrella. I feel a utopia rising within me."

WHAT NOT TO SAY: "Shall we play Monopoly instead?"

Melancholy ■

Samuel Johnson called it "the black dog," and so, in his turn, did Winston Churchill. Nick Drake also had a dark hound of foreboding but only described its black eyes and the fact that it knew him by name. But all three did much the same job; namely, to act as the feral metaphor for an oncoming fug of wild melancholy. You could call it a result of changeable weather, you could say it's a hangover from the decline of the empire or even a necessary by-product of a natural hardiness, but a significant proportion of the residents of the British Isles do seem to walk around underneath their own personal rain cloud all the time.

It has also been referred to as "the English disease," but then, so have other such Anglified maladies as hypochondria, rickets, football hooliganism, and putting spaces into compound words when writing in Dutch (no, really!), so let's maybe stick with the black dog thing for now.

It's not that the Brits are any more prone to dark moods or genuine mental illness than anyone else; it's more that they simply don't trust things that are 100 percent happy. Actually, they don't trust any simple emotions, but happiness—being uncluttered by anything except a giddy awareness of itself—is clearly accessible for only the simpleminded and people with no foresight and no memory for the heartbreaks of the past. It is not for rational thinkers with real lives, heads out of clouds, and feet on the ground.

Having said that, sadness is just as troublesome. As far as the Brits are concerned, being noticeably sad is an affectation largely played out for effect and attention. All that wailing and rending of garments, all that pulling of hair and sobbing openly so that people can see. Well, it might be all right in Europe, but not in Britain.

So if you had to find a way to define a certain reserved, unavailable, undemonstrative, and generally unforthcoming British state of being, that's melancholy. It's deep in the national psyche, peeping out mournfully and souring the milk.

They have a royal family who don't look like they enjoy being in charge; they have celebrities whose principal role in the world of show business is to be perpetually disappointed by other people; they invented Morrissey and fog-soaked folk music and Winnie the Pooh's grumpy friend Eeyore and Tony Hancock and Coldplay and Keats and Philip Larkin and Alan Bennett and the shipping forecast and the Kinks and Johnny Rotten and stone-faced comedians like Jack Dee and Stewart Lee. The greatest British romance is *Romeo and Juliet*, and while that does not end well for either party, it is still somehow considered an enviable passion. They are a nation for whom the glass is neither half-full nor half-empty, but *once-full*, and that's the way they like it.

So it's not that they enjoy being sad, or yearn to be happy; the way the Brits carry melancholy is as they would a heavy bag or tight pair of shoes. This is something that one simply endures. Not from a position of denial, far from it, but from the certain knowledge that there is very little anyone can do to shift it, beyond momentary distractions like drink or sex or crosswords. The trick is to make those moments last as long as humanly possible, which says a lot about how much the Brits like drink, and sex, and crosswords.

To summarize: You've heard the voice of Marvin the Paranoid Android from *The Hitchhiker's Guide to the Galaxy*? That's the English interior monologue. Give it a pleasing burr, round out the vowels, emphasize the *r* sounds, and add some sharp expletives and it's also the Scottish interior monologue. The Welsh interior monologue is, if anything, more dour and exasperated, but it sounds less so because the accent is friendly; and the Northern Irish interior monologue does not wish to be associated in any way with the English one. Oh, wait, some of it does. No, now it doesn't. Oh, now it's arguing with itself.

Or to put it another way: if the Brits had made *The Lego Movie*, the theme song would be "Everything Is Awful" and it would sound like Radiohead.

WHAT TO SAY: "Oh, dear, one of those days? Fancy a pint?"

WHAT NOT TO SAY: "Cheer up, love, it might never happen!"

All the news that's fit to print. And some that is not.

This topic is messier to unpick than a jumper made of wet dog hair, and just as prone to unpleasantly sticky patches, but the tabloids are as palpable a presence in British society as, well, that same wet dog in an immaculate hallway. The trouble is, in print journalism nothing is quite as straightforward as it seems.

There are lots of very good reasons to hate the British tabloid press (or, to give full credit where it is due, the British press). They inflame as much as they inform; they intrude when they should observe; they take themselves out of the situations they have created and then ask innocently, palms aloft, how such a thing could ever have come to pass. Worst of all, they set an agenda of campaigning cynicism, pitting communities against one another from both sides of the political divide and inflaming deeply held prejudices—sometimes using only the most convenient of facts, if any—so that politicians feel they must react to a made-up situation or risk a speedy death at the polls. Their influence, in other words, is untempered by the consequences of their actions. They can always say they told you so, but rarely admit to being wrong.

There again, all that power comes from somewhere. Ask a political blogger with a small audience to what extent he or she feels able to influence government policy and you will get a hollow laugh in return. Give that same blogger an attentive readership of millions, and the response will be entirely different. So the tabloids, and the broadsheets too, give their people what they want. And because their papers sell (they reason), they must not be doing anything wrong.

It's not unlike the argument about exploitative photographs in celebrity magazines. Ask the public if they think magazines should continually run shaming editorials about celebrities gaining or losing weight, or send paparazzi to lie on the floor and try to get shots of Emma Watson's knickers, and they will fairly uniformly say no. Ask them to stop buying the magazines that contain those editorials and pictures and they will also say no, quite firmly too. What is a magazine to do?

And then add in the fact that British people really do want to have an inquiring and critical press. They want fraud and criminality to be exposed. They want shady dealings to be brought out into the light and subjected to a thorough examination. They also know that the life of a tabloid hack involves a great deal of righteous dirt-digging. Even during a period when the public was exposed to some of the darkest, most exploitative techniques of information retrieval in journalistic history—as exposed during the Leveson inquiry into, among other things, the hacking of mobile phones—the consensus was that these were the acts of bad apples, under pressure from bad editors and un-checked by a regulatory body with any teeth. The public perception of the work of actual dedicated newshounds, while never openly admired in the way the work of a firefighter might be, did not suffer unduly.

That's because they love newspapers. They love them on their morning commute. They love them at lunchtime, spending a half hour with the crossword or giggling at the spectacularly bad advice given by experts on the problem page, and they love them all the way home. And if anything, that love is more intense at the weekend. Few plea-sures can match a Sunday morning sitting at a big table with a pot of coffee and a pile of newspapers to wade through. The Sunday papers are thick enough to provide a week's worth of reading in one hit, and still have a section or two left over to line the cat's litter tray with, and they cover hard news, lifestyle, sports, gossip, and culture in perfect nuggets that shouldn't take too long to finish, in between buttering toast and applying marmalade. You just pick the editorial flavor that most suits your taste and away you go.

Then there are the campaigns. These are the largest muscles a newspaper can flex. They can be inspirational or hateful, principled or bullying, and always play out on the front pages, usually with a spe-cific political outcome in mind. It might be a campaign to prevent road deaths for cyclists or to rescue an unhappy rhino from a cruel zoo (see: Animals). You'll find the *Daily Mail* or *The Sun*—Britain's top two popular newspapers—running stories about rampant immigration, fraudulent benefits claimants, or the antics of Russell Brand (he really seems to get on their nerves), and within a very short space of time, new government policies are announced that seek to tackle immigra-tion, to reform the benefits system, to curb the excesses of Russell Brand's hair. The newspapers can claim to have the ear of the people and the throat of the government and will use their popularity to shout and squeeze with some violence.

Not that this means they aren't campaigned against in turn. *The Sun* faces stiff opposition (no, really) to the daily topless model on page 3, and the *Daily Mail*—with the biggest traffic for any newspaper website in the world, thanks largely to a sidebar featuring celebrity women and their tiny, tiny flaws—fairly consistently tiptoes down the fine line between "saying what we're all thinking" and "inventing appalling opinions for attention" with all the deftness, grace, and elegance of a boulder landing on a wedding cake. For all that the *Mail* can muster troops to complain about the mistakes of the BBC and the NHS, there are no shortage of people ready for a counterattack on the occasions when it steps out of line.

There again *again*, none of the above applies to celebrity journalism. That's an entirely different fish tank of maggots. In celebrity journalism the exploited and the exploiters switch sides with such breathtaking speed it's hard to be sure what's really going on. You may find suspiciously staged photos of a young actor or would-be pop star out for a jog, because he or she wants to be seen in the paper. You may find that same star arguing with a photographer outside a nightclub, or angrily tweeting about being harassed, later that same week. But some stars are tabloidworthy only because their work is enormously well liked. They have never courted that attention but they get it nevertheless, and they're largely expected to deal with the intrusion with good grace. Some of them even manage it. And the journalists often use the excuse that they're well paid and in the public eye, so why should they complain? This line of reasoning only bears what little weight it can because the hacks are once again appealing to the people who really pay their wages: their readers, who are neither famous nor rich, but who will buy papers.

And that's really what the British tabloid press are all about: the bottom line. They write those things and they take those pictures because there's a willing audience that wishes to see them and believe them. The tabloids and the broadsheets aren't like that because they're run by evil masterminds bent on world domination—although that may also be the case—but because that is the way their readers want things to be, even those who buy the papers just to be appalled by them.

All we can say with any certainty is that Brits enjoy having their feelings whipped up by the press; but there again again *again*, maybe if the media were more honest about their own involvement in the news stories they cover, if they allowed themselves to be seen in the rooms they describe, things might be different. Do you agree? Text YES to this number . . .

WHAT TO SAY: "And you can read all about my sensational life in this week's *Mirror*."

WHAT NOT TO SAY: "No comment."

Cars and *Top Gear* ■

You don't have to be cruising down the freeway with the top down, or leaning out of a meandering Cadillac looking over the top of your sunglasses at a pretty lady (or pretty man), to have a soft spot for cars. In fact, there's almost as much romance to be found winding your way down Cheddar Gorge in an asthmatic Morris Traveller, rolling obliviously up the A1 with a caravan (and ten-mile tailback) in tow, or making furious revving noises in a souped-up Ford Focus while waiting at the traffic lights at the Hammersmith roundabout. Almost.

In Britain, as in every other country in the world, most people think cars are nice—helpful even—but find it hard to muster the enthusiasm to keep theirs clean. We don't need to linger on this middle-ground view for now, beyond saying you don't have to obsess over mpg or torque to have a bond with an automobile. Nor is this the moment to consider the views of the people who actively wish to ban the internal combustion engine on ecological grounds, as the overwhelming majority of people care only about the usefulness of the vehicle and try not to think too hard about its fuel.

However, some people do take their passion to an obsessive degree. Roger Taylor from Queen, for example, who wrote the song "I'm in Love with My Car," and meant it too. It's a languid, unsettling snog between man and machine that only really makes sense (note: it doesn't really make sense) if you take the view that the automobile in the song is a metaphor for a sexy lady, or if you consider that Roger Taylor from Queen is very much the kind of rock star who would buy the kind of car that a rock star might find erotically stimulating. One that purrs.

Not that you have to be a rock star either. Talk to any of the Brits attending bank holiday rallies in which everyone who has the same sort of a car—Minis, VW camper vans, Beetles, Citroën 2CVs, vintage steam tractors—gets together in a field to admire their vehicles and the subtle differences in color, design, performance, and . . . ah . . . did I say design? Then there are the admirable obsessives who maintain and drive the oldest cars in existence and take them out on the first Sunday in November for the London to Brighton Veteran Car Run. This is the longest-running motoring tournament in the world and is emphatically not a race, more a chance for a communal parade of a private passion. Should you be considering turning up with your De-Lorean or knackered old Volvo, you should be aware that cars are eligible only if they were built before 1905.

That's not to say the British are too genteel a nation to enjoy the thrills and spills of a good race. In fact, they've even invented some of the hairiest circuits on the planet. Never mind Formula 1, the Isle of Man TT race comes from the era of putting high-performance vehicles (in this case motorbikes) onto public roads and letting the chips fall where they may, and that's still an underlying attitude taken, if not by the organizers themselves, then by the participants, and definitely by the audience. The risk of injury, or even death, can't be removed from the thrill of the spectacle and that's partly why people love it.

Did I say never mind Formula 1? Strike that; Formula 1 racing is something of a national obsession, making household names of not only the best drivers but the TV commentators too. The BBC's Murray Walker is the name most associated with the sport, although he has now retired. But in his prime he had a voice like an engine revving furiously in too low a gear, one that could cut through the sound of a pack of finely tuned performance cars doing exactly the same thing. At the same time, the TV coverage made a permanent link between Formula 1 and the coda section on the Fleetwood Mac song "The

Chain," the bit that starts with just a bass guitar and the pitter-patter of tiny drumsticks on a snare.

So to sum up after the briefest of stone-skims across the surface of the British love affair with cars: there is a firm meeting point between motors, leering sexuality, smashing stuff up, and classic rock music, and that's the place in which you will find *Top Gear*.

Top Gear isn't really about the science of cars, although it does feature a lot of technical information, delivered with the giddy glee of schoolboys who don't seem to fully grasp the significance of the specifications they strongly trot out: it's more of a talk show than a torque show. That's why they bring famous people in for a chat and a drive around their racetrack. Once you get past the secret entry door that is their winking claim to be a useful consumer guide—easy to disprove just by looking at the prices of the cars they overwhelmingly tend to favor—it's clear that the purpose of the show is to treat automobiles as a kind of Swiss Army knife with hidden tools.

"I know what this thing is supposed to do," the makers of the show insist. "I'm supposed to point it toward the place I wish to get to, and assuming I have enough petrol in the tank and the traffic isn't too unforgiving, I'll get there in the end. But this is a TV show! We need to make things more interesting. What else can we make it do? What can we race it against? Who can we put in it? What if a car was a boat? What if a car was an airplane? What if you could wear two cars as shoes? What if you could use a car to play football? Or ice hockey? Or poker? Or send one down a ski jump? *Ooh! Ooh! I know! What if we could put a car into space?!*"

And then they attempt all of these ideas and many more besides, but they don't bring in the guys from *Pimp My Ride* to do any of the refurbishing work properly, because (a) that would cost a lot of money and this is a BBC TV show and (b) it's better to show the three presenters bodging their way through it as best they can, and failing. This also applies if all they are trying to do is get from A to B, where A is one side of a desert/mountain range/ocean floor and B is the other. Throw in a bloke in a white Formula 1 outfit who never takes his helmet off—all we know is, he's called the Stig—and your formula is complete.

The other thing *Top Gear* does is remove the veil of British reserve from an equally British kind of impatience. The show's three best-known presenters—James May, Richard Hammond, and especially Jeremy Clarkson—have all displayed a Mr. Toad attitude toward things that obstruct their view of the open road and what should be allowed on it. Caravanners, people who drive the wrong sorts of cars, cyclists, parking attendants, speed cameras, foreigners, women . . . anything and everything that stands, rolls, or officiously puts a barrier between them and putting their pedal extremity to the pedal to the metal is given short shrift. This does not always make them friends, but to a certain mind-set, it also feels a lot like cocking a snook at sensible kill-joys who can't relax enough to enjoy a spot of ribald humor—this, as you can imagine, causes quite a lot of debate—and so the aggro caused by their worst tuts and slanders is often matched and even bested by the warm glow of approval from adoring fans (see: Cocking a Snook).

But the secret ingredient to *Top Gear*'s success is that it doesn't really matter about the cars at all, because the show is about mates being mates and doing matey things together, matily. You, the audience, are one of the mates too, if you want to be. And actually it would be the same if the show were about cosmetics or DIY or if all the presenters were speed cameras dressed as foreign women in a caravan. So long as you have friends openly mocking each other while smashing up the things they claim to love the most, it's *Top Gear*.

WHAT TO SAY: "I know—what if you could use a car to get stones out of a horse's hoof?"

WHAT NOT TO SAY: "Say, why do you guys drive on the wrong side of the road anyways?"

Chocolate That Tastes of Chocolate ■

Selected highlights of British cand— Sorry, chocolate.

The Belgians and the Swiss may claim to have the best chocolate in the world, but when it comes down to everyday candy, the kind of sweets you can eat between meals without ruining your appetite (as the commercials for British Milky Way used to say), the Brits tend to prefer their own.

Granted, you can get some chocolate foodstuffs that are common pretty much everywhere. M&M's, for example, although the idea of little chocolate buttons covered in a colorful sugar shell already existed in Britain; they are called Smarties and Minstrels. Smarties are like classic M&M's (but made with Cadbury chocolate and without any of the variants that include peanuts or peanut butter or coconut, etc.) and Minstrels are bigger and coinier—although not as coinlike as the shell-less Cadbury Buttons—and have Galaxy chocolate inside. This is important, because while each brand of chocolate tastes noticeably different from the other, the one thing you can definitely say is that they both taste of chocolate.

If that seems like an odd distinction to make, remember that Hershey's products have also made their way over to the UK in the form of the Kisses and whatnot, and, well, let's just say the Brits now understand why Americans call their chocolate bars candy bars, 'cos they sure don't taste of chocolate.

Or, to be strictly accurate, they sure don't taste of the ratios of cocoa solids to sugar that British palates have grown accustomed to in a milk chocolate confectionery, given that the real taste of pure chocolate is richer, deeper, and more bitter than you would find wrapped around a Snickers bar, wherever it may be from. If you're looking for that kind of chocolate, and you're in a supermarket, the brand to look for is Green & Black's. Theirs is chocolate for grown-ups and they do not make anything that resembles M&M's.

Some candy bars vary by region. Mars bars in Britain have no nuts, the peanuts having been left to their sister bar, the Marathon (which changed to the more familiar Snickers in 1990). The British Mars is basically the bar that Americans know as the Milky Way—caramel and nougat inside—and the British Milky Way is the same as a 3 Musketeers. There's no British equivalent for the Baby Ruth, Butterfinger, or Mr. Goodbar.

Other creations from the Mars family include Twix (two finger biscuits with caramel on top and coated in chocolate); Topic (a hazelnut Snickers, but shorter in length and taller); Bounty (a coconut and chocolate creation that is an equivalent to the unpleasantly pooishly named Mounds; blue wrappers have milk chocolate, red have plain); and Maltesers, which are malted honeycomb balls in chocolate. They can also be found in a bag of Revels, which is an assortment of chocolate balls stuffed with something—a raisin! toffee! coffee! just chocolate!—best eaten by really fussy people for a Russian roulette thrill.

Mars also makes Galaxy chocolate, which is available in bars and slabs and with various nuts and extras. Galaxy is sold as Dove chocolate around the world, but, again, the Brits remain loyal to the local version only.

And some products are only available locally, such as the decidedly grown-up Fry's chocolate bars, all of which are made with plain chocolate and contain soft centers with either chocolate, peppermint, or orange flavoring. Fry's also make the Turkish delight, in which some Turkish delight (rose-flavored jelly, essentially) is dipped in chocolate. These are not everyday treats. Nor is Terry's Chocolate Orange, a ball-shaped masterpiece of confectionary architecture; this tends to come out at Christmastime, where the ritual of banging it on a tabletop to loosen it into segments can leave unpleasant dents on your furniture.

Rowntree was a real giant of British sweet making during a golden age of discovery and innovation (and hyperbole). Theirs was a Wonka-like kingdom where chocolate was just one of many flavors to explore. The company has been bought out by Nestlé now, and therefore is subject to fewer local quirks, but in its time Rowntree created some of the most beloved of all British candy.

There are Smarties, yes, but also Tooty Frooties; Fruit Pastilles; Fruit Gums; Polos; Rolos; After Eights; Aero (with bubbles, effectively chocolate with added less!); Yorkie bars you could break your teeth on; lumpy Lion bars; twiggish and elegant Matchmakers; the solid-but-dollopy Walnut Whip; and the immortal Kit Kat. We've had the Kit Kat tested by flavor experts (people with mouths) and it seems the British version is empirically better. Not Swiss chocolate better, but it will do fine for a perfectly good elevenses, thank you.

Nestlé also gave us the white chocolate Milky Bar, as advertised by a blond cowboy with spectacles called the Milky Bar Kid who would regularly give whole boxes of the product away, provided he had bested some six-gun-totin' hoodlum first. A most curious marketing strategy, that . . .

But the real chocolateering slog was and is performed by the British end of the Cadbury brand. As well as simple delights such as the Dairy Milk bar (just chocolate), the Whole Nut bar (chocolate and hazelnuts), and the Fruit & Nut bar (almond and raisin), Cadbury is responsible for the Crunchie (honeycomb in chocolate); the Wispa (like an Aero only with tiny bubbles in chocolate); the Picnic (biscuit, nougat, caramel, nuts, puffed rice and raisins in chocolate); the Time Out (fingers of flaked chocolate between wafers, in chocolate); the Twirl (flaked chocolate in chocolate); the Boost (weird burrito of crushed biscuit rolled in caramel, rolled in chocolate, sometimes with added guarana); the Starbar (same but with exciting wrappers); the Chomp and the Curly Wurly (both chewy caramel in chocolate but in markedly different shapes); the Caramel (runnier caramel than a Chomp and in chocolate-covered segments); and the Freddo (frog-faced chocolate for kids).

Cadbury has come to define the British run-up to Easter too, by allowing its Creme Eggs (yolky sugary goop in a chocolate eggshell) and Mini Eggs (like egg-shaped Smarties but with an eggshell finish) to be sold only from around Christmas to around June. This means the Brits can effectively live a binary year: it's either Creme Egg time or mince pie time.

The Flake is a crumbly creation that has two uses: it's notable for being jammed into the piped ice cream cones you get from the ice cream van, a concoction known as a 99, which children particularly enjoy. However, the adverts for Flakes were always a bit "sexy girl puts something in her mouth slowly, yeah?" leaving the ice-cream-less kids to assume this was a grown-up affair and opt for something far less troubling, like a Fudge with its entirely worry-free song: "a finger of fudge is just enough to give your kids a treat."

What? Who's giggling? Stop it at once.

WHAT TO SAY: "Haven't Mars bars changed size? They used to be bigger."

WHAT NOT TO SAY: "I prefer crisps."

A moment of historical vertigo kicks in when thinking about any of the great Neolithic sites that can still be found in overlooked corners of the British Isles. Stone circles like the ones at Avebury, or the Ring of Brodgar on Orkney, and curious edifices like the gigantic picnic table of Cornwall's Lanyon Quoit are proof that humans were active and busy and productive thousands of years before there ever was such a thing as England or Wales. And in the case of the most famous circle of all—Stonehenge—the evidence indicates that the area around Avebury in what is now Wiltshire has been occupied continuously for over ten thousand years.

Even taking into account the astonishing evidence that suggests it spent fifteen hundred years evolving as a constructed site, Stonehenge itself is only somewhere between four thousand and five thousand years old, of which a little over one thousand have been spent in a country called England. Before that it was in a land of warring kingdoms and battling barons—and the Romans—and back beyond that is all myth and legend and not writing enough stuff down.

And it's the lack of scientific understanding as to what these Neolithic sites were truly for that drives a chunk of the mystery. Some stones in some circles appear to be aligned with the rising of the sun or the setting of the sun on key dates of the year. So it could be that

Lanyon Quoit: You need a very impressive chair to sit at this table.

they're nothing but solar calendars, designed to help farmers work out what needs doing in order to secure the best harvest. And in a way this makes as much sense as the idea that they exist for ceremonial purposes, because the two things that, to this day, are likely to make a community band together in common effort are ceremony and commerce (and war, but it's unlikely anyone would have built Stonehenge as an act of aggression, unless Neolithic humans were big on metaphors or had a system of writing that spelled out insults that look like a big stone lowercase *n*).

Consequently, all manner of pagan and neo-pagan rites have been enacted among standing stone circles by neo-druids. There's a huge celebration at Stonehenge for the summer solstice (June 21) and an equivalent one in winter (December 21) because that's how the site is laid out, to give a dramatic effect to the rising and setting of the sun at key moments of the year. It's clear some kind of ceremony would have been held on the site, and so antiquarians have resolved to try to imagine what kind of a thing it would have been, and then re-create it.

This might seem a little daft, given that there's no record of the kinds of things that might have been going on at the time, and should it turn out that any of them involved ritual sacrifice of human beings, the event may lose some of its appeal, but that's really the point. It's a way of putting the mind back beyond everything we know about, to a time when residents of the British Isles made their first permanent marks on the landscape.

But it's not all druids and incense. Popular culture is as obsessed with Stonehenge as anyone. Turner and Constable painted it, Wordsworth wrote about it in verse. Any retelling of the Arthurian myths will inevitably place some of the action within the stones—and maybe credit Merlin with putting them there in the first place (with the help of some giants, naturally; he's no builder). The movie *This Is Spinal Tap* depicts a typically dozy English rock band attempting to create a stage spectacle called Stonehenge but failing because of a catastrophic error in scale. *Doctor Who* set a particularly stirring speech there, during the Roman invasion of Britain, in which the time traveler invited a galaxy-ful of aliens to come and get him while standing in the center of the stones. This, remember, was still two thousand years after everyone who genuinely did build the place had died.

Not to mention the designs carved into the chalk hills, the white horses and lions, all of which are much more recent than any stone circle but still an attempt to reconcile the human population with the landscape that surrounds them.

The provocative artist Bill Drummond (formerly of the visionary postrave dance group the KLF) proposed a plan to buy the plot of land on which the Rollright Stones were situated, take all the stones and grind them into fine powder, then make that powder into cement and pour it into monolith-shaped molds. He then wanted to return the reconstituted monoliths to their original positions to see if he could jump-start the stone circle into doing whatever it is stone circles are supposed to do.

It's a challenging idea, and one that fair turns the stomach over when thinking about the damage he could have inflicted upon a site that had remained untouched for so many centuries. There again, who wouldn't like to see a fully working stone circle in action? Who knows what wonders could be achieved?

WHAT TO SAY: "It's a hallmark of a society that has become elevated above the day-to-day concerns of survival."

WHAT NOT TO SAY: "I bet it's a gateway to another dimension using the old magic that no one talks about because they are scared. Or maybe they were forced to forget by evil wizards! Did you think of that?"

Mousehole, home of Jerry, Mickey, and Mighty.

Please do not feel that a visitor to the UK would be made to feel unwelcome; Brits love tourists, providing they are a source of revenue for the local economy, they're part of a valuable cultural exchange between two proud nations, or they bring supplies of sweets you can't get in your local store. At all other times, it's total war.

Although, being Britain, the weapons used in the field of battle tend to be less physical (see the points above, particularly the one about revenue) and more lexicographical. There are three principal ways in which the Brits enjoy snickering up their sleeves at Johnny Not-from-Round-Here, especially visitors from the U.S. of A.

1. Mocking the way Americans spell stuff.

2. Deliberately giving streets and villages dirty names and acting like it's no big deal.

3. Mocking the fact that outsiders can't immediately pronounce British things that are not said the way they are spelled.

The first is a hangover from the days of Noah Webster, who rewrote the American English dictionary, taking out unnecessary letters like the *u* in *colour* and the *ugh* in *plough* (and then adding a *w*) and rearranging *theatre* so it looked less fancy. If there's one thing guaranteed to make a chippy Brit do that superior smile that boils the blood, it's making out that Americans don't know how to spell words properly, and that's because Noah Webster did such a thorough job of tidying them up.

Of course, it's an unwinnable argument, akin to saying that language should obey the rules of the supermarket queue: first come, best spelled. And it generates a lot of unnecessary friction, which is entirely the point. You can delve into the social psychology of the situation and say it's a kind of consolation prize; that making such a fuss about something so trivial is a way of culturally dealing with the fact that America is America and Britain just plain isn't (see: America), but actually they do it to everyone. And even though the split between Britain and the United States happened during a time when spellings were particularly fluid, with both countries only formally nailing their colours/ colors to the mast during the 1800s, the Brits will always act as if it is their language that you are spoiling with your color, your flavor, and your rigor.

And then, just to prove there is no pomposity that cannot be undercut with some good old-fashioned toilet humor, they will send you on an errand to Beaver Close or Shitterton and act like you're a child for giggling.

Some British place-names are obscene in an internationally understood way: Cockermouth, Crotch Crescent, Fingringhoe, Hornyold Road, Sandy Balls, Dick Court (sadly not in a district called Zipper).

Some of them sound rude only to Brits: Back Passage (arf!), Minge Lane (oof!), Fanny Hands Lane (because you see . . . ah, ha-ha . . . in Britain the word *fanny* means . . .), Twatt (precisely), and Bell End, which is a village that has double points for embarrassing foreigners. Not only is a *bellend* a term of abuse based on a description of the rounded tip of a penis in British slang, but also the village is in Worcestershire, which is pronounced "woostersheer." Get that wrong and you will be lightly mocked or, worse, corrected in a helpful and earnest fashion. The shame of it!

This brings us to our final unfriendly assault, the places that aren't pronounced the way they are spelled. You'd think, given the size of the world and the number of dialects and languages within it, that the Brits would be a little bit forgiving of any traveler into their community who has clearly only just read the name of the village they've never been in before. But no; never mind that most Brits think that the United States has two different states, one called Arkansas and one called Arkinsaw; never mind that the English rampaged across the world asking what things were called, not listening properly to the answers, and then making up words that seemed to fit the bill—Bombay, Kingussie, Carnarvon—if you wander into Bicester and call it "bichester" (it's "bister"), if you enter Cholmondeley without knowing it's pronounced "chumley," if you call Fowey "fowey" and not "foy," or you wander about in Barugh and fail to call it "barf," there will be tutting. You may not hear the tutting, you may not even see it happen, but rest assured it will occur.

And there are some crackers out there, words that have no business claiming to be related, let alone pretending that the word on the page is the same as the one in the ear: Godmanchester claims to be called "gumster," for heaven's sake! Woolfardisworthy wants you to consider referring to it as "woolsery," while Oswaldtwistle has given up all claims to its own sharp consonants and reclined into the buzz of "ozzlethizzle."

Mousehole, made up of two very familiar words indeed, is pronounced "mousle," like "tousle," while Stiffkey claims to be called "stewkey" and Tintwistle is "tinsel." Of course it is. Why wouldn't it be?

Reversing this trend, Towcester is "toaster," which might just be the best fact about the entire British Isles, apart from all those rude place-names above.

WHAT TO SAY: "Seriously? Spell Albuquerque and then we'll talk about your arcane local knowledge."

WHAT NOT TO SAY: "So why is Manchester not pronounced 'manster'?"

Outdoor Art ■

I know it's tempting to believe that British people all live in thatched cottages in tiny rural communities, gathering around the fire of an evening to spin yarns about the day's plowing and supping on mead. There are thatched cottages; there are rural communities; there is plowing and mead and fire; but for the most part the lure of the enormous television, surround sound, good local amenities, and decent Wi-Fi have thwarted all but the most dedicated yarn-spinner. And even she is considering starting a blog.

So what does it take to get Brits to leave the house these days when all of entertainment is available at their fingertips? Something involving the arts and the elements, that's what; and gambling, but not with money. It is true to say that some of the most prestigious events in the British sporting calendar—the ones that involve a big shiny animal running around a track with a little monkey-man clinging to its back—only exist so that gambling can happen. Gambling is a Stuff Brits Like. And not just the kind where you lose your shirt credit-betting on a jolly before you've even ponied up the beeswax; technology being what it is, you can do all that from your sofa anyway.

No, the real gamble for modern Brits is to book tickets for an outdoor arts event, then see whether their weatherproofing supplies will suffice. It's one thing to rock up at Glastonbury or Download or Bestival, or any of the enormous range of British festivals, with a massive bag containing wellies (those rubber boots that too few people call galoshes these days), waterproof trousers, a parka, gloves, goggles, and a snorkel, but quite another to realize all you really needed was sunglasses, cut-offs, a faded T-shirt, and ten gallons of factor 50. Time to tear up your festival betting slip and start again.

And it's not just the pop fans that fancy a flutter on the elements. All across the frequently rained-upon nation there are outdoor art events going on. The Globe, for example, is a re-creation of the theater in which William Shakespeare's plays were first performed, and one that is untroubled with a roof. To stand in the stalls (and it really is standing), one must be prepared for things to fall from on high, not least from London's pigeon population. Oh, and you're not allowed to take an umbrella because that would spoil things for everyone else.

You can see classic movies in public parks or surprise locations, watch opera on the grounds of stately homes, or visit the Minack Theatre in Cornwall—where the sets and costumes of theatrical productions are frequently upstaged by the astonishing beauty of the Cornish coastline, as the theater has been built into the side of a cliff. And that's before you consider the many, many public rituals, art happenings, and performances that take place all year round, as part of a long and noble tradition of doing odd things outside on public holidays: something the Brits take very seriously indeed (see: Weird Traditions).

And the experience of outdoor art is not all old stuff, fine art, pop music, and fields. Thanks to the pioneering work of street artists like Banksy, British cities now boast thought-provoking al fresco murals, whether they wanted them or not. And as a bonus, the gambling has all been done for you by the artists themselves, taking internal bets on whether or not they'd get caught defacing public property (see: Drawing Willies on Things).

WHAT TO SAY: "Have you brought the picnic hamper?"

WHAT NOT TO SAY: "I re-created the festival experience at home, by rolling around in the garden until I'm good and muddy, rescuing an unfinished burger from a rubbish bin, and queuing to get into my own living room."

Boot Fairs and Charity Shops ∎

Getting rid of clutter is hard, even for the most unsentimental and meticulous householder. You can't just throw stuff away; some of it might be worth something. Some of it could have great sentimental value or become a family heirloom, with time, and some of it might even be of use in the future, assuming there's a sudden and unexpected global crisis that can only be solved by a heroic act involving two types of unfashionable hat, a selection of tiny ceramic statues, and a huge pile of dog-eared paperbacks.

So, leaving aside that last option for the moment, what's a spring-cleaning Brit to do in order to get rid of all the old junk? There are three options and the first is to put the real rubbish aside for recycling.

For the things that could be of value to someone else, there are boot fairs (also known as car boot sales). The boot is what the British call the trunk of their car, and a boot fair is a gatheration of cars on a patch of open land, from which people can sell their belongings for a small donation. It's an incredibly popular pastime for buyers and sellers alike. The biggest boot fairs can take up several fields, and as there are very few restrictions on what you can buy or sell—although, clearly, cars are going to be problematic, and body parts are a definite no-no—it's remarkable what turns up.

That's not to say there aren't common threads. It's an unwritten rule that all sellers must set up a wallpaper pasting table in front of their car, to display their wares better without going to the trouble of investing in expensive shop fittings. People also bring clothing rails if they're selling the kind of clothes you can't display by laying them on the ground (almost all clothes, in other words), and they will spend a good portion of their allotted time rushing over and picking everything up after the rail has blown over for the twelveteenth time.

If you are selling, you'll encounter two principal waves of interest: one pleasant and good-natured, the other feral and scary. Sadly, the second one comes first. This tends to happen most noticeably at the larger boot fairs, but when sellers arrive, they have a certain amount of time to get everything out of the car and displayed, and then some kind of signal—a klaxon or a siren—will sound, and that means the boot fair has started and the customers are on their way.

Now, at this point, just before the deluge hits, you'll notice that some of the other sellers have started checking out what's on sale nearby, and some of them may even start digging in their pockets for money. These are seasoned boot fair attendees, and they possibly even rely on innocent house-clearing folk for the bulk of their stock. A lot of deals are made in the first minute of selling.

The second minute, and most of the next ten, you will spend fending off the first wave of buyers—the boot fair zombies—people who are desperate for a bargain and do not wish to spend a lot of time thinking about what they are doing. That's for later. They'll poke at the delicately arranged collections of books and CDs; they'll root through the "Everything for £1" bin with the frenzy born of total panic. It's as if they know one of the stallholders has accidentally put a golden ticket to Willy Wonka's Chocolate Factory inside a tatty old teddy bear or has put out a valuable diamond ring that they believe to be cubic zirconium.

The first wave of buyers at a boot fair makes the January sales look like a particularly well stocked and generous soup kitchen. It's like a plague of locusts wearing money belts and looking for tat. The only sensible way to process the carnage as a seller is to remember the aim of the game is to get rid of things you no longer want, not to become a junk magnate. Let the wave wash over you, sell what you want to sell, at prices you're not going to regret later, and prepare for the calm after the storm.

That's when the ordinary folks arrive, people who enjoy a stroll in the fresh air and don't mind looking for a few bits and bobs while they're out and about. They won't take anywhere near as much of your stuff as the first wave, but they will leave the skin on your hands as they walk away.

After a couple of hours of this sort of thing, it's time to pack away the remaining 50 percent of your original pile and go home to count your takings. This is the end of the part of the story that could turn you a profit. Enjoy it while it lasts but do not be tempted to buy more crap. Learn from your mistakes!

What you have left is a pile of stuff that no one wanted to buy from you, but that could still be worth something to someone. And the place to take that kind of stuff is a charity shop.

Brits adore thrifting. Apart from coffee shops, charity shops—which is what the Brits call thrift stores—are the most common type of retail outlet on British high streets. Towns that have a particularly large number of charity shops are highly prized, and sometimes shoppers arrive by the coachload. They may be pensioners with not much else to do, or students looking for old clothes for a wacky fancy dress, and the shops' individual pickings may be slim, but it's all in the thrill of the chase.

Of course, if there's anything left in your thrice-filtered pile after all that, the only place for it is the bin.

WHAT TO SAY: "How much for that first edition of *Northanger Abbey*?"

WHAT NOT TO SAY: "A pound? I'll give you twenty p if you throw in the car . . ."

So, we've established that sport equals ritualized fighting, yes? But what happens when the ritual also contains a lot of what must, to inexperienced eyes, just look a lot like fighting anyway? Does it still count as a game if players routinely come away with a face like a knackered leather handbag, ears red and swollen up like toadstools, and their teeth having been left in parts of other players? What kind of ritualized war is rugby, with its rucks and mauls, if it is also still a war?

To step back from this a second, it's important to start with the basics. Rugby (league or union) is the game American football likes to think it is. It's a rough, knockabout brawl, with particular focus on territory and passing and carrying and running, and taking an oval ball to a place, while an opposing team tries to make you dead with their arms and shoulders and feet and pummeling ham fists.

Aside from the various rules and customs of the two games, two key differences separate American football and rugby, and on the surface, it's the rugby players who come off looking the bravest.

The first and most obvious point is that rugby players wear no armor beyond a gum shield of the sort that boxers wear. Brits rather enjoy telling themselves that this means rugby is a real man's game for real men, not an elegant pastime for precious little darlings that need wrapping in cotton wool before they will consent to even pick up a ball. That's just payback for years of comments about whining limeys, and best ignored.

It's also not true. As with modern boxing, where the gloves cause greater damage to fighter's brains than bare knuckles would because the blows are far harder, the American football padding and helmet mean athletes can really do themselves a mischief (as the sports scientists would say) in ways that rugby players can only dream of. But hey, at least they don't get cauliflower ears.

The second difference is that in rugby the principal scoring motion, once past all the grabby trollmen and their big hands, involves actually making contact between the ball and the grass, using a hand. Dropping the ball won't count. And this is where sports language becomes stupid. The game that involves touching the ball down on the floor calls that action a *try*, when at the very least it should be called a *do*. The game that does not require players to touch the ball down anywhere calls their scoring moment a *touchdown*.

It should be reiterated at this point that these men risk brain damage on a match-by-match basis; confusing them with misleading words is just cruel. And that's before we even consider the fact that both games have the nerve to call themselves *football*, when really they should consider *carryegg* as the proper alternative.

Rugby also holds a class conflict that really doesn't exist in any other major British sport. It also plays out across nations in an interesting way. If you're from Wales, your national sport is not football; it's rugby union, which enjoys huge support from fans from every walk of life. There are over two hundred Welsh rugby clubs, all hoping to field players toward the national team to play in the annual Six Nations Championship and beat the English. Scotland, while being more football friendly, also fields a rugby union team in the Six Nations and hopes to beat the English. As do Ireland, France, and Italy.

England itself has a slightly complicated relationship with the sport because of class. Football is the most prominent working-class game; cricket is the most prominent middle-class game; and anything above that probably involves horses. But the playing fields of English public (meaning private) schools ring with the shouts of games teachers enforcing rugby union matches upon freezing young bodies in the mud. In fact, the sport was invented and named by former pupils of the exclusive Rugby School in Warwickshire. So, in marked contrast to Wales and the other countries in the Six Nations, rugby union in England is very much a game for the sons of the ruling classes, who will be trained for a life in the civil service and possibly as officers in the army.

But that doesn't mean the game has no working-class support, far from it. In fact, in the industrial north, players in the late 1800s, who were all amateurs at the time, were losing so much paid work in order to play they elected to go professional. The southern clubs, gentleman players with affluent backgrounds, declined to join them, causing a split between the two sets of teams and, ultimately, the formation of a new sporting body: rugby league, which developed in parallel with rugby union and has its own rules. So rugby has its own north-south divide, with the league teams in the north playing their own tournaments and developing their own customs, in parallel to the south.

What this all means, apart from the normal run of matches and playoffs, is that when the Six Nations rolls around, there's a chance for four nations with reasonable grounds for a grudge against the English ruling class (plus Italy) to beat the stuffing out of them. And of course, the thing to remember about the English upper classes is they are hard, and ruthless, so it's usually a fight worth watching.

WHAT TO SAY: "What time do the cheerleaders come out?"

WHAT NOT TO SAY: "Is that guy called a 'scrum-half' because he's half the size of the other players?"

Curry ■

An uncomfortable truth lies at the heart of British cuisine. The most popular dishes and beverages—with surprisingly few exceptions—are either imported or contain imported ingredients. The English (in particular) consider themselves a proud, isolated island race with passions and interests and vices that are uniquely theirs, but they did have to go off around the world and fetch them back, before drawing up formal adoption papers and then pretending they had been there all along.

Take a look at a roll call of great British foodstuffs. Tea isn't local. Nor are the potatoes in fish 'n' chips and bangers 'n' mash, or the carrots and broccoli in a Sunday roast. Grilling some tomatoes with your fry-up? Adding some beans, perhaps? Yeah, they're not from around here. And that's before you consider the more obvious imports, like pizza and pasta, Chinese takeaway, or the spices used to flavor HP Sauce.

But the greatest incorporated import of them all is curry. Whether it's a premixed sachet of powder in the cupboard, ready to give some leftover meat a boot up the jacksy, a sweating takeaway in a carrier bag on the bus home, or a hot sauce, pooled and dripping on a portion of chips, the Brits have a particular affinity for any spicy food that comes from the general direction of India.

In fact, they love curry so much that they have developed their own dishes. Chicken tikka masala—regularly voted the most popular meal in Britain—is barely known in India or Pakistan, having been created in an Indian restaurant in Glasgow in 1971 (or so the legend goes). Now it's available as a meal, a flavor of crisps, and even a pizza topping. Balti curries are also claimed to be a UK innovation, first credited to Adil's Restaurant, Birmingham, in 1977. And this was forty-two years after the arrival of Jubilee chicken, a salad dish made from chicken, mayonnaise, and curry spices that was created to honor the silver Jubilee of George V. When Queen Elizabeth II was crowned in 1953, the dish was given a culinary reboot by Constance Fry and renamed Coronation chicken. It remains hugely popular as a sandwich filling or a topping for baked potato.

Some homegrown attempts at creating curry have led to discoveries that have since been claimed as entirely English. One is the recipe handed to pharmacists John Wheeley Lea and William Henry Perrins, who failed to make it into a palatable curry sauce, as they didn't have the right ingredients, and left their concoction stewing in a barrel once they realized it had failed. This allowed it to ferment, and when they came back to it and tasted it again, they discovered they had accidentally created Worcestershire sauce.

Naturally there are British traditions around drinking and curry. Thanks to the influence of the immigrant families from southern Asia in the middle of the twentieth century, the Indian restaurant—known chummily as a curry house—fast became a stopping-off point on a big night out, or the last stop on a weavy, shouty journey home, to grab a takeaway and drop it on the floor of the bus.

Certain customs are associated with a visit to the curry house too. It's common for people to overorder and then share their food—common enough for sticklers and connoisseurs to have to dig their heels in and fight for sole access to their dishes—and there's an element of showing off, in ordering the spiciest dish on the menu, just to prove you can take it. There was even a hugely celebrated sketch about it on the BBC comedy show *Goodness Gracious Me*—written and performed by British comedians of Asian descent—in which a group of drunken Indian office workers barge into a restaurant demanding "an English" and asking for the blandest meal on the menu.

It would be lovely to be able to say that this appreciation for the various cuisines of southern Asia has led to greater understanding and tolerance between communities, especially in areas such as London's Brick Lane—home of an entire street of curry houses—or those parts of Birmingham, Bradford, Batley, Blackburn, Dewsbury, Keighley, Leicester, Slough, or anywhere that can boast a particularly significant Asian community.

Sadly this isn't always the case, although if anyone is looking for a good bread to break during a peaceful community get-together, naan seems particularly well suited to the task.

WHAT TO SAY: "Of course I can take it. I eat spicy food all the time."

WHAT NOT TO SAY: *"Water. Please. Or I shall have to stick my head in the fish tank."*

Moaning About Bureaucracy ■

D id anyone say decorum? Emotional reserve? Stiff upper lip? Pah! For all that the Brits will tell anyone who'll listen that they're a nation that prefers not to talk about feelings, the one emotion you can always rely on hearing about is mild irritation. It's there in John Cleese's comedy, as the spiraling fury of Basil Fawlty; it's there in the narkier songs of Half Man Half Biscuit; and it's there in every angry comment on the Internet that begins with an eye-rolling sneer and ends with "Open your eyes, sheeple!"

And the one thing that causes greater outbreaks of petulance and irk than any other is bureaucracy. Which may seem odd, given the international British reputation for properness and bookkeeping, but while few things are more conspicuously British than a well-written series of regulations aiming to prevent something bad from happening, the only people who are pleased about those rules are the ones who drafted them.

And it does not matter how reasonable those rules are. In fact, the more transparently necessary they are, the more withering the scorn for having to be told in the first place: "'Don't stick your head out of the train window?' I mean, what kind of idiots do they think we are?"

There's an enormous disrespect for health and safety legislation, one that borders on ingratitude (which, again, is something you'd expect a culture that bangs on about manners all the time to be a little more aware of). If at a clifftop car park an appalling accident occurs in which a car drives over the edge, that's one thing. But woe betide the regional authority that seeks to prevent such an accident from happening again by putting up a sign suggesting that drivers be careful—"Of *course* we're not going to drive over the cliff! Who would *ever* do a thing like that? This is just another example of the nanny state telling people what to do. They can't help themselves . . ."

This mild apoplexy doubles if it's pointed out that such a sign exists so that the owners of the car park cannot be held responsible for such accidents, should they occur. Brits may love America (see: America), but the legal system in the UK is less happy handed with the compensation payouts than in the States, and this is a source of some pride. They hold a special place of utter contempt in their hearts for ambulance-chasing lawyers seeking to make money out of tragedy (unless they have experienced such a tragedy themselves, of course).

The irony being, had the sign not been there, but a strong fence put up instead—which is more draconian a measure, if we're talking freedoms being curtailed—that would be absolutely fine. It's the being told to behave that rankles.

The same problem occurs with matters of "so-called" political correctness. Now, I should state that I've put the speech marks there on purpose, partly because you can't say "politically correct" without hearing air quotes in your mind, but mostly because it also calls to mind the sound of someone who is more angry than clever prefacing the term with "so-called" because he or she thinks it's doubly damning. It's not a great rhetorical tool or even a convincing way to start an argument, but it does happen often.

In general, it would be fair to say that everyone understands the basic idea behind political correctness, which is that certain terms and phrases were coined during a period of intense unfairness for the majority of people. Not minorities; that's bull. Women account for more than 50 percent of the world's population before we've even started tallying up everyone else involved: people of non-Caucasian ethnicities and alternate sexualities, people with disabilities, and so on.

It's natural for language to evolve, for terms and expressions to come in and out of fashion due to changing priorities in culture. That's a process that never stops happening, and it only benefits and strengthens language that this is the case. So if a term comes from a position of extreme injustice, and it still carries the luggage of that injustice, it's probably a good idea to retire that phrase from public use. It's not as if there's a shortage of words that can be used instead. And for anyone who holds a residual fondness for those old words and is reluctant to give them up, it's sometimes useful to wonder if that's because you got away with it then and you know it.

But the problem is not the idea of dropping unacceptable words, it's being told to drop words that may (or may not) be unacceptable. That's what causes the irritation. And the process is not helped by spurious media reports about well-meaning councils that have banned words like *manhole, blackboard,* or *Christmas* to appease "the PC brigade." That most of these stories turn out to be either grossly exaggerated or flatly untrue is of no consequence compared to the appealing idea that this is just something the council bloody *would* do. It's just typical!

This can lead to some delightful legends springing up, such as the time trains were canceled after a heavy snowfall in 1991. When explaining that the problem was not in clearing the lines, but that the unusually dusty snow was getting into the electrical systems of the trains and causing them to short-circuit, a British Rail executive fell on the wrong side of a BBC interviewer, whose barbed response— "Oh, I see, it was the wrong kind of snow"—set the tone for the subsequent media coverage. This did not linger long on the electrical side of things, favoring the suggestion that "the wrong kind of snow" was corporate doublespeak for "we can't be bothered to clear the tracks properly."

So whether it's out of a sense of frustration that everything in the world is not run better, or a natural chippiness about being told what to do, the one guaranteed way to truly irk British people is to try to prevent them from killing themselves. They hate that.

WHAT TO SAY: "Oh, look, we can't stand here. I expect there's a good reason for that."

WHAT NOT TO SAY (PLEASE): "It's so-called political correctness gone mad."

Pub Quizzes ■

I t's not enough that the pub is the hub of all social interaction in British communities (see: Pubs, Inns, Bars, and Taverns). Once you're through the front door, you've greeted the bar staff, ordered your drinks and settled down at a table, what are you going to do?

Traditionally, pubs have offered quite a few ways to pass the time. There are the old traditional table games, such as shove ha'penny, tabletop skittles, and dominoes, and the championship games, such as darts, billiards, and pool. But these are all restrictive affairs, designed for only a few players and offering no chance to unite the room in one common endeavor.

So, assuming there are no football or rugby matches to watch and the karaoke machine is broken, one of the most popular ways for Brits to spend their evenings is to engage in a group quiz, often with the chance to win a free meal at a local restaurant or a plate of meat from the butcher's.

Pub quizzes are popular at all points of the compass and they all follow a broadly similar format. People arrive, get the drinks in, and sort themselves into teams. Some teams are formed from groups of happy friends who wish to have a fun night out; others are formed of experts who wish to dominate all pub quizzes forever.

But whether novices or veterans, all the teams will attempt to come up with a funny name that either mocks their collective intelligence, strikes a saucy tone, or cleverly combines the twin pastimes of drinking and thinking in a pun. Genuine examples include: Alcohooligans, the Three Must-get-beers, Clitoris Allsorts, Don Quizote, DENSA, Agatha Quiztie, and Eddie Quizzard.

Some will fail, and they may resort to being called "Tom, Barb, Jimmy, and Jackie" or "Table Six," but having a good pub quiz team name is like going to Oxbridge: it provides the kind of start that will ensure you have the confidence to succeed.

Then the quizmaster steps up to the microphone. It's a terrible microphone, very muffled and with a marked tendency to create howling feedback at the drop of a question about a hat. The quizmaster will have spent a week preparing fiendish questions, organized into rounds by topic. The objective is not to pander to anyone's misguided self-belief about their specialist subject; it is to crush and humiliate, to sort the addled-but-capable from the entirely-incapacitated and to ensure there is only one winner at the end.

To that end, it is not uncommon to be faced with an entire round of questions that would befuddle a top crime scene investigation team led by Sherlock Holmes himself. Subjects might include: "Pop music from before 'Rock around the Clock'," "Coins of the Roman Empire," or "Some of the things my mother said to me yesterday between lunch and her afternoon nap."

And it is equally common for frustrated quiz-ateers to make up silly answers to the questions they cannot fathom, just to break the tension. However, most teams have at least one member who cannot see the funny side, and a frosty silence can develop, punctuated by hissed arguments and bad-tempered shushing.

At the end of each round, the teams swap answer sheets and mark each other's papers. This is an opportunity to keep your rivals at bay, so any spelling mistakes, any attempt at levity, any deviation from a perfectly expressed correct answer will be marked as incorrect. The foolproofedness of such a plan lasts just long enough for each team to receive its own sheets back and discover that everyone is marking to the same impossible standard.

Then the scores are tallied and the quizmaster reads out the leader board in reverse order, giving all of those hilarious team names a good airing, with cheers coming from various different points around the pub, even for the teams at the very bottom.

And that's it, save for a few bad-tempered arguments between the quizmaster and various pedants and experts who can't believe their correct answer was marked wrong because the question was badly phrased (or the answer given is, in fact, incorrect), and a possible tie-break round at the end.

By this time all the funny team names have lost their giggly allure and become entrenched in the collective mentality, as if they've some-how acquired the status of minor republics in the United Nations, with superpower status being allocated to the final two, no matter how pre-posterous their names may be.

WHAT TO SAY: "Actually the song is called 'Make Me Smile—*brackets*—Come Up and See Me—*close brackets*,' so . . ."

WHAT NOT TO SAY: "Dunkirk! It's *definitely* Dunkirk! Unless it's Dieppe . . ."

The England that is shown in *Kes* doesn't exist anymore, but unlike, say, *The Railway Children* and *The Great Escape*, it most certanly did while the film was being made. So while it was originally shot as a contemporary view of working-class life in the mining communities of Yorkshire—among some of the lowest-paid workers in the country at the time—it has now become a snapshot of a particular moment in English history, as loaded with significance as a sepia-tone shot of pioneers settling the Wild West.

Kes was filmed during that period when the 1960s was just about to turn into the 1970s—the same year the Beatles walked tetchily over the zebra crossing outside EMI (later renamed Abbey Road) Studios—but no one had thought to tell the people of Barnsley. The long hair and flares of Swinging London had still not permeated far enough north, so all the grown-ups wear beehives or comb-overs, and everyone gathers in the workingmen's club for a drink, a saucy sing-along, and a knees-up just as they always have. There are no teenagers here, just insolent kids and angry grown-ups. There's a bit of pop music, but it's already out of date—musicians dressed like the Searchers in the era of Jimi Hendrix—and there's no youth explosion.

That's not to say progress has not happened. In fact, there's a long speech from a truculent headmaster about the youth of the day, declining standards, and the beneficial effects of tearing down the old slum housing and building new estates and new schools. But the new estates have the same reputation for trouble as the old ones, and the headmaster is merely justifying his indiscriminate use of the cane, even on the hands of a boy who only came into the office to deliver a message.

Kes is also one of the first of those films where working-class people—usually children—are lifted out of the drabness and unpleasantness of their everyday environment by something spiritually enriching. In *Billy Elliot*, thirty years into the future, it would be ballet. For Billy Glover in *Kes*, stuck in 1969 and running from paper round to school yard and back home again without his games kit or a proper uniform or even a clean pair of ears, it's a stolen kestrel that he can encourage and train.

It's also a film about the wild, but not the wildness of nature. The rolling fields around the housing estates of Barnsley and the trusting kestrel that Billy raises carefully with instructions from a stolen library book are a civilizing influence when compared to the brutality of the humans. There's the savage elder brother, Jud; Billy's wayward mother; the fierce headmaster; the belligerent sports teacher with his Manchester United T-shirt and preening ego; and various untamed children to the left and right.

Two weeks from leaving school and looking for work, and terrified of becoming a miner like his brother, Billy spends his life in a series of battles with people who think they know best for kids like him, or with his classmates. Only in the stolen moments with his bird does he blossom into something else; just for a short while, his potential is reached. It's a beautiful metaphor for the anticlimax of reaching adulthood.

Kes was Ken Loach's second film, after spending a good deal of the '60s making gritty dramas for TV about social issues. His films are down-to-earth, unsentimental, funny, and tragic at the same time, and that's something that suits a certain British taste. Some people prefer escapism and robots on their cinema screens, but many Brits prefer to see life as they understand it, in accents that are close to their own. The films of Mike Leigh and Bill Forsyth also work in a similar way, as do the songs of Pulp, the Kinks, and Arctic Monkeys.

A moment about halfway through the film shows one of the first times Billy experiences the support of his peers. Bullied into telling his English class about Kes, his enthusiasm starts bubbling out, and he winds up gabbling away ten to the dozen about this hawk, and how he trained her to fly to his glove from the edge of a field, and his classmates are rapt, his teacher enthused and sympathetic for the first time. It's the "hey, troubled kid, I didn't know you could rap" moment, only far less cloying.

Naturally the next thing that happens is Billy takes a hiding from a bully in the school yard and winds up rolling in a pile of coal while the whole school runs to watch. But because of that moment earlier, his teacher takes pity for the first time, visiting him and Kes in the field, and Billy's world starts to make a kind of sense. He gets free scraps from the butcher to feed the bird; people stop him in the street to ask about it. For a while the wildness recedes.

And then, because this isn't *Billy Elliot*, because of that British mistrust of easy sentimentality, the wildness returns. Billy fails to put two bets on for his brother, spending the money on a fish supper instead. Jud goes looking for Billy to give him a good hiding, and when he finds the kestrel instead, he kills her.

The final scene of the film is Billy quietly digging a grave for his hawk and tamping the dirt down, all questions about his future still unanswered, his moment of hope extinguished.

Taken as the story of a young man adrift in adult company, *Kes* is a British answer to *The Catcher in the Rye*, with Billy as an inverse Holden Caulfield. Instead of a self-obsessed and rather whiny privileged kid, he's an underfed waif with nothing but misery for company; and rather than swan about acting aloof, he chooses to invest all his time and creative energy working with a genuine force of nature, because after everything he has experienced, he's only comfortable with a creature that can't be tamed.

WHAT TO SAY: "Are we supposed to find this bit funny?"

WHAT NOT TO SAY: "Those accents are impenetrable. I can't understand what they're saying."

Mythical Beasts ■

While the Loch Ness Monster may cast the longest imaginary shadow and create the most opportunities for tourism and Scooby-Doo specials—the twin props of any thriving first-world economy—there's an undiscovered zooful of mythical creatures still on the prowl in the British Isles, one that is entirely resistant to the dispelling effects of science, religion, and photographic equipment. Some are dark and fearsome, some are haunting and strange, and some are bloody and weird. This is what the rural Brits were doing in between building stone circles and inventing cider.

First, there are the black dogs. Not an allusion to depression this time (see: Melancholy) but actual sooty hellhounds with scarlet eyes and pin-sharp fangs. In the northern counties of England he's called Barghest or Gytrash; in Leeds he's called Padfoot; in Wales he's Gwyllgi; and in Scotland he's Cu Sith. There's even a hybrid ape-dog called Shug Monkey in Cambridgeshire, but for a good portion of the middle of England, one dog rules them all, and his name is Black Shuck.

This is the dog that chases catastrophe into your path, and your only protection is to close your eyes and pray. Not that this helped the congregation of Blythburgh church, Suffolk, in 1577. In a contemporary account, Black Shuck charged in with a storm at his heels and killed a man and a boy, then left with such startling velocity the steeple collapsed and there were scorch marks on the door.

Still at least they had firm evidence that something had happened. When it comes to hellcats, particularly those said to roam the moors down in the southwest, the reports get a little hazier. Exmoor is said to be the home of a big black cat, something like a panther or puma, that kills grazing sheep. Another one has been sighted on Bodmin Moor in North Cornwall, and a third way over in Brighton, on the southeast coast. Then there's the Fiskerton Phantom, a ghost panther (or possibly bear) seen near a campsite in Lincolnshire.

While we're on big animals, what about the Owlman of Mawnan, in Cornwall? This Spring-Heeled Jack–type figure is a recent arrival— first seen in 1976, last seen in 1995—and seems to be either a man with wings, claws, and a beak or an owl as big as a man, with the requisite red eyes and pointed ears: a hellowl, in other words.

Then there are the beasts that are like horses, only nasty. The Nuckelavee is a demonic Scottish brute said to resemble a composite horse-and-rider in one, only entirely skinless. It lives in the sea—which must sting something rotten, given the no-skin thing—with breath bad enough to spoil an entire crop and sicken a cow. Mother Supernature can be cruel sometimes.

Kelpies are perhaps better looking, in that they're big black horses, with backward hooves, that live in lochs and freshwater pools; but they're no less fearsome, because they eat people. In Aberdeenshire, the kelpies have manes of snakes, and the ones in the River Spey can sing travelers onto their backs, at which point they become stuck fast. Oh, and they can elongate their backs to fit more people on, because why not? They're mythical.

Grindylows do not look like horses, but they do like to drag children into their watery, boggy homes if they come too close. Shellycoats, knuckers, and the Tiddy Mun are also best avoided, as is the eachy, which is either a humanoid lake monster or a thirteen-foot-long, three-humped, snake-faced beast. There are also asrai, which are water fairies or river mermaids, but they will die in direct sunlight, so it's probably best to leave them be. In fact, if you're by anything watery and you see movement of any kind (especially if it's an underwater horse) just leave.

It's a bit safer on land. The worst you'll get from being conned into riding a brag is a dunking in a nearby pond, and if you climb aboard a dunnie, it'll take you to the muddiest stretch of road and then vanish, followed by a wet plop (that's you).

But not all mythical creatures are out to cause trouble. Some are even helpful, especially if you're a miner by trade. Bluecaps are tiny fairies on the English-Scottish border that aid miners to find the best deposits, help to push tubs of coal, and warn them if the ceiling is about to fall in. They're not unlike the Cornish knockers, who are paid in pasty crusts for their hard work.

Redcaps, on the other hand, are rotten goblins who look like old men with red eyes and live in ruined castles (in the same area as their helpful blue cousins) and kill anyone foolish enough to visit. Like Smurfs gone bad, they then dip their caps in the blood of their prey, which have to be kept moist or they will die. Mythical evolution is clearly even more bizarre than the real thing.

Then there are brownies, hobs and hobgoblins, elvish imps who all look broadly similar and do household chores, providing you don't get on their nerves. Brownies are especially useful around the home—assuming no one is looking—and will take their wages in honey and porridge, provided this is not considered a payment. Lubberkin offers a similar service, even though he is far bigger and hairier, and has a tail. Oddly, he prefers a saucer of milk to porridge.

A similarly house-proud spirit was said to occupy Dryburgh Abbey in Berwickshire, Scotland. He would stamp the moisture from the air using heavy boots and was given the Jaggerish title Fatlips. On the more unhelpful side, boggarts will work in your house, but they'll sour your milk, lose your stuff, and make your dog go lame. And occasionally steal your children. Spriggans occupy ruined buildings and are horrific thieves. They can also inflate to huge sizes and might steal your kids too, so steer clear.

Then there's Black Annis, an old woman with a blue face and iron claws who likes to wander around Leicestershire looking for tasty young humans to skin, eat, and then wear as a belt. Or Reynardine the werefox, who roams the mountains looking for maidens to abduct.

But the most grotesque story of them all is the tale of the Ratman of Southend. This terrifying creature, heard in scratches and moans late at night, is either the feral rat-faced child of the Mayor of Southend, kept in a cage in a specially built underpass, which he often escapes, or he's a supernatural grotesque, the reanimated corpse of a homeless man who was kicked to death by a gang of kids (in the selfsame underpass) and feasted upon by rats.

Either way, I'd rather take my chances with Black Shuck.

WHAT TO SAY: "Right, I've got my holy water, my Bible, some honey, and a broken shoe for mending; all I need is some black dog biscuits and I can go for a stroll."

WHAT NOT TO SAY: "Why any rational person would choose to believe in this supernatural mumbo jumbo is beyond me. Oh, look, is that a horse?"

The Theater ■

Generations of British schoolchildren have experienced the deadening confusion of the "improving" trip to see a production of a Shakespeare play, the highlights of the trip invariably being a minor argument between best friends over who gets to sit next to whom and widespread incredulity as some members of the audience loudly guffaw at some incomprehensible business onstage in which a woman dresses as a man (see: Cross-Dressing), pretends to be her own brother, and ends up fending off the attentions of an amorous woman who has fallen for him (meaning her). Then those same people begin ostentatiously sobbing at a beautifully orated, but quite confusing speech in which the words seem to rise up like an angry snake and then fall back on themselves like a wet earthworm on a pavement. It is not the best way to encourage a love of the Bard.

But this does not mean that, as grown-ups, people feel a sense of hostility or unease about the theater in general. It's true that Shakespeare is a monolithic figure to get around—in much the same way that Everest is a monolithic mountain to get around—not least because he invented so many words and phrases that are now used every day by English speakers all over the world. And even if he had not, his plots and characters—scheming Iago and jealous Othello, angsty Hamlet, mad old King Lear—are the bedrock on which theater rests.

Even if we had no Royal Shakespeare Company or National Theatre in Britain, his works would continue to play out across stages and screens for as long as there are stages and screens. There's a quiet satisfaction to that even for the most greasepaint-phobic of British citizens.

And even if they refused to set foot in a theater ever again, they would still be well served by those who do so regularly. The biggest and best British screen actors and actresses got started by treading the boards, and they still nurse a quiet aspiration to get back there as soon as they've finished their latest project: playing an evil genius, a sarcastic detective, a black-hearted cop, or a sarcastic evil genius supervillain cop detective . . . in space. In Britain, acting is a theatrical skill, one in which you have to learn to talk quietly with enough clarity to still be heard by everyone in a large room.

This transfers to television and the movies because that kind of authority, that quiet intensity, becomes mesmeric in front of a camera. Just look at Ian McKellen—as magnetic playing Gandalf in *The Lord of the Rings* and *The Hobbit* as he is playing the genuinely magnetic Magneto in the X-Men franchise. And it's the same for Tom Hiddleston, Emily Blunt, Patrick Stewart, Helen Mirren, Benedict Cumberbatch, Helena Bonham Carter, and so on. And that resonant delivery shares a tone of voice with the great British novels, so it suits television adaptations of the works of Jane Austen, Charles Dickens, and the Brontë sisters. That's the intermediary stage for all British actors between the theater and Hollywood.

More recently, a hugely popular trend has been to film theatrical presentations and present them to cinemagoers as a special live-but-not-live event. This saves people the trouble of traveling all the way into London to see the as-Shakespeare-intended productions at the Globe theater, and it circumnavigates the expense of trying to get hold of hot tickets. The extra bonus is this arrangement often guarantees a better seat in the house, which, in the case of the Globe stalls in particular, means any kind of seat at all.

Sometimes a cultural event happens that draws all the great theatrical performers together like gnats on a fruit bowl. The Harry Potter movies did that very thing, acting as a kind of end-of-year collaborative class project for the British theatrical tradition at large. It was also a rare collision of profitable circumstances, driven by a worldwide expectation from fans. J. K. Rowling's stories were so popular they created a guaranteed audience waiting to watch them come to life in a cinema, and their expectations were threefold: (1) that all the characters in the books would be included (and there are loads), (2) that the magic look magical (which costs money), and (3) that everything be as British as Marmite butties. This, thankfully, was not hard to achieve, given the talent involved.

And the list of great British actors who appeared in the Harry Potter movies is truly impressive. Skim a stone across the surface of a random selection and you'll hit Maggie Smith, Ralph Fiennes, Emma Thompson, Kenneth Branagh, Gary Oldman, Julie Walters, David Thewlis, John Hurt, Jason Isaacs, Imelda Staunton, Michael Gambon, Richard Griffiths, Fiona Shaw, Jim Broadbent, or Timothy Spall. And it was a two-way street, making future theatrical stars out of its three child leads: Daniel Radcliffe, Emma Watson, and Rupert Grint. And of course, international recognition of this sort doesn't just enrich the soul; it also brings money to the British economy, and with money comes state recognition. That's one of the reason why so many of the best loved of British actors, directors, and playwrights have appeared on the Queen's Honors List.

But most important, the success of Harry Potter gave those bored kids in the theater a taste for longer narratives and complicated words— credit where it is due, there's no difference between Shakespeare inventing *wild-goose chase* and J. K. Rowling inventing *expelliarmus*—and some even began watching the Bard voluntarily, on the BBC in the form of *The Hollow Crown*, which took his history plays and made them look like *Game of Thrones*.

WHAT TO SAY: "As with all theatrical presentations, it takes about a half hour to attune yourself to the language and wait for Dad to fall asleep, and then you're off."

WHAT NOT TO SAY: "Dude, where's the popcorn stand?"

Banter ■

Let's clear up any confusion from the start: *banter*—also known as bantering, bantersaurus, bant, bants, bantz, top bantz, underbants, bantarctica, bantastic, bantam roastering, and bantasmagoria—is a terrifically overused word.

It is most often used to describe a group of friends, work colleagues, or strangers sharing a joke. Or several jokes. It may once have meant sharing a joke at someone's expense, and certainly that is the version that causes the most problems, but any fine detail has been worn so thin by overuse it now includes everything from indulging in prank phone calls to tossing a pun into a Twitter hashtag game. If you have sat around a bottle of wine or jug of beer with mates and thrown around competitive one-liners on any topic, congratulations! You have indulged in banter. It's a nice thing to do, but as with all nice things to do, overuse or misuse can lead to unpleasant situations.

There are two schools of thought around banter and its manifold applications pertaining to the crunching gears of contemporary British life.

One claims that a little bit of light mockery does everyone a power of good and if you can't take a joke you shouldn't make them and if you're not making jokes what kind of a person are you? Let's call this the tightrope school, because you're always one false step from being hit in the face (by a rapidly approaching floor).

Graduates of the tightrope school enjoy the idea that they are speaking to friends, who automatically understand whether they believe what they are saying or not. This allows for a thrilling frisson whenever the conversation blunders over traditional boundaries of taste or decency, as these banterers pretend to be just like stand-up comedians—or the presenters of *Top Gear*—for the night.

It comes from the same corner of the brain that understands that mutually understood sarcasm is a form of honesty (see: Sarcasm) and that affection can take the form of pretend abuse—providing the abuser and the abusee are both in on the joke—and the Brits, being suspicious of public displays of emotion, are rather fond of it. You can't tell people you love them by saying "I love you," because that would be rank sentimentality; you should instead embark on a really long and systematic dressing-down, taking in all of their foibles and failings, followed by a drinks order. That's banter.

The opposing school holds that banter is a pernicious umbrella and a convenient mask for people in positions of power—white people, men, straight people, straight white men, etc.—to wear so that they get to say horrific things about anyone they like and pretend that they don't really mean it to avoid taking the consequences of their own unpleasant views. This tends to come up as a point of conflict in communities where all context has been shorn from the original comments. Jokey thoughts are one thing when shared among friends, but they look very different when, for example, broadcast on social media. This doesn't mean it's fine to say whatever, whenever, but Twitter is no place for nuance.

Antibanterers tend to be hostile to the idea that context is key to working out if someone is genuinely being a rotter or not. How, they wonder, could someone even think of those things, or use horrific terms of abuse, if they don't really mean them? What kind of a person would say unsayable things if they didn't wish them to be said? That's banter of the ringmaster school, in which the speaker has the red jacket and the whip hand and if anyone doesn't like it, they can always send in their clowns.

The truth, as any fool could predict, is somewhere in between. By which I mean it's not banter's fault that spiteful sods with a grudge now have a word for their most revolting comic instincts. A comedy roast is still just a comedy roast, even when it's really near the knuckle, but sometimes using humor as a kind of escape vent for bleak thoughts allows other things to travel the same path. And it would be wrong to try to halt the little bit of laughter that releases a lot of tension in what are, after all, very tense times.

That said, it's abhorrent to claim that everyone should just put up with abuse just because the abuser has claimed banter as a free pass. The idea that social taboos need to be dissected by humor, while appealing in the hands of expert comedic surgeons, only betrays the rubbery scalpel edge of the tools used by most pub boors.

And if things do go badly, the idea that "I'm sorry you found that offensive" could even be considered as a real apology for any offense caused is beyond laughable.

WHAT TO SAY: "My comedy is about challenging social norms and forcing people to examine their own prejudices, yeah? Now get me a pint."

WHAT NOT TO SAY: "Easy, love, can't you take a joke? Jeez!"

Ampersand Foods ■

British cuisine has long been the subject of international derision. Many Americans like to make jokes claiming that British chefs think the way to prepare any meal—from Christmas dinner to cornflakes—is to take the basic ingredients, whack them in a pot, and boil them for nine hours, then dollop everything onto a plate in a pool of rapidly cooling water, with a sprig of parsley as a garnish.

This is patently unfair, especially coming from a nation that seems to believe that a reasonable dressing for any dish—including dessert—is cheese. The British Isles can boast some world-beating recipes, and some of the best of them are made with a secret ingredient they have always been very fond of: the ampersand.

It's there in some of their best-known dishes: not just fish & chips*—the full title of which should really be fish & chips & mushy peas—but also firm favorites like bangers & mash (sausages and mashed potato and gravy), pie & mash (eel pie, mashed potato, and a parsley-based sauce called liquor), and the ever-popular steak & kidney pie. And it's particularly prevalent in some of their most beloved food brands too.

---

* Yes, yes, yes, it's fish 'n' chips, not fish & chips. But let's face it, what is the immortal 'n' if not a rock 'n' roll ampersand? Nothing, that's what.

The mighty fish & chips (& mushy peas & tartar sauce).

It now seems incredibly quaint to look back on a time when the makers and purveyors of foodstuffs would simply name their companies after their founders, especially in an era of one-word corporations like Innocent and Starbucks and Monster. It's not unlike Coldplay calling themselves Martin, Buckland, Berryman & Champion, which they almost certainly would have done had they formed in 1972.

There's Marks & Spencer, whose food hall contains many wondrous delights. Some are precooked and ready to eat; some you take home and bake in the oven. Marks's is any Brit's absolute reliable standby should one attempt to throw a dinner party and then panic over what to serve. Even the queen would find herself pleasantly surprised by a table groaning with its food.

Mind you, she's probably more of a Fortnum & Mason girl. They're the people who make the hampers wealthy people send to each other at Christmas (if popular fiction is to be believed). Never mind the ready-to-bake three-bird roast, a hamper from Fortnum's will come with startling delights such as pickled quince and Piccadilly piccalilli, with variations tailored for any occasion (apart from a children's birthday party where they're expecting Happy Meals for everyone). There are hampers for him, hampers for her, hampers for mothers and fathers and lovers and fighters. Cheap(ish) hampers and plush hampers. It all depends on the statement you wish to make.

One item that will probably make an appearance in either retail establishment is Worcestershire sauce (which, as any fool knows, is pronounced "woostersheer," just to save an impatient look from a British shop assistant). This peculiar condiment—most famously used in the creation of the Bloody Mary—adds a brackish tang to any dish, is entirely unique, has carried the Queen's Warrant as a sign of purebred British quality, and is made by Lea & Perrins.

Crosse & Blackwell does not have the Royal Warrant, but its creations are no less singular and no less popular. Specializing in preserved food—whether that's tinned beans, dehydrated soups, or chutneys and pickled items—this is the company responsible for making Branston Pickle, which is to chutney what Shakespeare is to the theater. There will always be other pickle relishes, and some of them are wonderful, but Branston is the one you're most likely to find in a plowman's lunch. If any relish were to take on the mantle of Sole British Pickle, Branston would be top of the list.

Should you be looking for something of a more pulsey, nutty, or vitaminy nature, the place you'll need to go is Holland & Barrett, which will sell you an enormous jar of weightlifter's protein powder with your Bombay mix and multivitamins. It's that kind of a place.

Huntley & Palmers used to rule the world with biscuits. At one point it had the largest biscuit factory on the planet, with its own internal steam railway network, churning out four hundred different varieties of biscuits and exporting them all over the British Empire in colorful tins. The firm had the kind of market penetration that McDonald's has now, only it amalgamated with rivals Peek Frean and Jacob's to form Associated Biscuits. That's like creating a McTucky King. Although once the & was gone, so was the market dominance. Coincidence? Well, probably.

Tate & Lyle specialize in sugar, with Lyle's Golden Syrup proving to be a particularly iconic piece of British packaging, thanks largely to the green and gold tins featuring an illustration of a dead lion with a swarm of bees above it. This is not as unsettling as it sounds; the image comes from part of the Old Testament, in which Samson kills a lion and later discovers a bees' nest, complete with honeycomb, in the great beast's carcass. The inscription on the tin—the same now as it has always been—is taken from Judges 14:14 and reads, "Out of the strong came forth sweetness."

All of which just goes to underline a simple point: while an ampersand may not be the only thing required to make truly great British food, having a couple in the kitchen will certainly come in 'andy.

WHAT TO SAY: "Care for a dash of Worcestershire on your pie & mash?"

WHAT NOT TO SAY: "So wait, Lea & Spencers does . . . what?"

Conkers ■

This game has taken on legendary—nay, mythical—status as a totem of childhood fun, most commonly for British boys, although that's probably as much to do with the legend as the reality. And that's an important distinction to make, because the British love of conkers is all about the memory of conkers, the legend of conkers, and there are two important reasons for this:

1. It's only really played by children from around the age of eight until the age of eleven and, even then, can only be played for a short period, during the early weeks of autumn. This means most children, even the keen ones, have perhaps two or three seasons as conker players. So to think back as adults, on that time between the full blush of childhood and the shaky onset of puberty, is guaranteed to provoke a rush of fond memories.

2. Thanks partly to concerns over playground safety, but mostly to the rise of handheld electronic devices, very few children actually play conkers anymore. There are exceptions and enthusiasts, although they do tend to be pushed by adults seeking to re-create that innocent rush for their own children (or grandchildren).

The rules of the game are simple, but some preparation is key:

Choose your conker—a horse chestnut—preferably harvested in the first flush of autumn during a walk through the fallen leaves in your wellies. Having found a suitably tough nut, drill a hole through it and thread a bootlace through the hole, tying a hefty knot at the end. Hold the other end of the string, and make a few experimental swings with your conker, as if using a flail. Now you are ready to play.

Find a suitable opponent with his or her own weapon and face off. Player one dangles his conker at arm's length and waits. Player two winds the string over her knuckles until there's about five inches left and, keeping the string taut, swings her conker at the other, attempting to smash it to bits. Then the positions are reversed and it is player one's turn to let fly, whether contact has been made or not.

The game of conkers (first position).

The conker that eventually survives intact gains a point, becoming a *one-er* (new conkers are all *none-ers*). Subsequent victories add to that conker's tally, moving from a *one-er* to a *two-er* and so on. In some areas conkers take on the scores of the conkers they beat, so a *one-er* smashing a *two-er* will become a *four-er*: adding one for the game, as well as the two points belonging to the smashed conker. The former *two-er* is now just a smashed horse chestnut on the floor.

The preparation of the conker for battle has also taken on the status of a mythic quest. If you ask most British people of a certain age, they will tell you about baking conkers to make them harder, or soaking them in vinegar, or even keeping them in a drawer for a year before using them. Of course, these methods are to conkers what performance-enhancing drugs are to the Tour de France, but a lot of enthusiasts claim that the stamping-out of these traditional methods of one-upmanship has contributed to the decline of the game in school playgrounds. These are clearly not smartphone users.

But even if the only people who play conkers are those who are too old to play conkers, the myth of conkers is what will endure. Despite being less than two hundred years old, conkers feels both ancient and traditional and also very eccentric. Three qualities most Brits find very hard to resist.

A related game in Peterlee, Durham, is played with hard-boiled eggs, held sharp side up. It's called egg jarping, and the town even plays host to an annual World Jarping Championship, although there probably aren't that many teams coming from too far afield (see: Weird Traditions).

WHAT TO SAY: "No conkers? Okay, who wants to play British bulldog?"

WHAT NOT TO SAY: "You've cooked this one—I can smell it."

T hings have changed in the smoke-blackened continuing drama meeting room since we last visited. It is now the early 1980s, and *Coronation Street* has been dominating the TV schedules for over twenty years. It's been the subject of some rivalry from a show called *Emmerdale Farm*—later renamed *Emmerdale* to steer the story lines away from cattle, feed, and threshing—and another called *Crossroads*, but no one has managed to create a serious contender for *Corrie*'s crown. The people sitting around the fabled table have been having a serious go, though. This time, instead of paper there's a whiteboard, which is becoming increasingly mucky at the top as successive ideas have been abandoned and scrubbed away before they can even be fully explained. Sometimes the titles are enough: *Victorian Boxing Club, Zookeeper Nation, Eldorado* . . . it's a sorry state of affairs and by now some of the senior executives are openly sobbing into their ties.

At the dark end of the table, the shadowy man has begun to clip his latest and fattest cigar, sighing at some volume. He is starting to lose what little patience he ever had. Then a brash voice pipes up from behind the whiteboard. It's a cheeky little fellow in an outsized bottle green frock coat and tatty top hat, and his face appears to be lit from within.

"If I may be permitted to speak, your honor?"

"What? Who are you?"

"Dodger's the name, sir. I'm what you might call a jack-of-all-trades. Sometimes I can be found relieving hardworking gentlemen, such as yourselves, of their heavy wallets; sometimes I'm delivering packages and messages for my personal sponsor—a fine fellow who only ever hurt those what he don't like—and sometimes I'm away down the boozer to neck the gin. But today I have the answer to your prayers . . ."

"I . . . have *prayers?*"

"O'course you do, sir. 'Course you do. You want a new soap opera—"

"If one more person calls them soap operas, so help me I'll have you all shot. They are 'serial dramas,' or 'continuing dramas,' and—"

"I know how it goes, guv'nor. I calls myself a toff sometimes too, but it don't make me posh. A soap opera is a soap opera and there ain't a thing you can do about it. Now, it strikes ol' Dodger that what you needs is a slice of working-class life, with a community of people what lives on top of each other in a big city and meet up in the pub for drinks and plotting and romance and fighting. That's what the people want."

"They do want that. And they get it. It's called *Coronation Street.*"

"No, no, no, me old china. I'm not talking about your northerners and their flat caps and whippets and all that rubbish. I'm talkin' about your proper Londoners. Y'know, salt of the earth, happy to greet you with a smile and a hearty handshake while emptying out your pockets and throwing you in the canal. That lot."

"So this will be set in the past? Like Dickens?"

"Like *who?* Naw, mate, this will start right now, in the mid-1980s, in the East End of London, in a made-up borough called Walford and a place called Albert Square. We'll have a decent mix of characters—gossipy laundrywomen, brassy barmaids, ruthless businessmen, and a couple of wannabe gangsters, that sort of a thing—and we'll have them all mix together in the pub in the middle of the square. Let's call it the Queen Victoria, Gawd save 'er.

"Then we'll have a market just outside the pub, and a café by the market, so there's a lot of movement and people can see what's going on from all sorts of different angles."

"And let me guess: we'll need to get the tone of the dialogue just right . . ."

"Woss the matter with you, sir? Are you simple? The dialogue? Dialogue, is it? Don't talk daft! Alls we need is a lot of action and some hard-hitting story ideas. We need issues! We need a schoolgirl to get pregnant with an older man. We need gay characters . . . with HIV! We need acts of betrayal, drug addictions, prostitution, alcoholism, sex trafficking, racism . . . the lot! We need to show London as she really is, and then get rid of all the la-di-da bits, like galloping house prices and all the museums and stuff, until all that is left is unmitigated misery and the occasional singsong around the old Joanna."

"Old . . . Joanna?"

"Strewth! Where you been all your life? The piano! In the pub! Anyway, eventually your soap will become every bit as popular as *Coronation Street*. The two soaps—and don't get uppity with me, sir, 'cos that's what they is—will compete with each other for the greater ratings, which means bigger issues, harder-hitting story ideas, and more heartache for everyone. It's gonna be a right set-to and no mistake."

"And what will we call it, this endless parade of urban misery?"

"There's only one thing we can call it, sir. If we let slip the idea that this is a dramatic presentation—and not real urban life as she truly is—people won't believe a word of it, as God is my witness. So it's got to be *EastEnders*, with two capital *E*s, because it's a doubly capital idea."

"Before I decide, can I ask one thing, Mr. . . . ah . . . Dodger?"

"Whatever pleases you, your worship . . ."

"Could you please take your feet off my conference table?"

And with that, the cigar is stubbed out, the lad looks crestfallen, and silence falls for a final time.

WHAT TO SAY: "Of course, it will all go to pot when Dot Cotton dies."

WHAT NOT TO SAY: "Buddy, I've been to the real East End and they've got the ethnic mix *all* wrong."

This is a delicate topic, because there's a fine line between laughingly mocking other communities in the spirit of healthy regional competition, and outright racism. Popular tastes change over time, faster than language does, and so words are often left in common use that are a throwback to an era when prejudices were so heavily ingrained in culture that it seemed impossible to shift them even if the will was there. No matter how lightly thrown a word like *jock*, *taff*, or *sassenach* may be now, it can land like a brick made of flint. And even the slightest of laughingly competitive terms can be thrown around angrily by frustrated people with a nasty agenda, because that's how bullying works.

So while the Brits tend to pride themselves on playing fair, this by no means prevents some of them from bickering among themselves in quite an unpleasant fashion or finding fairly insulting ways to demean their neighbors. That's not to say there's no fun to be had whatsoever, just a note to say tread carefully before you let fly.

Of course, nothing gets the creative brain fizzing like a war, and over the course of two world wars, and a lot of time spent waiting around in trenches with little to do, Allied troops managed to come up with a colossal backlog of nicknames for the Germans. These included: Dutch (a derivation of *Deutsch*, as in "Pennsylvania Dutch")

Cabbage Eaters, Krauts, Fritz, Jerry, the Hun, Atilla (as in: the Hun), the Boche, Ludwig, Gerboy, Germhun, Square-Heads, and so on.

Some of these were quite hard to drop once peacetime arrived. In the early 1970s, when German youth were attempting to create a new musical form out of the psychological debris left by the war, they left language behind, preferring to create long jams with a theme of space exploration. And what did the British rock press charmingly decide to call this radical movement? Krautrock. Because it was made by the Krauts, you see.

The Brits do it to themselves too, of course. It's part of that inherent tribal thing, the bonding together against a common foe that fuels all sports. Some of the names come from without; some from within. So the residents of Birmingham will be called Brummies, Liverpudlians are Scousers, the residents of Newcastle are Geordies, and nearby well-to-do Durham has Posh Geordies. Manchester has Mancunians, Sunderland has Mackems, London has Cockneys, Glasgow has Weegies, Sheffield has Steelies, Leeds has Loiners (or, magnificently: Leodensians).

(Deep breath.)

Middlesborough has Smoggies, Plymouth has Janners, Nantwich has Dabbers, Bristol has Ciderheads, Dumfries has Doonhamers, Oldham has Yonners, Barnsley has Tykes, Chesterfield has Spireites (thanks to a wonky old church spire), Coventry has Godivas, Southport has Sandgrounders, Weymouth has Kimberlins, Walshall has Saddlers, Tarbert has Dookers, Sutherland has Cattachs, and Kirkcaldy (pronounced "kirk-aw-day," locally) has Langtonians (pronounced "lang tone ians"), so named because it's quite a long town.

The people of Wiltshire are called Moonrakers, thanks to the county's location on the main smuggling route between the southwest (supply) and London (demand). One legendary night, some smugglers were retrieving their stash when a representative of Customs and Excise found them; playing dumb, they claimed to be trying to rake in the moon's reflection, so as to get some cheese, and this apparently worked.

Oh, and one for the insectophobes: creepy Crawley has Insects.

But that's not all. Thanks to the intense rivalry brought on by football and rugby, the supporters of the local team in Blackpool are called Donkey Lashers (referring to the donkey rides on Blackpool beach); Milton Keynes, home of several bovine statues, has Plastic Cow-Jockeys; Leigh has Lobbygobblers (lobby being a local stew made with corned beef); while people from nearby Wigan, where they make a lot of pies, are all Pie-Eaters.

Bolton went one stage further up the food chain, ending up as the Trotters, possibly because their training ground used to be next to a pig farm (this may be a fib, but it's a good one), and if you want to offend someone from Burnley, call him or her a Dingle. This is a reference to a farming family in the British soap *Emmerdale*, and it is not a complimentary one.

Hartlepool has the best of the lot. They're called Monkey Hangers, thanks to the possibly apocryphal tale of a monkey in a French army uniform washing ashore from a shipwreck during the Napoleonic Wars. Local myth has it that the monkey was tried as a French spy—because the locals hadn't seen a monkey or a Frenchman before—and then executed.

Some names are even shared. Because of their fishing heritage, the residents of Grimsby and Arbroath are both called Codheads (due to the Scots accent, the latter is often spelled *Codheids*). Whitehaven and Workington are both Jam-Eaters, and should you be blessed with a West Country accent, even if you live in Southampton or as far as Norfolk, someone will probably call you a Carrot-Cruncher.

And finally, if you're not from around here and you're in Cornwall, you're an Emmet. If you're not from around here and you're in Devon, you're a Grockle.

WHAT TO SAY (WHEN IN CHESTERFIELD):
"Go, Spireites!"

WHAT NOT TO SAY (ANYWHERE): "Excuse me, are you a Monkey Hanger, by any chance?"

The kebab in its natural environment.

Some decisions make sense only when you are drunk. Under normal circumstances it's entirely possible to resist the charms of a doner kebab. It's only a hot sandwich, after all. Very nice in its way, but only one of a huge selection of potential meals available in the cafés and restaurants of Britain's towns and cities. There's no reason why it should be favored even over other kebabs. The shish is very nice, for example, or the shawarma sandwich, which observes the same basic principles of construction as the humble burrito.

So it's not as though one tends to see British people in business suits queuing up at a sandwich bar every lunchtime, making the painstaking demand that a pita bread be stuffed with a little too much salad, too much leathery sliced meat, and a generous helping of *chilli* sauce (with two *l*'s, thanks awfully) and packed in a soggy, easily torn paper bag to take back to their desks. That would make very little sense at all. It probably happens a bit, but not to any significant degree.

But if you wait just a few hours, until all trading has ceased save for the passing of cash over pub counters, and the exchanging of liquid refreshment for mental confusion, you'll see those same business-folk making their way to a brightly lit shop with a meat cushion rotating in front of an electric heater in the window, as if that cushion were a beacon, a grail to be tracked and claimed. The pub may have called last orders, but the night is not over, not while there's a kebab to be had.

Some people swear by the postpub curry; some eat crisps all night long and are too stuffed to eat anything, no matter how drunk they are; and others are too far gone to push anything else into their rebellious stomachs, and have to find a quiet spot in which to exorcise their inner demons all over the floor. Rewarding as all of these pastimes can be, none casts the shadow of expectation like a kebab. It's like waving a leash in front of a dog's face; suddenly there is a very intense focus where previously there was just amiable chaos.

So, the Brits are out on a spree and the barman has called last orders. Everyone is standing up, slightly wavily, and trying to work out what to do with all the excess exuberance they've got sloshing around in their heads. Someone suggests going on to a club, but this is a divisive move. Not everyone wants to go dancing; others are mindful that there are important things to be done in the morning and don't wish to see a diverting experience turn into an appalling shambles.

That said, it doesn't feel as if the night has truly finished. After all, those crisps were nice, especially the way everyone opened the packets out so they were shareable, but only a couple of people really sated their appetites and now for the rest of them the booze is starting to clamor for something to soak into. You can't just go home and eat drunken cheese on toast, that's boring. Right now, everything in your nervous system is telling you that you are some kind of superhero/comedian/pop star hybrid and that's the kind of mindset that deserves a celebration. Never mind the blood pressure tablets, bugger the diet, it's time for a kebab.

It's worth mentioning that many other options are open to the postpub diner; chips being several of the main ones. There's chips and curry sauce, cheesy chips, chips and gravy, and a chip butty using a kebab pita; you can even have just chips, with or without salt and vinegar. Then there are regional bread-based delicacies like stotties (the northeast and Newcastle), barm cakes (Lancashire), bread cakes (Yorkshire), cobs (East Midlands), bannocks (Scotland), nudgers (Merseyside), and batches (Shropshire). Any one of them could take something meaty or chippy, depending on your requirements, but at this point in the evening, none of them have quite the gustatory tractor beam of the doner kebab.

Suddenly the only righteous thing to do (providing you are not a vegetarian, in which case see the paragraph above for options) is to visit that strip-lit palace of disinterested greasy delights: the kebab shop. Here is where you find out that the difference between medium and large is just how much stuff gets thrown on top of your order. Here is where the meat—it's lamb, by the way, pressed into a shape and then skewered on an industrial spit—is sliced from the rotating cushion and thrown carelessly into a metal pot. Here is where the pita is heated up on a griddle and then filled with too much salad. Here is where you will be asked if you want garlic or chilli sauce, or if you want "everything." It's best just to say yes.

Here is where coleslaw may or may not be applied, and the meat is shoved into and on top of the rest, which is already spilling out of the bread. Here is where they dig out a huge anemic-looking pickled pepperoncini and jam it on the top, like a pale green cherry on a very strange cake.

It's not the breakfast of champions or the dish they serve to the Viking soldiers of Valhalla, but to tipsy Brits—male and female—a messy, opulent kebab is all the feasting a drunken warrior needs.

WHAT TO SAY: "Extra chilli sauce on mine, please. I'm feeling defiant."

WHAT NOT TO SAY: "Is this place even hygienic?"

Downton Abbey and Sunday Night Nostalgia TV ∎

The big night for British television is traditionally a Saturday. That's when the bells and whistles are brought out, when there's a stench of gunpowder from the confetti cannons and a vinegary whiff of excitement and peril.

Entertainment shows like *Strictly Come Dancing* and *The X Factor* are on, as well as big family dramas like *Doctor Who*, *Merlin*, *Atlantis*, and *Casualty*. There's a reason for this: Saturday TV is about glitz, glitter, glam, and glory; it's about Things Happening and Life-Changing Moments and Going on a Journey and generally making the most of your weekend. It's important that the audience at home feel as if important things were happening directly to them, even though they have not so much as left the comfort of their sofa to fetch a snack.

Some of the audience will be getting ready to go out; some will be enjoying the fact that they don't have to get ready and go out. Either way, they will be being served excitement and potential and optimism and jeopardy, because Saturday night is that kind of a night.

Sunday, on the other hand, is a night for consolidating what has already happened, putting new discoveries away, fixing that which is broken, wallowing in the past, and generally preparing a psychic shield for the rigors of the week ahead. It's not a night for fresh information or worries about what the future may hold, and Sunday night TV caters to this need immaculately by focusing heavily on the past.

There are two long-running TV shows that could only exist on a Sunday night. More specifically, they could only exist on the BBC on a Sunday night. One is *Songs of Praise*—essentially just footage of people singing hymns in a cathedral, but it's been running since 1961—and the other is *Antiques Roadshow*. This is a program in which Brits visit a stately home carrying an item from their house—a family heirloom or a charity shop bargain, usually—that they believe might be worth a bob or two. It is then given the once-over by an antiques expert, who offers a valuation, which may or may not please the owners. Sometimes they go away happy, and sometimes they go away pretending to be glad they found out the interesting facts that they did, but secretly wishing for more cash. That's about all the jeopardy anyone in Britain can handle at this point in the weekend.

Also on Sunday are the big nostalgic drama presentations, scheduled for just after the kids have been packed off to bed: *Call the Midwife, Downton Abbey, Heartbeat, The Royal*. Each one a step back from the worries of the present day, so viewers can worry instead about things from the olden days that have already happened. *Downton Abbey* is the most successful example of this type of show, being so rooted in the past and riddled with the etiquette and hidebound traditions of Edwardian England it could also have been called *Antiques Roadshow*.

And what drives it is partly the ripeness of the characters—Maggie Smith's Dowager Countess with her flinty judgments taking center stage—and partly the skill with which that lost world, and its attendant class structure, has been re-created. There's nobility and savagery, comedy and tragedy, high-mindedness and low cunning, all set in a society with values that are not those of the modern era, so no one has to worry about what it says about nowadays.

So while huge modern (bleak) detective procedurals do come along later in the evening—*Prime Suspect, Broadchurch, Cracker, Inspector Morse*—Sunday night nostalgia TV tends to avoid stories that end in utter misery for everyone concerned. Even when a terrible event happens, it will usually be leavened by some lighthearted japery from some of the less-photogenic members of the cast who are largely there for comic purposes. These will most commonly be refugees from a soap opera: household names in face only, and good for a daft subplot about a get-rich-quick scheme or some dodgy theater tickets (*Call the Midwife* specializes in this sort of thing). For the most part, gritty realism is not required on a British Sunday, not if anyone is to get a good night's sleep before Monday rolls around.

Also, Sunday night dramas are all rooted in the world of work as it used to be. This is another psychological trick to encourage viewers to prepare for the week ahead, and they do this by setting up scenarios across all boundaries of class. You'll see policemen from the past driving around on old motorbikes in order to arrest local ruffians for stealing antimacassars from Lady Sourmouth's dayroom. You'll see a servant discussing how best to cook the hare the poacher left on the kitchen table when he came round at 1:00 A.M. to pitch woo at the wayward chambermaid. You'll see a doctor stub out a cigarette before going to attend a dangerous birth at the bedside of a plucky but weak working-class housewife who worries how she'll make ends meet, now her Sid is up in front of the beak on charges of wearing his hat in a saucy manner in front of a copper.

All of which are suggestive of the stresses of work without actually causing any pangs of worry about genuine modern-day work stuff. Throw in a modern drama with e-mails, balance sheets, or that report that was due last Thursday and the week is ruined before it has even begun.

WHAT TO SAY: "I see Lord Favourable's invitation has been sent to the wrong Lady Famished. This is precisely the kind of crisis they employ Blenkins in order to prevent."

WHAT NOT TO SAY: "Who wants to watch *Breaking Bad*?"

Weird Traditions ■

As the natural world ticks along its endless cycle of birth, growth, and death, there is much to celebrate, much to commemorate, and much to be superstitious about. The Brits have had a long time to work up their own unique reactions to these moments, and their customs and traditions can loosely be split into two subjective categories: those I grew up with and understand (and are therefore Not Weird) and those I do not recognize and do not understand (and are therefore Weird). Of course, if you're not from around there, they're all weird.

Let's start with the customs around New Year. In first footing, someone has to knock on the door after the stroke of midnight, but there's some local disagreement as to whom. In some places it should be the darkest and most handsome young man, and he must return with gifts—money, salt, bread, or coal—to ensure a prosperous and healthy year ahead. In Yorkshire, they'll settle for any man, unless he has red hair, and in Worcestershire he needs to be singing a Christmas carol. Yorkshire also has the tradition of people intoning "black rabbits" three times just before midnight and "white rabbits" three times just after.

Wales has an entirely different New Year tradition, based around the *calennig*, a small decorative twig sculpture not unlike a tripod with an apple at the top, which is coated in dried fruit, nuts, and a sprig of conifer. This is displayed for good luck (presumably until the apple goes off). On New Year's Day (*Dydd Calan*), children carry their *calennig* from house to house in the early morning and sing songs, for which they are given sweets and gifts and not, for example, a firm talking-to for waking everyone up after a hard night's drinking.

The more fiery New Year's celebrations include Northumberland's Allendale Tar Barl Festival, where guisers (not to be confused with geezers, who are just normal blokes) carry burning tar-filled whiskey barrels on their heads. Up in Comrie, Perthshire, a similar procession takes place but there are just eight burning torches, which are ceremonially dumped into the River Earn to cast out wicked spirits.

These are not to be mixed up with the straw bear (or strawboer) celebrations a week later. On January 7, in the Fenland borders between Huntingdonshire and Cambridgeshire, a man dressed from head to toe in straw goes from house to house, offering to dance for money, food, or beer. That's how they get the farming year started. On Shetland, there's a great big Viking party called Up Helly Aa that lasts all day and all night, the peak of which is a torchlit parade in which a specially made Viking longboat is dragged through town, and then all the torches get thrown inside and it burns to the ground while they sing a song called "The Norseman's Home." That's how they mark the end of Yule.

Then it's relatively quiet until May Day, the biggest red-letter day in the calendar of strange local customs. In the ancient Celtic communities in Scotland, Wales, Ireland, and Cornwall the first of May was called Beltane, and it marked the first day of summer. To celebrate the end of the hardships of winter, the people would have ritual fires and dances, and these are what current May Day traditions are largely based upon. The theme is very much one of sex and reproduction, across humans, livestock, and crops. May Day dew was said to have magical properties for a young girl, allowing her to see her future husband in the mirror, or to use as a love potion if collected in a jar. The Maypole may look suggestive, and the dance may be one intended to stimulate a good harvest and healthy, productive livestock; any recreational pleasures that may arise in the process of all that drinking and dancing are merely happy by-products, honest.

Speaking of which, on May 1, the Wessex Morris Men lead a parade of suitably engorged revelers on a merry dance up to the Cerne Abbas Giant, to welcome the arrival of spring and life blossoming before them.

The best known of all the springtime observances is the cheese-rolling competition on Cooper's Hill, near Brockworth, Gloucestershire. This dates back to the fifteenth century and may have evolved from a Beltane-style ritual of rolling burning bundles of wood down this dangerously steep incline and scattering bread and biscuits on the land. Nowadays they have no rolling fires, but the scattering still happens, and then there's the small matter of the eight-pound wheel of mature Double Gloucester cheese that is ceremonially rolled down instead, reaching speeds of up to seventy miles per hour. Competitors are invited to chase the cheese down the hill, which is so steep they invariably fall over and roll down, breaking bits of themselves in the process. The first to catch the cheese wins the cheese. It says something about local commitment to this event that during the privations of the Second World War, they had to craft a ceremonial cheese out of wood in order to keep the event going. Never mind that the contestants were risking their own usefulness in the war effort by deliberately falling down a hill; that was a secondary concern.

And then it's Easter, time to start acting out a battle between St. George and the Black Prince of Paradine in the middle of the street. The Pace Egg plays, once common Easter entertainment for the whole of England, were later revived in the north as a cross between street theater—St. George battles someone and dies, then is reborn—and a pub crawl, which may explain their popularity. They also feature some slapstick, some buffoonery, and a cartoonish villain or two to boo at. In some places children also get to go house to house (again) and are given painted eggs to roll down a hill. Oh, and the Pace Eggers have bequeathed at least one permanent addition to the English language. Amid the common characters—Owd Bett and Miss Kitty Fair (both men dressed as women), Owd Beelzebub, Derry Doubt, and the Doctor—is the fool Toss Pot, whose name lives on as a term of friendly abuse (see: Grade-B Swearwords).

On Easter Monday, the rival villages of Hallaton and Medbourne in Leicestershire take part in bottle kicking, a ritualized battle that appears to have started with a genuine punch-up two hundred years ago. The version that exists nowadays involves parading a big hare pie (see: Innuendo) through the streets of Hallaton, then taking it up to the top of a hill where it can bear witness to a big brawl in which representatives of both villages try to prevent their rivals making off with one of two barrels of beer by any means necessary, short of eye gouging. They had to make a rule about the eye gouging. In a similar party/punch-up between the villages of Haxey and Westwoodside in Lincolnshire, the fight is over a silk hood and involves the ceremonial contributions of characters called the Fool, the Lord of the Hood, and the Boggins.

There are even weird old traditions around the planting of parsley. Some claim that the herb will only germinate if planted on Good Friday by a woman, in rows aligned north to south; others say a successful crop will curse your family to have only daughters. Parsley is clearly a male chauvinist sprig.

A more recent addition to the list comes from the Bottle Inn, in Marshwood, Dorset, as a result of two farmers bragging about the height of the nettles on their land. As things do, this chat became competitive, and eventually one farmer said he would eat the nettle from his rival's land that could beat his tallest stalk. And so he did, and before you could say, "Hey, that hurts!" the pub had created the World Nettle Eating Championships, in which contestants scoff the leaves from two-foot-long nettle stalks for an hour, and the winner is the person who has consumed the most.

Brighton has its own winter solstice celebration, another fire festival, called the Burning of the Clocks. In a parade numbering up to a thousand, people carry decorative lanterns made of willow and paper, then burn them on the beach. Similar lantern parades—albeit without the fiery finish—take place at different times in different locations across the country, from Truro to Dumfries. And then there's bog snorkeling. This is another product of idle minds: organizers in Llanwrtyd Wells, Wales, dig a 120-foot trench in a peat bog; contestants then have to swim the length of the turbid water using only flippers as propulsion.

But the prize for the most unorthodox of traditional gatherings has to go to Egremont Crab Fair—named not after the first most likely interpretation of the word *crab*, or the second, but the third: crab-apples. There's a parade with an apple cart, with apples being lobbed into the crowd, while the fair itself holds such delights as the climbing of the greasy pole, a pipe-smoking competition (the winner being the person who sucks the most, presumably), and some Cumberland wrestling (not, sadly, with a sausage). But that's just the entertaining preamble to the main event: the Gurning World Championships.

Gurning is hard to explain. It's essentially a face-pulling competition, and to frame the distorted fizzogs of the people involved they put their heads through a horse collar (or braffin). The best gurners can fold their faces up like an old leather purse, making deep ridges and strange furrows appear where there previously were none. It's an astonishing sight, although would-be gurners should know that it does help if you've lost a few teeth along the way.

WHAT TO SAY: Nothing, just go with it.

WHAT NOT TO SAY: *"Sir! Sir! Please keep away from me with that tar barrel, as it is on fire and I do not wish to be disfigured."*

Real Ale ■

Ale: Not cold, not fizzy, on purpose.

The way the British like their beer is one of those standing jokes based on foreigners' shocked firsthand experiences. It's warm, it's flat, it's served in those dimpled mugs, and it doesn't taste like beer, it tastes like the backwash from a sluiced-out bread bin.

And of course all that stuff is broadly true, or at least it probably was forty years ago, and the reputation has stuck. The thing is, this is only a problem if you're expecting your beer to be lager. British beer—the stuff in the dimpled glasses, at least—isn't lager, it's ale, and ale differs from lager in much the same way that coffee differs from soup. They're not even brewed in the same way. Lagers use bottom-fermenting yeast (which, disappointingly, isn't a cure for trapped wind) that sinks down into the barrel and converts the malt and sugars into alcohol from there. Ales use top-fermenting yeast (which, disappointingly, isn't a cure for baldness) that floats on the surface and does the fermenting from there.

A good many ales are less carbonated than lager, so this thing about them being flat isn't a sign of poor quality, it's simply what the drink is. If you want a nice frothy head from a beer, drink something with a big creamy lid on it, like stout or porter. If you want to try the taste of a British best bitter, do without the bubbles; and if you want a really fizzy drink, try British lemonade.

On the issue of temperature, yes, the beer isn't ice cold, but here's the thing: British ale drinkers treat their beverage (let's be honest: beverages) with the same reverence and appreciation as wine drinkers do. They aren't necessarily after a drink to throw down their necks as fast as possible, for maximum refreshment. In fact, the true aficionados don't even drink ale in pints, but halves (and quite possibly out of a pewter tankard, because real ale is not, repeat not, about looking sophisticated). It's all about the flavor, and that means the smell as well as the taste. Colder drinks are harder to taste, and don't have that heady aroma, and so, in order to fully savor all the hoppy hops and the yeasty yeast, real ale is served at room temperature, just like good red wine. This also allows the ale to continue fermenting in the cask, and that's something real ale drinkers particularly approve of.

So far from being hairy-handed country simpletons with no taste buds, drinkers of real ale (they even call it real ale, to distinguish it from cheaply made, easily processed beers) are true connoisseurs. They even formed a pressure group to protect the central place of the British pub in communities—be they rural or urban—and to protect the beverages they sell. The Campaign for Real Ale (CAMRA for short) was formed in 1971, and far from being a society that just seeks to have members stick a teaspoon in a row of beer glasses and sip 'n' spit their way down to the end, it's been working to maintain a certain kind of British pub atmosphere (see: Pubs, Inns, Bars, and Taverns). This involves keeping six or seven casks of real ale behind the bar, and very probably a couple of local ciders too, particularly if the pub is in the West Country.

On that note, it's important to state that not all ciders are the same either. At one end are your mass-produced bottles of ice-cold Magners, served with ice, and at the other there's scrumpy, flat, and cloudy and sold in plastic vats like campsite water. Scrumpy is the West Country psychedelic; it's a locally produced, enormously potent beverage that can, when taken in the right amounts, alter the very fabric of reality.

There's also a tradition for giving real ales—which are by their nature not produced for supermarkets or other family-friendly retail outlets—risqué names. These will either be daft and sexist (Top Totty, Old Slapper, Booby Trap), daft and suggestive (Dog's Bollocks, Ginger Tosser, Dorset Knob), or just plain daft (Vicar of Dribbley, Village Idiot, Fiddler's Elbow, Wobbly Bob).

And there's been a recent crossover between brewers and rock bands. Iron Maiden, Elbow, Enter Shikari, and Status Quo all have their own signature beers, in the same way that Beyoncé, Katy Perry, and Britney Spears have their own signature perfumes. Because it never hurts to extend your brand with a product your fans would be buying anyway.

So the important lessons to draw from all this are that British beer is everything it is internationally mocked for being, and all the better for it. It's also worth pointing out that chilled lagers of every description are also available in British pubs, and they're incredibly popular too. It's not as if the Brits are all devoted ale-ophiles. It takes a while to get used to the taste, after all.

But if you're still tempted to nudge elbows with your drinking buddies and giggle about British beer, consider this: no one looks good coming out of a French restaurant complaining that their bottle of vintage red was too warm and it didn't fizz like the champagne back home, so maybe it's time to let ale be ale.

WHAT TO SAY: "Two pints of Bishop's Finger, Cheryl, and have one yourself."

WHAT NOT TO SAY: "It's Miller time!"

Putting Union Jacks on Things ∎

Only to be worn on the last night of aprons.

The British have had a turbulent relationship with their own flag over the years. For some it's a statement of overbearing nationalism, for others a symbol of national pride and a line in the sand that people from other nations cross at their peril. Mods love it because it's sharp and bright, in highly contrasting red, white, and blue. It's brought out at the Last Night of the Proms and at sporting events where Britain competes as one nation, rather than as England, Wales, Scotland, and Northern Ireland. It has flown all over the world in times of victory and in despair, so it's bound to have picked up some cultural baggage along the way.

Until recently it was considered bad form to refer to the flag as the Union Jack, as that name applies only when it is flown on a ship. Put the same design on a mug and it's a union flag. But no one ever gets this right, so that particular line of pedantry has been gradually, and officially, phased out. For the purposes of clarity, let's just make a mental note of this distinction, call it a Union Jack, and move on.

And it's not even a fully representative flag. The red cross of England's St. George is in there, as are the blue saltire of St. Andrew for Scotland and the red saltire of St. Patrick for Ireland. The Welsh flag—depicting the Red Dragon of Cadwaladr, King of Gwynedd—is not represented because (and this must be particularly annoying for the Welsh) Wales was considered legally part of England when the flag was made. For similar reasons there's no space for the Cornish cross of St. Piran, which is white on a black background. When the Scottish took a vote in 2014 on becoming independent from the UK there was a lot of talk about what the flag may look like if they decided to leave, and even though they voted to remain part of the United Kingdom for now, it's unlikely that the flag will remain as it is forever.

Of course, the net result of all this bickering is the flag has become a potent symbol within pop culture, and not just on merchandise for tourists in London, although heaven knows there is enough of that too.

One early putter of a Union Jack on a thing was Pete Townshend of the Who. He—and his manager Kit Lambert—had one made into a sports jacket in the band's first flush of chart success. It was 1965, and London was the eye of a musical storm that had ravaged across America, dragging the rest of the world in its wake. England swung, everything British was automatically cool, and here was a skinny kid with a big nose wearing the national flag as a coat, sticking an imperious two fingers up at the elder generation (who had fought a war under that very flag) and smashing his guitar on the floor. It was quite a sight.

During the early '70s the most prominent use of the design outside of proper ceremonial purposes was Tim Brooke-Taylor's Union Jack waistcoat in the comedy show *The Goodies*. And he was playing a stuck-in-the-mud conservative. But in 1977 the queen celebrated her Silver Jubilee, and there were street parties and cakes and bunting and all manner of red, white, and blue things everywhere. Because of this, punk rockers took to wearing it sarcastically; with Jamie Reid tearing his up to make Sex Pistols tour posters and generally mock the authorities. Before long, right-wing groups like the National Front were making use of both extremes—the patriotism and the righteous fury—to rally gangs of skinheads under the flag to antagonize and harass people from the Caribbean, India, and Pakistan who had come to live and work in the UK.

For most of the 1980s, the Union Jack remained a polarizing symbol, still tainted by association with the National Front, but given fresh boosts by the British victory in the Falklands War and a continuation of the more traditional, less worrying strains of patriotism, especially in the affluent southeastern counties.

But then a curious thing happened. During the 1990s a huge upswing in cultural confidence, similar to that of the Swinging Sixties, gave the flag a whole new context. It didn't mean racism or stuffy patriotism anymore; it meant British fashion, Britpop, Britart; it meant a thriving multicultural nation (the key word being *union*) and being really good at theater and music and films and football (see: Movie #3: *Trainspotting*).

So it was as a natural extension of this mentality that Noel Gallagher had a guitar made with a Union Jack on it. It was proof of his mod affiliation too, and soon Union Jacks were cropping up on T-shirts and scooters and badges and more guitars in an entirely unironic way. Nowadays the right-wing English groups rally under the flag of St. George, having decided that the Union Jack is a bit too broad for their tastes, and this has freed the union flag to appear on everything from cupcakes to Converse shoes without all of that ideological weight to carry. It's not untainted by the past, but then, what is?

And they still wave it at the Last Night of the Proms, Bruce Dickinson of Iron Maiden has one onstage every night, someone made a Union Jack cake on *The Great British Bake Off*, and the relaunched Mini came with a Union Jack roof. There are Union Jack playing cards, pens and pencils, gloves and coats, leggings and scarves, haircuts and tattoos, socks and pants. There is even a Union Jack Dalek toy for *Doctor Who* fans, and those guys won't get paint jobs for anyone.

Tim Brooke-Taylor's waistcoat suddenly seems conservative for very different reasons.

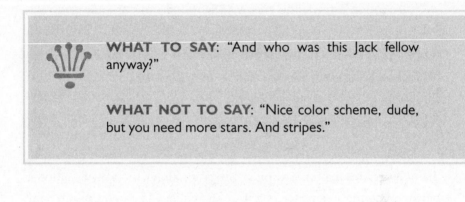

WHAT TO SAY: "And who was this Jack fellow anyway?"

WHAT NOT TO SAY: "Nice color scheme, dude, but you need more stars. And stripes."

Stags, Hens, and Having a Do ■

O nce upon a time, the correct way to toast any friends and relations who were about to jump the broom would have been a
night in the pub. Just one night, just one pub, and no speeches. That's
what a stag night was; it's what a hen night was too. And the night in
question would have been the night before the wedding. One last little
blowout, a moment of total freedom before the greatest day of your life
and an assured future of domestic servitude, er, bliss. Job done.

Unfortunately, just like a licked lollipop rolling down a dusty hill,
drunken traditions tend to pick things up along the way. So once it
became a common jape to try to lure the hapless bride or groom as far
away from the church as humanly possible, tie him or her to a lamp-
post, and take his or her trousers off (actually more of a groom thing,
now I come to think about it), sensible would-be-weds started to move
their prewedding parties further and further away from the big day
itself, if only to give themselves time to get back from (or to) Aberdeen. And once you've moved the day, you're no longer taking advan-
tage of the fact that everyone is together in one place at the same time,
so you have to start thinking about accommodation for people who
simply have to be there but live farther than a late-night taxi ride away.

So, if people are going to be making a big effort to be there, it
seems daft to start the occasion in the evening. Really it makes far

more sense to extend it a little and make a real do of it, maybe start with lunch, and stay over somewhere. And actually, we don't have to meet in just the one pub, not when we can do something nice beforehand, like have a nice meal all together. Or go paintballing or visit a spa or go to a comedy show or a gig.

Tell you what: we should make a weekend of it. Hang the expense, let's get everyone together in a holiday resort and hit the town like an invading army. We can go white-water rafting, cage fighting, basket weaving—it really doesn't matter so long as all the girls are wearing glittery pink cowboy hats and angel wings and those L plates you put on a car to show there's a learner driver behind the wheel (eh? eh? learner driver, yeah?) and all the boys wear specially printed T-shirts with the groom's face and a risqué slogan on the back, or dress up as Ghostbusters, and everyone gets very drunk in the evening and plays silly games and drinks and drinks and drinks and eventually we all get barred from our own hotel and have to spend the evening asleep in a park.

At some point along the way, some gifts of an alluring or sexual nature may be exchanged. This could mean a nice garter belt or a chocolate penis for the girl or a whip and handcuffs (unisex) or a pot of vitamin supplements with a name like Horny Goatweed or Leviathan for the boy. The inference is the same as it would have been if the stag/hen do were the night before the wedding: these items will be of use when the time comes. Oh, and there may be strippers, but some of the people in each party will be quietly judging the people who booked them.

The terminology for these events is exactly the same whether it's a full weekend in the Mendips or a single night in someone's flat around a solitary bottle of wine. You're having a do. You could have a do for any occasion, from birthdays to retirements, but stag and hen dos are particular and special.

One last note: it's not a shower; that's not really a thing Brits do terribly well, although the baby version is taking off a little. Bridal showers just seem like extra gift giving, and bearing in mind gifts have already been bought for the big day (and all the money spent on the hen do as well), it's all a bit much.

No, as things stand currently, a bit of a do will do just fine, thanks awfully.

WHAT TO SAY: "So I thought we'd all get massages and play laser tag. Who's in, fellas?"

WHAT NOT TO SAY: "A stag and a . . . hen? Is that even biologically advisable?"

Make no mistake, not everyone in Britain loves this film. It's posh, it's sentimental, and it plays up to national stereotypes about charmingly befuddled men with floppy hair that inadvertently paved the way for Colin Firth to woo Bridget Jones and for Matt Smith to take the lead in *Doctor Who*.

Okay, so that last one probably counts as a plus, and actually, so does the one before it. In any case, the Brits are buggers for claiming that sentimentality is bad and then communally weeping into a tissue—one tissue each; they're not animals—when a noble man reads a sad poem in a Scottish accent and can't quite get to the end without becoming overpowered by sobs. The funeral section of *Four Weddings* (and it's always called *Four Weddings*, by the way; we're on first-name terms) is the bit that justifies all the soppiness above and beyond. It's no coincidence that the poem John Hannah reads—"Stop All the Clocks" by W. H. Auden—has gone on to regularly star at the top end of any quest to find the nation's favorite poem.

Mind you, that first point about it being posh is useful too. Start a movie with an impressive twelve or thirteen goes at the F word with a bugger on top, but put in the mouths of working-class hard men or a line of council house mums, and you're dealing with gritty realism.

Have two posh friends running late for a wedding while saying "gosh!" and "heavens!" and it's just a typical drawing room farce. Posh people really having a good old swear, though . . . that's comedy.

And that's just the introduction. The movie fizzes with smart ideas like the bubbles in a bride's champagne. Here's just one: In order to make Hugh Grant's character, Charles, stand reluctantly in front of an entire congregation at his own sham of a wedding and say the words "I do" in such a way that it breaks his bride-to-be's heart and brings the whole affair crashing down around him (which, to anyone who has not been to a British wedding, is not what usually happens), Richard Curtis didn't write a conventional soliloquy, where the hero suddenly realizes what a ghastly mistake he is about to make and brings himself out of it. No, Charles's self-awareness speech comes at the hands of his brother, David, who objects to the marriage and explains why, using sign language because he is hearing impaired. Charles has to translate what David is saying, which is lengthy and well argued and ends with a gag about flies being left undone, and Charles condenses it down to, "He suspects the groom loves someone else," to which the vicar asks, "And do you?" and Charles replies, "I do." That's clever.

Four Weddings wasn't supposed to be a global hit. Only the Brits really knew what lineage Richard Curtis was working from: that he'd been one of the two guys who wrote the hugely beloved *Blackadder*; that he'd written *The Tall Guy*, a movie in which Jeff Goldblum's character falls in love with Emma Thompson's; and that he'd cowritten *Mr. Bean* and *The Vicar of Dibley*. British TV comedies don't often make the leap to movies that well, and certainly not so well that they become enormous successes in America, essentially making the careers of everyone involved and spawning pop singles that stay at number one in the charts for sixteen weeks (Wet Wet Wet's cover of "Love is All Around" by the Troggs). And yet that's exactly what the movie went and did.

This uncorked a bottle marked "Confidence" and suddenly comedies would aim to make you feel other things between the laughs. One way to do this was to reverse the class trick *Four Weddings* had pulled off. Instead of having posh people swearing like a Cockney docker at the soccer, British films started to show working-class people engaging in the fine arts. In *Little Voice,* L.V., the eccentric daughter of a wayward mother becomes a top-notch cabaret artiste for one night only. A troupe of unemployed steelworkers find a curious form of dignity in becoming male strippers in *The Full Monty,* and in *Brassed Off,* a colliery brass band makes it all the way to the Albert Hall; there the bandmates beat off all comers (not like that), shout at everyone (with, it must be said, some more swearing), then take an open-topped double-decker bus on a tour of London . . . at night.

And those are just the rational juxtapositions, based on well-meaning attempts to use art to alleviate pain. Before too long British comedies were awash with stranger cross-pollinations, like the suburban zombies in *Shaun of the Dead,* the sympathetically predatory schoolteacher in *The History Boys* (not strictly a comedy, but certainly not *not* one either), or the Plasticine machines and Claymation cheese in *The Wrong Trousers.*

Some of these things would have happened even if Hugh Grant had never dropped the F bomb, but *Four Weddings* remains high in the affections of British people for being the movie that suggested that even posh people with problems that aren't really problems can be lovable goofs.

WHAT TO SAY: "Charlotte Coleman, RIP."

WHAT NOT TO SAY: "I prefer *Notting Hill.*"

Look, boys, don't pull that face. You got all that stuff about sheds earlier, cozy little man caves with toolboxes and drills and lawn mowers and all that stereotypical stuff. This is simply the other thing to that thing's this thing, plus you get to see a grown man risk certain death by taking apart an explosive subject with inexpert tools. I mean, I've definitely done that elsewhere in the book, but this time it's more blatant.

The thing is, a few years ago there wasn't as much feminism in British popular culture as there is now. There was a lot of talk of ladettes and a giggle at Geri Halliwell's "girl power"; a bit of a poke at the glass ceiling, perhaps; a certain amount of concern over sexualization and sexual assault; and a fairly regular check on where we all were on using certain words with strong female associations, the C word and the B word in particular. But not actual feminism that you could put on a banner.

Now there is loads of feminism. Feminism has had enough of life in the sidelines, an embarrassed decline into worthiness, and decided to come out fighting. And boy, is there a lot of fighting. The thing is, the last time there was a lot of feminism about, people who didn't like it had to go to some trouble to tell the feminists their feelings, using personal interactions, and it was risky. Because going up to someone who is angry and righteous and threatening them to their face is a risky business, certainly compared to reaching into your own pocket, pulling out a smartphone, and tapping it repeatedly.

So while this new feminism has a greater platform, so do the people who wish to keep women in their place. They're going to have a job, though: the buggers are everywhere, asking awkward questions and causing trouble (by which I mean asking awkward questions and being repeatedly told off on the Internet, something that happens a preposterous amount; in fact, if it wasn't such a drearily reprehensible act, telling women off on the Internet would have to have its own chapter—possibly its own book—because there is just so very much of it).

This does at least work in both directions sometimes. The social media hashtag #everydaysexism, coined by the writer Laura Bates, simply asks people—men and women—to note when they see an imbalance, from the estate agent who always favors eye contact with the man of the house to the overexcited men catcalling women in the street and worse. And it's been a source of power; women feel their experiences, the ones that make them feel diminished, are worth sharing, maybe even worth tackling head-on.

What has been astonishing is the vitriol that comes after the sharing or the tackling. Emma Watson makes a speech in front of the United Nations and—as if by magic—becomes a lightning rod for Internet aggro. Recently journalist and campaigner Caroline Criado-Perez asked a seemingly straightforward question about whether, as the five-pound note was being redesigned (taking Elizabeth Fry off the nonmonarch side, where a place is reserved for admirable Brits, and replacing her with Winston Churchill), there might be space for a prominent woman elsewhere. During the ensuing row (in which the Bank of England acquiesced to the request with plans for a Jane Austen ten-pound note), Criado-Perez was the subject of such sustained harassment—the quoted figure was fifty threats an hour on Twitter, at the peak—that Twitter had to review its own procedure on dealing with complaints. All for a question and answer that deserved no more ruckus than you might get asking someone to move his or her car.

Then there's Caitlin Moran, the pie-eyed piper of British feminism. Her enormously successful book *How to Be a Woman* arrived just as feminism was shaking the dust off its boots and giving the old knees a try for the next round; and her second, semiautobiographical novel, *How to Build a Girl*, gave Moran the rock star status she so clearly was made for, despite being a funny writer and not a musician. She cleverly wove her own ideas about where women sit in society (wherever they want to, thanks) and what moral code they should follow (their own, dummy) with autobiographical details and tales from her own unorthodox life. So she could comfortably discuss her minor epiphanies and major tragedies within the context of her own feelings about feminism, and then make knob gags, because that's who she is.

And that sense of fun and personality is key. Whenever worried men ask questions about whether it's okay to describe themselves as feminist or call women *ladies* or open doors (because apparently that is still a thing), it's to a global panel of all-women, with their all-women opinions and all-women responses. And the feminism that we've got so much of at the moment isn't like that. It's like a release of pent-up energy from a thousand different directions at once, and all that energy is being put to useful purposes, but none of them are the same purpose. So as a unified movement with goals and aims and intentions, this feminism is a bit ragged, because it is made up of individuals, and that's exactly as it should be.

If there is going to be bickering, there should be laughter too. Provocative statements appear to be welcome, as are reasonable demands, outrage, and silly jokes. There should be fury and debate and disgust and unease and nothing should be too certain or feel too hard to achieve, and it should all be dazzling to watch, and that's exactly what it is.

WHAT TO SAY: Helpful stuff.

WHAT NOT TO SAY: Unhelpful stuff.

What kind of idiot enjoys waiting in line? And before you say, "a British idiot," just be aware that they really don't. They're no more keen on queuing than anyone else; it's just that there's no better way to ensure that the people who get to a thing first can get in first than standing in a queue. It's not ideal but it's all we have, and, that being the case, why fight it?

There again, what does it say about a country that the people who live there enjoy an international reputation for being quiet and docile when waiting in line for something they really want? Does it suggest that this is a nation of living, breathing, red-hearted, and vibrant individuals or a community that feels comfortable only when everyone knows exactly where they fit in relation to one another? And isn't it a form of international disgrace to be recognized as a nation of queuers, when waiting in line is something that happens all over the world? Of all the things to be considered to be really into, who in their right mind would pick waiting in line well?

"Look at the Brits," says Johnny Faraway, "they love to line up. They love it so much they have a word for it, made almost entirely of vowels, and if you whisper it, it sounds like an angry way to tell someone to leave you alone. And it's the French word for 'tail'—I heard that people actually used to call braided hair a queue for the same reason—anyway they call a line a queue because that's what a line of people waiting to get inside a building looks like. It looks like the building has a tail. I love that. Don't you love that? I mean, like, mind . . . blown . . . y'know? Totally . . ."

On and on he goes, but do the Brits care? They do not. They're too busy pretending not to hear him and wondering how much longer before they can shuffle forward an inch or two and wishing they had brought headphones with them.

But please, don't carry around the idea that the Brits are into queuing because they're supernaturally patient or they're so into manners that they simply cannot abide unfairness taking place on their streets. No, the reason the Brits sink gratefully into a queue is because of social awkwardness. The same social awkwardness that creates the eternal sorry flurry (see: Apologizing Needlessly), that's the driver here.

There's only one way to approach a queue: from the back. So the first mild panic is to work out where the back is. If this is a store with a helpful sign, or an airport with a twisty maze of belts on poles, the back is easy to spot. If it's a pub with a special till in the middle just for food orders, things can get stressful pretty quickly. The famously flustered internal monologue of socially awkward Brits will be sending out conflicting information at this point. One strand hopes desperately that this is the right place to stand; the other will be issuing panic bulletins every time it looks slightly as if the people immediately in front are just standing there and chatting. Because if they *are* just chatting, this means someone is going to have to ask them if they're in the queue, and the problem with this is that you're the one next to them and the people who have joined the queue behind you are relying on you as their leader to keep the thing going. If it turns out they are just chatting, you'll need to find out sharpish, or someone may abandon the fake queue and join the real one ahead of you, and that would be unfair. But then in order to ask if they're just standing there chatting you'll need to interrupt them, stop the talking, and ask, "Excuse me, are you just standing here chatting?" to which the only sensible answer is, "Well, we were, before you butted in," and that's not ideal either. So the only thing to do is say, "Excuse me, are you in the queue?" and hope they say yes, and not "What queue?" because then it will be a free-for-all and you'll end up at the back behind all those people who arrived after you did, and that's simply not fair.

As I say, only the first panic, and it's a mild one. Everything about queuing is stressful, and the only comfort is the sure and certain knowledge that everyone knows what the rules are and everyone is too socially awkward to break them, because to be challenged over cutting in (the Brits call it pushing in) would be a faux pas of a magnitude similar to using the wrong butter knife to flick peas at a duke. Queuing is about everyone knowing their place and sticking to it, secure in the knowledge that this is all for the common good (see: Talking about Class).

And what you may find is that socially confident Brits, the ones who don't really care about the common good or what other people think of them, are more likely to push in or to march up to the front and demand access based on some spurious reason, such as being a footballer, a pop star, or a minor member of the royal family. They will congratulate themselves that the venomous looks coming their way are to do with status envy, but really it's because the entire fabric of British society has been insulted. "Who are these people?" the stares insinuate. "These nonqueuing people? Don't they remember we once beheaded a king? They should."

WHAT TO SAY: Nothing. Just slip into a meditative state and be at one with your queuing brethren and sistren.

WHAT NOT TO SAY: "Come on! How long has it been now? What's the holdup? I can't wait all day! Tsk, tsk!"

A selection of delicious British beverages (and none of them are tea).

One of the great joys of foreign travel is to go into any supermarket or corner shop and just look at the chocolate bars and soft drinks on sale. The jolt between the familiar environment of a shop and the unfamiliar packaging, ingredients, and flavors on sale is just as exciting as a trip around areas of great cultural interest or outstanding natural beauty.

So, to save on plane fares, here's a very brief guide to the fizzy drinks you can expect to see in British shops—the ones that are not either big global soda brands like Coca-Cola (or Pepsi) or based on global soda brands like Coca-Cola (or Pepsi). The Brits have those, and they love them as much as you do.

Oh, before we get started, it's important to say no one in Britain calls a soda a soda. There is soda water—which is just carbonated water, used as a mixer—and soda bread, but not soda. The stuff in the cans and bottles used to be called pop, or fizzy pop, but is generally referred to as a fizzy drink, if not called by name.

That said, one of the more old-fashioned cans of fizzy pop you can still buy is called cream soda, and it is principally vanilla flavored. It's like drinking a carbonated milk shake, only far less thick in texture. But for everything else, the word *soda* is conspicuous by its absence.

It's also odd to note the omissions in terms of fruit flavors. While cherryade and limeade have been staples of pop flavoring for decades, there's no grapeade, apart from in imported cans. Pineapple and grapefruit have been combined into a drink called Lilt—with suitably Caribbean marketing that describes it has having a "totally tropical taste"—and, worst of all, there's no root beer.

The nearest equivalent is dandelion and burdock, a drink that has roots (pun intended) that go back to the Middle Ages and is considered a classic of olden days pop. Originally a lightly alcoholic beverage, made from the roots of the two plants in its name, dandelion and burdock shares a common flavor base with sarsaparilla and root beer, beverages that were believed to derive medicinal qualities from their ingredients, even though nowadays the drink is concocted entirely from flavorings. It's not a hugely popular drink, but you can still find it on sale if you look. It's beloved by the kind of plummy Brits who say, ". . . and lashings of ginger beer," in tribute to the Famous Five stories by Enid Blyton.

Some drinks were originally sold as tonics or pick-me-ups before they made the jump to general consumption. Certainly Lucozade—so named because it is riddled with glucose and is fizzy—was once marketed as the sort of drink one might deliver to a relative in hospital. It even came wrapped in a translucent orange plastic sheet, to facilitate the idea that it needed to be kept sterile before serving. Now it is marketed exclusively as a sports drink, for athletes who need a sugar rush immediately after, before, and during exercise. In this respect Lucozade has become the energy drink that (possibly) won't give joggers heart palpitations or gastric trouble. Mmm! Refreshing!

Then there are the drinks that, by blending or other means, managed to depart from conventional fruit flavors into another realm entirely. One that is quite hard to define by taste alone, and their names do not help matters.

Take Vimto, a name suggestive of vitamins and sunshine combined. It began as a cordial, like the eternally popular black currant Ribena, and is still widely available in both fizzy and ready-to-dilute form (as well as ice lollies, sweets, and even on draft in some pubs), and if it were widely known that it is supposed to be a mixture of grapes, raspberries, and black currants (with a few extra herbal bits and bobs thrown in to keep things mysterious), maybe it would be less of an enigma. As it is, the key fact any schoolchild knows about Vimto is that the name is an anagram of vomit. A most unjust state of affairs, given that the drink is so popular that some traveling rock stars—like Eddie Argos of the band Art Brut—take a supply on tour, as a reliable taste of home.

Another form of patriotic fervor comes from rusty Irn-Bru, which basks under the glorious advertising slogan "Made in Scotland from Girders." It is the most popular soft drink in Scotland, effortlessly outselling such giants as Coke and Dr Pepper, and commonly referred to as Scotland's second favorite drink (after whiskey). Its efficaciousness as a hangover cure is just one of the many reasons for this incredible popularity. Bright orange in hue, but not remotely orange in flavor, Irn-Bru has a taste that is entirely its own, being a soft drink equivalent of licking a battery (only, y'know, nice).

Brits who came of age in the 1970s and earlier will have fond memories of taking the reusable glass pop bottles back to the shop in which they were bought and claiming five pence or ten pence back. It's a reassuring nod to this prerecycling past to note that across Scotland, A. G. Barr, the manufacturer of Irn-Bru—as well as cream soda and a variety of other beverages—has kept this tradition going.

Barr is also responsible for making Tizer, which is bright red and has a taste that is equally hard to define. It's sort of sweet and medicinal, the kind of taste you'd expect from a herbal extract that claims to cure indigestion in four hours. And in fact its name derives from the word *appetizer*, under which it was originally marketed. Definitely one to add to your fizzy pop tick list.

You are making a fizzy pop tick list, aren't you?

WHAT TO SAY: "Two D&Bs and a Vimto chaser, straight, no ice."

WHAT NOT TO SAY: "Haven't you got any Mountain Dew?"

Tribute Bands ■

For all that the British feel intimately connected with the pop and rock explosion of the past fifty years or so, they nonetheless have a niggling suspicion that the real action is always taking place somewhere else. And often that somewhere is America. While any touring global superstar would be foolish to overlook a couple of dates in Britain, even London is not so spoiled for choice that music fans can afford to just sit back and wait for the big gigs to happen, and there are always punters who require entertainment when Bruce or Beyoncé is otherwise engaged, or too expensive. This need is only increased when the singer, rapper, or group in question is no longer available for any kind of performance.

Enter the tribute artist, a chance to show off on three simultaneous levels at once: dressing up, naming the act, and the performance itself.

Dressing up is a key aspect. Whether it's Elvis or the Beatles or the Spice Girls, you want to create the idea that this is an alternate version of reality, one in which the real Elvis neither died nor continued to thrive, but somehow lost his fortune and the bulk of his fan base and ended up doing gigs in local pubs around Britain for the cost of a hotel, a meal, and the petrol to get to the next one. His movements, his look, his Elvis-ness, have to be in some sense intact, albeit slightly lost in translation thanks to the physical limitations of his alter ego: a podgy plumber from Barnsley called Neil.

But that's part of the fun too. If drama is all about the willing suspension of disbelief, tribute acts are Shakespearean in scale and emotional heft. It doesn't matter if you're not the right age for the star you're attempting to be; it doesn't even matter if you're not the same gender or the same race (actually, the race thing matters a lot, but only in one direction; even with that willing suspension, blacking-up is still blacking-up). All you need to do is stand on a stage and say, in a firm voice, "I am Elvis," and the powers of Elvis shall be yours.

So the performance becomes about commonly understood mannerisms. More Elvis tribute acts appear in white rhinestone jumpsuits than any other costume, because that's the Elvis most people know. Beatle tribute bands without collarless jackets and 1963 moptops (or fluorescent *Sgt. Pepper's Lonely Hearts Club Band* army uniforms) are not going to get repeat bookings. And if they don't bother to talk to each other in exaggerated Liverpool accents between numbers, that's weird too. Not as weird as using the wrong guitars, but still unsettling.

But the real creativity in being a tribute act—and this is something the British are particularly fond of—lies in creating a name that somehow refers to the original performers, while making it clear that this is not them, and wrapping the whole thing up in a clever pun. The Bootleg Beatles, the Australian Doors—these are good descriptive names for a handbill or a poster, but they're not funny. Not like:

Elvish Presley, Not the Hoople, Blackest Sabbath, Antarctic Monkeys, Forged Harrison, Oasish, Motorheadache, Surely Bassey, the Police Academy, the Fillers, the Counterfeit Stones . . .

And that really is the tip of the iceberg. Such a list could easily be entirely populated with Beatles tribute bands alone.

So while people need to see those songs performed in a live situation, while people enjoy reliving their wild youth (or imagining they are at the Cavern Club in '62), the tribute act takes what was once an expression of individuality, youth, and charisma and makes it a parade of vaudeville fun, pitched somewhere between a reminder of days gone by and a resurrection of something the audience is too young to have seen the first time around. What you lose in danger and spontaneity you win in verisimilitude and shared nostalgia.

There are even tribute band festivals, for which the tickets are far cheaper and the lineups beyond your wildest imaginings. And of course the festivals are as susceptible to punning names as the bands themselves, the most notable being the perfectly titled Glastonbudget.

WHAT TO SAY: "I've always wanted to see Nirvana live and now I can!"

WHAT NOT TO SAY: "Of course, the real Paul is left-handed . . ."

The Boat Race

As a title for a sporting event, it's hard to top "The Boat Race." Every word is key. It's a race, between boats, and it is the definite article. All other boat races, even the big ones between sailing boats that go, y'know, all the way to over there and back again, they pale to alabaster nothing next to The Boat Race. You never hear sports journalists or TV presenters discussing a fixture called "The Football Match" or "The Running Race," do you? That's because there are too many examples with a claim to being definitive. Even Wimbledon, which has some claim—from a British perspective, at least—to be "The Tennis Tournament," is bereft of that lofty title.

The Boat Race is also one of the few notable British sporting events in which all the participants are students. There are a lot of interuniversity sports, of course, but nothing that permeates the wider consciousness; and none of these participants got a place at college based on their ability as athletes. But there appears to be something magically enticing about an annual grudge match between two eight-person rowing teams—representing the Oxford University Boat Club and the Cambridge University Boat Club—on a bendy stretch of the River Thames in London. This is an annually televised event that reaches millions of homes, which is more than can be said for almost any other student activity that is not a news story about exam results featuring photogenic female students jumping up and down and/or crying.

While The Boat Race was first held in 1829, it wasn't until 1854 (practically last week by British historical standards) that it became an annual event, taking place on either the final weekend of March or the first weekend in April. And make no mistake, the Brits who are partial to this kind of thing take it incredibly seriously. Only outbreaks of world war have interrupted the racing, and when disruptions have occurred—a couple of sinkings, broken oars, two prerace mutinies, and a protester interrupting the race in 2012—the drama is given the reverence and scrutiny one might expect of a troubling murder trial. After a particularly fractious time preparing for The Boat Race in 1987, the Oxford team faced an ultimatum from American oarsmen who refused to take part if a fellow countryman who had been cut was not reinstated. The team that entered, patched up from the reserve team, went on to win. It is a measure of how seriously some Brits take this stuff that there have been two books written (and published) about the events leading up to that one race.

The match is rich in traditions. In stark contrast with most team games, both teams wear the same color—blue—it's just that the blue of the Cambridge blues is a lighter shade of blue than the blue of the Oxford blues. While the race itself is quite short, it's the kind of sporting event that encourages spectators to make a day of it, and as it's by the river, there are no shortage of picturesque pubs into which fans can cram, lingering before and after, and after again. On that note, critics sometimes complain that The Boat Race is little more than a posh picnic for the upper classes, an impression that is in no way dispelled by the fact that the teams pick which side of the river to row on by tossing an 1829 gold sovereign. A fifty-pence piece would simply never do.

Oh, and the tradition of lobbing the winning team's coxswain into the river is pure beefy public school high jinks, akin to Formula 1 winners spraying champagne everywhere. It's just a bit of fun, old thing, why the sour puss?

The most interesting thing about The Boat Race, however, is that in all that time, the results between the teams have been remarkably even. At the time of writing, Cambridge currently has the edge over Oxford, but only by a couple of wins (the time in 1877 when a tie was declared does not count). There have been wider margins of success between the two teams down the years—Cambridge won thirteen years in a row, in the 1920s and '30s—but this period of balance serves a useful purpose, in that it means outsiders can't go wrong by just picking a side they fancy and supporting them. Knowledge of boats, past form, and rowing is no barrier to enjoying the full majesty of the event, or the lack thereof; it is, after all, only a boat race.

WHAT TO SAY: "Isn't *boat race* Cockney rhyming slang for 'face'?"

WHAT NOT TO SAY: "Come on, you blues!"

Crisps and Other Deep-Fried Foods ■

One of the international legends of British cuisine states that the Brits, particularly those in the north and in Scotland, have only two methods of cooking, and both involve boiling liquid: water or oil. That's nonsense, but there's just enough evidence for the prosecution to keep the jokes coming, especially when it comes to deep-fried foodstuffs. Even if you take fish and chips out of the equation (and you would be wise not to even attempt such a thing), you've still got a world of oily boiled joy to explore.

Let's start with crisps. We all love a crisp, don't we? Although, as with all things, the Brits have managed to inject a note of class consciousness into their appreciation of them. By which I mean, depending on the situation, some flavors and brands are more welcome than others.

So while the full range of Walkers crisps, from salt & vinegar to cheese & onion (see: Ampersand Foods), would be suitable to serve to any guest, beggar or prince—although possibly not prawn cocktail; it's tacky—the cheap corn-puffed Space Raiders would be unwelcome in any social situation beyond a child's birthday party (and even then it depends on the child). The far plusher Kettle Chips, on the other hand, are wasted on children, party or not, and don't even bother to open the oven-roasted root vegetable mix, because they'll be too busy scoffing party ring biscuits to care.

You can even cut this down to individual flavors within the same range, with smoky bacon and tomato ketchup crisps being notably more plebeian than any sour cream and chive or Worcestershire sauce options, with pickled onion being the lowest of the low. Having said that, one snack is even further down the food chain—it should come with a public health warning—and that is Smiths Scampi Fries. You know how the scent of certain snack foods tends to linger on your fingers? Imagine if that scent wasn't something relatively wholesome like cheese or vinegar, but fish. Dirty, dirty fish. After eating a pack of Scampi Fries, it's not uncommon to find yourself locked in the bathroom for hours, methodically trying to scrub that fishy whiff off your digital extremities and vowing never to go near them again. Not a snack to put out if the queen visits, that's my point.

Then there are Skips, a tapioca approximation of a prawn cracker, in the shape of a buttercup. These delicately flavored snacks rather fancy themselves as a cut above the average roast-beef-flavored Monster Munch and are probably terribly embarrassed by their gaudy yellow packaging. There again, Twiglets—knobbly wheat sticks that taste of Marmite—are simply too down-to-earth to care. And compared to almost all other savory treats, they're practically health food.

Of course, with all these snacks attempting to re-create or improve upon the chip shop experience in a convenient and portable way, the chip shops themselves have had to fight back by bunging newer and more interesting things into their hot fat to see what comes out. Scotland received international acclaim by inventing and popularizing the deep-fried Mars bar, having already been battering haggis and black pudding and white pudding for years. The Scots then went on to innovate further with deep-fried Cadbury's Creme Eggs. Now even Nigella Lawson has published a recipe in which she takes a beloved high street chocolate bar (in her case it's a Bounty) and gives it a damn good frying, and she's not even Scottish.

This fondness for frying that which should never be fried has saddled Scottish cuisine with an international joke reputation that everyone seems perfectly happy to play along with. Take an egg, wrap it in a ball of sausage meat, coat the ball in bread crumbs, and deep-fry it, and it's called a what? A Scotch egg. Take a circle of batter and whack that in the fryer, then sugar it and frost it, or inject it with jam, and what's that called? It's called a doughnut. Everyone has those.

In fact, that deep-fried Mars bar was conceived as a one-off gimmick by one chippy in Aberdeen: the Haven Chip Bar, in Stonehaven. The only reason we know about it is because the local press marveled at such gastronomic gall, and the story spread. Other chip shops simply followed suit, because it would improve business, and now this joke thing is a real thing; the greasy genie has slithered out of the bottle and the hunt is on for the next battery masterpiece.

Deep-fried pizza has already happened, as have fritters of all descriptions—from banana to mushy pea to spam. But there's still scope for a few late additions. How about a deep-fried lettuce? Or deep-fried After Eight mints? Who would like to try deep-fried hummus? Or perhaps a deep-fried ice sculpture of the Proclaimers?

Mind you, a bit of batter around those Scampi Fries would definitely help.

WHAT TO SAY: "Maybe we should just get a salad."

WHAT NOT TO SAY: "And where can I get hold of this human-breast-milk ice cream I keep hearing about?"

The Cheese Map of Britain ■

Since time immemorial, there has been a foolproof way to give directions in the British Isles. Long before GPS, before Google Maps, before properly signposted roads and the satisfying solidity of tarmac underfoot, should someone wish to know the way to a place, the clearest directions are always by pub.

"Take a right at the White Hart. That'll lead you down Tickley Road toward the Queen's Head. Once you get there, you want the third left, just before you get to the Red Lion. Follow Touchstone Avenue for two miles until you reach the Old Cock and look for a dead tree on your right. Directly opposite is a one-lane track—Squeezeguts Lane—that will take you all the way to the main road. It comes out in the car park of the Coach and Horses, so watch how fast you take that corner. Turn left as you come out, follow the road for a mile, past the Open Season, and your friend's house is sixteenth on the right."

But if you have farther to go, if you're covering some serious distance, you're going to need a larger scale to your map. Never mind pubs, never mind motorways, cheese is the only way to travel. Leave your A–Z behind; these curds will show the whey.

According to the British Cheese Board (and please, can we have a moment of reflection and applause here for the governing body for British cheese having the wit to call themselves that? "Would you like to see the British Cheese Board, sir?" "No, thanks, I'll just have

The actual map (cheese not pictured).

coffee."), over seven hundred British cheeses are registered and produced in the UK and a good portion of them are named after the
place from whence they came. You'll already be aware of Cheddar, no
doubt, and Stilton, Gloucester (double or single), Leicester, and possibly Cheshire. But as a collection, these are only the thin end of the
cheese map wedge.

As well as acting as an almanac of British cheese-making towns
and counties, reading through the list of location-themed cheeses is
like a roll call for the lesser members of Robin Hood's merry men. Try
reading them out loud; every name rolls off the tongue as pleasingly as
the cheese rolls on.

There's Davidstow, Swaledale, Harlech, Duddleswell, Coquetdale,
Buxton, Cotswold, Berkswell, Goosnargh, Wensleydale, Red Windsor, Coleraine, Harbourne, Dunlop, Appledore, Lancashire, Beacon

Fell, Bowland, Rothbury, Dunsyre, Teviotdale, Brinkburn, Caithness, Garstang, Cotherstone, Croglin, Dorstone, Derby, Lanark, Hereford, Tintern, Dovedale, Barkham, Bonchester, Chevington, Woolsery (see: Embarrassing Foreigners), Appleby, Parlick Fell, Whitehaven, Allerdale, and, of course, the Stinking Bishop.

Granted, that last one isn't a place. The cheese does whiff, though. It's very tasty but it won't win you the affections of any Maid, nor will it help you Marian.

And while some of these names are too specific to be as useful for guidance as, say, a decent map of the major British motorways, that's a small price to pay for the sharp tang of history, on a cracker. Possibly with chutney.

Among the cheeses that aren't affiliated with a specific location, there are names that read like another roll call; this time it's hobbits setting off for a picnic on a summer's day.

Picture a member of the Baggins clan with his feet up and a pipe lit, muttering to himself, "Well, bless my braces if that's not young Radden Crowdie back from his dovecote with a basket of oatcakes in his hand; Gevrik and Tesyn the pasty-makers are already halfway to the old stones; Slipcote Gallybagger seems to be heading out too, even though he should really be hard at work, doing chores for the Lord of the Hundreds; and is that Black-Eyed Susan, she with the daintiest hairy feet of them all, skipping daleward without so much as a backward glance? The scuttlebutt has it that she is courting the lothario of the Shire, young Master Pantysgawn . . ."

That last one is genuinely the name of a cheese, by the way, so don't snigger. It's an organic goat cheese, for proper cheese connoisseurs, and the name is taken from the Welsh farm where it is made.

Which leads us to a final note of caution: while there's some fun to be had with Welsh names, be aware of local sensitivities around identity and culture. Should you wish to make fun of the Welsh, proceed Caerphilly.

WHAT TO SAY: "Who's the most popular rock star in Cheddar? Curd Cobain."

WHAT NOT TO SAY: "Really? Cheese puns? From the nation that gave the world Shakespeare? For shame."

National Treasures ■

uperlatives are so lightly thrown around at the moment that anyone who has managed to remain relatively well-known for more than a fortnight without enduring any public disgrace has a legitimate claim on the title of National Treasure and all the benefits that come with it.

Okay, there are no benefits. It's just a term that gets bandied about to show a kind of uncritical approval of anyone whose cultural credit is firmly in the black, sometimes not even that firmly. However, some people appear to have given more than their fair share to the British communal pot, the kind of people who act as ambassadors for Britain just by being (a) British and (b) really good at what they do on a globally recognizable scale. If (b) turns out to be a bit of a stretch, they'll have made up for it with lots and lots of (c) charisma. These people are so embedded in the nation's enjoyment of itself that even death can't sever their eternal reputation, although time will definitely have a really good go at it.

Peter Cook was a national treasure, and so was his comedy partner Dudley Moore. Morecambe and Wise are preserved as national treasures on archive tape forever more. Paul McCartney still is one (although he is starting to wear out the welcome for "Hey Jude" at national events) and John Lennon's posthumous status has been firmly nailed in place by the beatification—Beatlification?—of generations. Judi Dench must surely qualify, although she's spoken very firmly against it—comparing national treasure status to being exhibited behind glass—and so must Emma Thompson. Then there's everyone else, dead and alive: J. K. Rowling, David Frost, Helen Mirren, William Shakespeare, Jane Austen, Alan Bennett, Victoria Wood, Jarvis Cocker, Maggie Smith, Charles Dickens, Emily Brontë, Vivian Stanshall, Elizabeth Taylor, Sean Connery, Kate Bush, Michael Caine, Virginia Woolf, Stephen Hawking, Julie Walters, Trevor McDonald, Trevor Nunn, Trevor Nelso . . . oh, sorry, that's from a different list: National Trevors.

The two people most commonly referred to as national treasures are Stephen Fry and Sir David Attenborough. The former because he resembles the kind of posh, fluffy, and rather fearsome uncle that one might come across buried in a dusty old book at an aged relative's house. He is a man who wears many shoes: he's an expert on consumer technology; he's the elegant Jeeves in the best-known TV adaptation of P. G. Wodehouse's tales of the raffish gadabout Bertie Wooster; he's two generations of the family Melchett in the TV comedy *Blackadder*; he's a documentary maker, with films on endangered species and mental illness (from a highly personal perspective, as he lives with bipolar disorder); he's Oscar Wilde in the biopic *Oscar*; he's a celebrated author of novels, an autobiography, and a guide to writing poetry; he's a creator of wildly daft sketch comedy with Hugh Laurie—the future Dr. House and the Wooster to Fry's Jeeves; and he's the (mostly) genial host of *QI*.

That list of improbable achievements, each one a gem, is why the Brits love him so. And despite taking his place in a line of genuine idiosyncratic English characters who continue to fascinate down the ages (see: Quirks, Foibles, and Eccentricities), he's simply too ripe as an individual to possibly be available in real life.

Sir David, on the other hand, is very real indeed. As the British broadcaster of natural history programs, he is possessed of three entirely admirable qualities that set him apart: nerves that do not flap even when he is being cuddled by wild mountain gorillas, a childlike sense of wonder when faced with any natural phenomenon, and a quietly authoritative voice that regally unicycles down the boundary line between awestruck observer, hoarse with reverence, and travel-hardened expert.

He's the man with the hobby he can't seem to let out of his mind for as much as a second. He's the kind of person one suspects would allow conversations to happen around him in any direction they care to wander, and then find a way to divert them back to his particular field of interest. In Sir David's case, this means the natural world, although at one time he was a controller of an entire television channel—BBC Two—at a time when there were only three of them, and the man who commissioned *Monty Python's Flying Circus*, *The Old Grey Whistle Test*, and snooker on TV, among other things.

And as if all that weren't admirable enough, in 1972 Sir David let go of his management responsibilities, turning down the chance to become the director general of the BBC, in order to write and present enormously popular TV shows about animals and plants and fish and birds. He's not just a boffin—and, my word, the British love a boffin, especially one who is equally unafraid to have his hair ruffled by an elephant as he is to appear in an app with Björk—he's the boffin who abandoned the rat race in order to race with rats.

WHAT TO SAY: "So Sir David Attenborough is Sir Richard Attenborough's brother? Imagine the family arguments over *Jurassic Park*!"

WHAT NOT TO SAY: "Stephen Fry was in *National Treasure*, wasn't he?"

t is probably no coincidence that the United Kingdom and the United States both have a long-standing tradition involving fireworks, a fondly anticipated night in which everyone gathers to ooh and aah themselves closer together. It's no bad thing for communities to spend a moment watching the heavens explode, although the events that inspired each celebration, and the emotion that drives them to this day, could not be more different.

Independence Day is a reminder of the birth of the United States, the moment at which a nation was founded and an imperial force overthrown. The fireworks are an acknowledgment of the tumult of war and a glimpse of the excitement of the future. Whereas Bonfire Night, or Fireworks Night, or Guy Fawkes Night, commemorates an attempt to blow up the palace of Westminster, more commonly known as the Houses of Parliament, for sectarian reasons that are not often discussed anymore.

To put the event into proper historical context, in the early hours of November 5, 1605, guards were instructed by King James I to search the cellars underneath the House of Lords. He had been shown an anonymous letter sent to Lord Monteagle, warning him and all good Catholics to stay away from the state opening of Parliament. The guards found a man leaving an undercroft just after midnight and, in the undercroft itself, thirty-six barrels of gunpowder, hidden by coal and firewood.

Under torture, the man admitted his name was Guy (or Guido) Fawkes and that he had been waiting there to light the fuse once the king had entered the building. He and twelve other men had conspired to kill the Protestant king and place his young daughter Elizabeth on the throne, once she had been kidnapped, brought up as Catholic, and married to a Catholic husband. They had leased the undercroft, filled it with gunpowder, and were just waiting for the right moment to strike.

The public, outraged that their king's life had been threatened in such a way—by Catholics, who were not popular in British society at the time—lit public bonfires in the wintry air to celebrate his good health. Once the plot had been fully uncovered and explained, and the plotters executed, these impromptu celebrations were enshrined in law, in the Observance of 5th November Act (which, impressively, remained in force until 1859), to ensure a public day of thanksgiving that the king's life had been spared. The celebrations included fireworks, food, and commemorative bonfires on which effigies of Guy Fawkes—and sometimes the pope—would be burned.

This has lasted as a tradition for over four hundred years. There are huge public fireworks displays, accompanied by a massive bonfire on which a figure is often burned, although not always by any means. In Ottery St. Mary, Devon, people run through the streets with burning tar barrels on their backs too. There are tiny backyard bonfires too, with children waving sparklers and potatoes roasting in the embers. Kids used to make their own Guys too, and until relatively recently many could be found on the streets asking strangers for money: "A penny for the Guy?"

Even people who could not name the king whose life had been spared (and there are a lot of us) grew up with this rhyme, to be intoned darkly:

Remember, remember the fifth of November
Gunpowder treason and plot
I see no reason why gunpowder treason
Should ever be forgot.

And it has not been. Alan Moore used Guy's status as a folk anti-hero when he created his graphic novel *V for Vendetta*, in which V, a lone terrorist in a Guy Fawkes mask, overthrows a British fascist state. The anticapitalist movement seized upon this idea, using V masks to secure their anonymity at protests. There again, the right-wing blogger Paul Staines uses the pseudonym Guido Fawkes to write a gossip blog about Westminster, claiming the name as a tribute to "the only man to enter parliament with honest intentions. The intention being to blow it up with gunpowder."

So, rather than being a day to commemorate the first steps of a new nation, or the overthrowing of an imperial regime, Bonfire Night is a wilder event entirely. It's an exorcism of folk demons, and while it has lost most of its anti-Catholic sentiment (although some traditions die harder than others), it still carries the idea that somehow someone should be punished for something. There's a rude celebration at play, a sense of irreverence toward figures of authority. In places where a Guy is to be burned, he may be just a nondescript and makeshift man built of old, stuffed clothes, but he could also be Simon Cowell or Osama Bin Laden or Lance Armstrong or Margaret Thatcher. Whoever the local community deems to be the devil of the moment (see: Cocking a Snook).

And if there's no one else, Guy Fawkes himself is always there, ready for another roasting.

WHAT TO SAY: "Have you checked the bonfire for hedgehogs?"

WHAT NOT TO SAY: "Of course, this is just a modern recasting of the ancient pagan festival of Samhain."

Quirks, Foibles, and Eccentricities ■

There's a knack to being eccentric. It's not simply a matter of growing a half beard; answering the phone with a hearty "good-bye!"; wearing a wetsuit to the office; and painting all your eggs to look like planets before you eat them. That's just bad grooming, bad manners, a recipe for a nasty rash, and an overactive God complex, respectively. And showing off.

However, there are few things Brits enjoy more than individuals with genuine quirks and foibles. The lawyer who writes only with a red pen, the postman who spends his weekends happily pretending to fly a Spitfire from the replica cockpit in his garage, the woman who collects toy frogs and displays them all over the house—these are all people who may not have the buffer of extreme wealth or a country estate in which to blossom into the full fullness of themselves, but they do it anyway. It's easy to be unorthodox when you're in charge. Sir George Sitwell had a sign in his mansion requesting that guests should not contradict him, lest it interfere with his digestion and prevent sleep. He also created a miniature pistol for shooting wasps—much harder to carry off that kind of thing from a tiny flat in a heaving metropolis.

They also like their experts to act as if knowing a lot about a subject has taken a toll on their ability to blend in with everyone else. This seems, in some way, to be a fair swap for the extensive knowledge they now possess. The television astronomer Sir Patrick Moore, for example, always had the air of a man who simply did not have enough time to care whether you found his manner bizarre—imagine being told about space by a stern human owl with a monocle—because he spent his entire time looking upward through telescopes or (and this is the key detail) playing the xylophone.

Sir Patrick also comes from the tradition of the Great English Eccentric, one that takes in some truly marvelous oddballs, whose most unorthodox instincts were cushioned by extreme wealth, like Willam John Cavendish-Bentinck-Scott, Fifth Duke of Portlant, who dealt with his natural shyness by electing to live in a network of chambers and tunnels, one of which led directly to Worksop Railway Station. He would travel there by carriage—blackened windows, naturally—have the carriage loaded onto the train, travel to his overground home in London, and then hurry to his private study while his servants were ordered to keep their distance.

He'd have hated the more ostentatious Baron de Rothschild, whose carriage was drawn by four zebras, and who trained a tame bear to slap women guests on the bum. Actually, that's not eccentric, that's just creepy.

Lord Rokeby simply wanted to be a fish, and he spent a good deal of his life immersed in water, either in the sea or in his private swimming pool, in which he took his meals, his enormous beard bobbing on the surface. Lord North was, by contrast, an otherwise unremarkable man whose sole quirk was that he would go to bed on October 9 and not get up again until March 22. He even conducted dinner parties from his bedroom, which can't have been awkward at all.

C. B. Fry, enormously talented world-class sportsman across the disciplines of cricket, football, rugby, and the long jump, may have been beautiful enough to earn the nickname "Almighty" in the press, but he is most fondly remembered as a man who, with very little prompting, could jump backward from a standing start and land on a mantelpiece.

That's the kind of tradition a true eccentric can really work with, especially as none of these people were doing it for the attention. Particularly not Lord William.

The same can't really be said for Quentin Crisp, although his motivation was far from self-aggrandizement. Born Denis Pratt, he simply wanted to express what would nowadays just be considered natural flamboyance and the desire to kiss a few boys, at a time when it was physically dangerous, not to mention illegal, to do so. So he changed his name, painted his nails, dyed his hair, and stepped out to meet his destiny. He famously never cleaned his home, claiming the dirt did not get any worse after the first four years, and when his memoir *The Naked Civil Servant* was made into a popular TV drama starring John Hurt, he became a celebrated figure—in his own words, "the stately homo of England."

There are people who have turned their quirks into art, like the inscrutably suited Gilbert and George, the singer and comedian Vivian Stanshall, and the dour performance poet Ivor Cutler, and people whose quirks actively obscure their art, like Lawrence, lead singer of the indie bands Felt, Denim, and Go-Kart Mozart, who, it's been said, never lets any visitors use his toilet and refuses to eat vegetables. And then there are people whose art is a kind of running commentary on some of their quirks. The bulk of Russell Brand's stand-up act is about what happens when he is allowed to follow his instincts—even though they get him into trouble on a regular basis—and it is a narrative he delivers while gesticulating wildly and speaking in a peculiarly mannered manner that could almost be a caricature of the Great English Eccentric Lords of old.

He, however, is most definitely showing off. It's only the fact that he's doing it in a quirky way that saves his bacon. Not that he eats bacon, of course.

WHAT TO SAY: "So how did Quentin Crisp make a cup of tea?"

WHAT NOT TO SAY: "I've started a Facebook campaign to make every January fourteenth National Winking Day!"

B race yourselves: one of the food products in this chapter has a name that, had the product been developed today, would not have been considered on grounds of public decency and supermarket giggling. And you may find that it temporarily distracts you from the matter in hand, which is to be a brief discussion of a couple of nighttime hot drink alternatives to Ovaltine. This is only natural, and nothing to be ashamed of. But to help create a frictionless reading experience, let me just say the word *Horlicks* and leave you to process it for a second.

Horlicks. I know. Amazing.

Actually the name comes from the brothers James and William Horlick, and it should be relatively familiar to anyone in the Chicago or Wisconsin area, as that is where they created, patented, and manufactured the drink that bears their name to this day. And because it's a brand name that has become so familiar in the UK, entirely stripped of any alternative meaning the individual syllables may carry when taken one at a time, *Horlicks* is actually used as a safe alternative to the comparatively far less racy *bollocks* (see: Grade-B Swearwords). You'll hear bar wags mock-gallantly trying not to swear in front of the ladies by describing what a "total Horlicks" someone has made of parking their Jag outside. Or describing a rugby match in which one of the players got an elbow "right in the Horlicks" that took him off the pitch for a couple of minutes.

In 2003, the British foreign secretary Jack Straw famously referred to the dossier of evidence for weapons of mass destruction that led to British involvement in the invasion of Iraq as "a complete Horlicks," which cast the term in a far less charming light. Had he opted just to swear mildly instead, who knows what would have happened?

While you're mulling this over, and we're on the topic of names, did you know that Ovaltine was originally called Ovamaltine? It's made with malt; that's a key part of the brand. But a faulty label on a packing note when shipping cases from Switzerland—where it was originally developed—to the UK caused a total rebrand of the product, one that now leaves the original name sounding not unlike Homer Simpson singing "saxamaphone" to the tune of Beethoven's Fifth.

So, Horlicks, then. Like Ovaltine it's a malted milk drink in powder form, beloved of people who need something hot and filling just before bedtime. The ingredients are different, in that Horlicks is closer to being a ground-up biscuit or cake than being just a powdered mix of malt and milk powder, but that's by the by. The point is people drink it before bedtime to aid restful sleep. But what you may not know is that even the people at GlaxoSmithKline, which manufactures Horlicks, have no idea why it may work. There's something about the malt being a way of keeping the stomach full overnight, but they're as much in the dark about the effects as anyone.

You don't even need to drink it hot. In fact, in Hong Kong cafés Horlicks is served chilled with ice, much as you'd drink a malted milk. And in India, where the drink arrived with returning soldiers from the First World War, it represents 85 percent of GlaxoSmithKline's revenue in the entire country. Horlicks is second only to water in popularity.

Back in Blighty, people who find the choice between Ovaltine and Horlicks to be too restrictive can also choose Milo, a third malted beverage, created in Australia and similarly ready for nighttime use. Due to a manufacturing quirk, Milo maintains a gritty texture, even when fully dissolved in water or milk, and some people even sprinkle the powder on ice cream as a garnish. It is made with chocolate, which means it has a sweeter taste and may even prove to be a slight stimulant.

This makes it better suited to an early evening drink on a cold day, rather than a replacement for hot milk and cookies at the end of an evening. And certainly the advertising for Milo in Australia suggests it's a get-up-and-go drink, rather than a settle-down-and-snooze one.

Mind you, if you're struggling to get off the sofa and get yourself to bed, maybe it'll provide just enough of a jolt to get you up the stairs.

WHAT TO SAY: "If I put whiskey in my nightcap, would that make me an alcohorlick?"

WHAT NOT TO SAY: "Can't sleep? Here, try this cup of hot bollocks."

Not everyone enjoys roughing it, especially not during a hard-earned holiday, without which some kind of internal pressure valve would blow, necessitating the purchase of a long-distance weapon—and as it's Britain, we're talking either a starter pistol with a toilet-roll barrel extension or a peashooter with telescopic sights—and a conveniently central and elevated location from which to unleash fiery (pea-flavored) vengeance on an uncaring world.

The prospect of going to a field; building your own home; and try-ing to maintain a safe, clean, and dry environment in the teeth of plummeting temperatures, howling gales, and soaking rain, is simply not a universally appealing one, no matter what Glastonbury veterans would have you believe. And yet, for the people who don't consider a hotel without room service to be on a par with living like cavepersons, camping remains incredibly popular.

It may be because of the chance to go for a bracing walk in the fresh air, which is an often-used British euphemism for "a grumpy trudge in the freezing rain, looking at the sky with hopeful eyes and sighing," or it could be a quest to defy the odds on the faint hope that one day it will be dry enough to light an actual fire and sit around it and roast marshmallows. That's the dream. But the most likely expla-nation is that camping is cheap and you have to be cheerful to endure it, and those two words have a magical effect on those Brits who still harbor an affection for the spirit of the Blitz. "Oh, come on," they'll say encouragingly, "it won't kill you, so where's the harm?"

And of course, Brits being Brits, a distinct class system has emerged among campers, albeit one in which each strand looks down upon the others: a kind of Mobius strip of snobbery under canvas.

To mark this onto a graph of elitism, the x-axis would be marked "home comforts" and the y-axis would be "proximity to nature." So people who own a static caravan in a campsite that boasts a leisure complex with a bar and restaurant and live entertainment have better resources than any of their campsite peers, a definite home away from home with electricity, a flushing toilet (within the walls of their dwell-

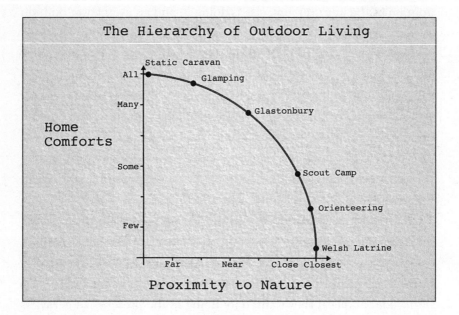

ing), and the ability to boil a kettle without striking a match. But they're not exactly at one with the environment.

Whereas, pitching a one-person tent in a field on a remote Welsh mountain where the only available electricity comes forking down from the very heavens and the only entertainment available is the satisfaction that comes from digging a latrine—that'll test the mettle, it'll irrigate the primal enjoyment cortex. Everything else exists some-where on the spectrum between these two extremes.

So if you arrive on a bicycle with a little pod tent in your panniers, that's one thing; if you're planning to decant a chillboxful of very drink-able Prosecco inside a year-round yurt and then head for the commu-nal supper and talent show, that's something else. Some people camp because they like to barbecue and drink and sing; others, because they have children and want them to spend their holidays running as wild as they can within certain clearly defined boundaries. Some like their temporary accommodation to be palatial; others huddle up together in the cold, telling ghost stories until late in the night and cooking ba-nanas in foil. The only two things all campers have in common is a low opinion of the way everyone else is doing it, and an even lower opinion of caravanners.

Not, I should add, people who live in caravans because of their culture, heritage, or ethnic background; they have enough of a rough time without accusing them of being poor campers. No, the real venom is reserved for the slowpoke road snails who carry their homes behind them on two wobbly wheels. They're looked down upon not just by the other campers; drivers also hate them for clogging up the A-roads, which they do with precision accuracy every bank holiday and for a good deal of the summer.

Somehow the act of taking all those mod cons along for the ride *and then* attaching a tent on the outside—like campers do—is enough to enrage temporary field dwellers of all stripes. But mostly those who sleep under canvas, those who know they could take themselves off into wilder climes if they wanted to. Being in the presence of caravans makes them feel not unlike the wolf that has been chained up in the back garden in a wooden house with "Poochie" above the door. They hate that.

Not that caravanners give a stuff. If they did, they would not be caravanners. Cool is not something that unduly troubles people who tow caravans to and from their holidays. They're too keen on the prac-ticalities, on the delicious joy of avoiding two key camping headaches that everyone else has to put up with, namely (a) cramming bedding and groceries and clothing into a car and (b) having to put up tents.

Although none of this lot is anywhere near as bad as the people who drive motorized caravans and tow a smaller car behind. A clearer argument for just bloody booking a hotel is hard to imagine.

WHAT TO SAY: "Let's just book four or five pitches next to each other and make a little enclave in the spinney, like explorers!"

WHAT NOT TO SAY: "We should just sleep under the stars, man. And if we wait here long enough, we're bound to see them eventually."

Driving to Wet Beaches and Sitting in the Car ■

"Oh! Looks like the rain's stopped. Fancy a stroll or shall we head back?"

Maybe there was a different plan to start with and it all went awry. Possibly it's just that all anyone needs is a view of the sea, without all that bothersome fresh air messing up an immaculate hairdo. Maybe there's a seagull phobia at work; but it's apparent, if you visit certain clifftop car parks and seaside lay-bys, that some Brits—enough to make this a clearly recognizable phenomenon, not so many that it feels mandatory—do enjoy a visit to the coast in inclement weather, so long as they don't have to get out of the car.

This isn't a recent development either. Since the earliest days of motoring—or, to be more accurate, motoring with a roof on—people have taken the old jalopy out for a spin at the weekends; and as Great Britain is an island, there's usually something scenic and coastal, or scenic and lakish, within fairly easy reach. On a sunny day, what could be nicer than a puff of bracing sea air and a bag of chips on a bench overlooking the beach at Weston-super-Mare or Skegness?

Trouble is, sometimes the elements are out to get you. A perfect day out could be ruined by poor weather, those chips left sodden and cold in a car park bin, that view of the beach left unseen thanks to screwed-up eyes to keep the wind out, and a permanent hunch to stop the rain running down your back. Now, some people may feel that the way to solve this is to buy a decent raincoat and umbrella. Others would suggest simply not going out at all, or taking a trip to somewhere with adequate facilities for entertaining indoor visitors. A clifftop café, perhaps, or, if we're resigned to getting wet, a swimming pool for splash-about fun.

To suggest such things is to miss the point somewhat. These trips are not to be made alone, and while there's a cuddly closeness in huddling under an umbrella with a loved one, it really is for the early days in a romance, rather than a long day out with someone whose physical proximity isn't always a thrill. And as for the café option, it invites the rest of the world into your private reverie, and perhaps that is not what the day is about either. Maybe you got in the car to get away from people, not to hear them loudly berate their children for upending a sugar bowl on a table next to yours. As for the swimming option, what kind of a relaxing activity is that? The pool will be cold, the changing rooms colder, and there are lanes now so you have to commit yourself to the act of swimming—you can't stop and chat—and besides, you can always go swimming in January, during the self-improving fortnight of resolutions following New Year. This is a day out.

Also, it is especially nice to make these trips out of the traditional holiday season. There's something terrifically pleasing about a bright and cheerful British seaside resort like Margate or Cleethorpes or Brighton when no tourists are there and nothing is working. It doesn't even have to be raining. All the seasonal shops with their gaudy displays are either shut or in denial, still offering seaside rock and postcards (see: Saucy Seaside Postcards) despite the gale blowing outside. And the fun-fair rides and amusement arcades sit quietly untouched under a layer of sand. What could be more melancholy, more peaceful, than a noisy place with no noise?

It is in this spirit that the British pack a thermos with tea, stick a packet of biscuits in a bag, and climb into the car. It's with the intention of going, but not taking part, that they find a nice place to park, with a decent view. And it is in the sure knowledge that horizons have been shifted and experiences have happened—within tiny parameters—that they pack up the flask, brush crumbs from laps, put their seat belts back on, and head for home.

WHAT TO SAY: "Look! Her umbrella just turned inside out! Can I have a custard cream?"

WHAT NOT TO SAY: "Come on! Let's get out there! It's so bracing!"

Slang and Making Up Words ■

As a patchwork nation made up of counties upon countries upon kingdoms, Britain wears its idiosyncratic quirks of language like fans wear the T-shirt of their favorite band. New communities mint new words on a daily basis, whether because they wish to hide something from the authorities—as is the case with almost all youthspeak, rhyming slang, and Polari, the secret gay language of mid-twentieth-century London—or because they want to find a way to discuss coarse matters in polite society.

Some slang fits neither brief, of course. Popular Britishisms like *cheerio* and *tickety-boo* and *fab* are just colorful ways to use language. And the Brits do love a bit of color in their social discourse. There's not enough room to cover every made-up phrase or invented word in the British English language, but here's a decent smattering, a last-minute glossary of possibly unfamiliar terms, to get you started.

Note: Not all of these are in common use everywhere.

Bairn—baby or small child
Banjaxed—broken
Bare—lots of, many, or really, as in "I'm bare drunk"
Bawbag—scrotum; but mainly used as an all-purpose insult
Beast—top-notch, very good
Bee's knees—the acme of excellence

Berk—idiot (affectionate term); taken from a slang term for
  vagina

Bevvy—alcoholic beverage

Blag—get something for free

Bob's your uncle—"and there we have it"

Bonce—head

Bonk—have sex

Candy floss—cotton candy

Cheerio—good-bye

Cheers—a drinking toast, also a fond farewell, also a
  thank-you

Chirpsing—flirting

Chuffed—proud, pleased

Chunder—vomit

Cling film—plastic wrap

Clinker, beezer, cracker—good

Cock-up—all gone horribly wrong

Codswallop—nonsense, piffle

Dicky—unwell

Dosh, wonga, spondulicks—money

Dry—no fun

Extra—over the top

Faff—(verb) waste time; (noun) fuss or bother

Fancy—find someone attractive

Fanny, quim, tuppence—vagina

Fit—sexy

Fizzog—face

Fringe—bangs, as in hair

Gammy—lame, sore or infected

Gipper—old person

Gobsmacked—surprised

Goolies, wedding tackle, meat and two veg—male genitalia

Grotty—disgusting, of poor quality

Gutted—very upset

Gyp—pain, as in "my gammy leg is giving me gyp"

Her Majesty's pleasure—prison

Hobbledehoy—a swaggering youth or awkward buffoon

Iffy—dodgy

I'll give you a bell—"I'm going to call
    you on the phone"

Jobsworth—overly officious official

Kip—sleep

Knackered—tired, as in "fit for the knacker's yard," where
    horses were taken to die

Knackers—testicles

Knob, todger—penis

Lost the plot—gone a bit mad

Lurgy—cooties

Lush—very good or very attractive

Minger—unattractive person

Numpty—idiot (meant as an affectionate term)

Nut—head

Off your chump—crazy

Oh, my giddy aunt!—"oh, crikey!"

Parking the tiger—throwing up

Plastered—drunk

Poxy—faulty or dirty

Quite—very, as in "quite sure," "quite finished," "quite cross"

Rat arsed—drunk

Rubbish—garbage, also nonsense, also poor quality

Scrumping—stealing apples

Scundered—embarrassed

She looks well in that—"she looks hideous"

Slag—sexually promiscuous person (usually a damning
    insult for a girl)

Slag off—talking smack about someone

Slapper—sexually promiscuous girl

Smart—well groomed

Smasher—attractive person; can also be used fondly to refer to nice friends, children, etc.

Snog—kiss

Sod it—"oh, what the hell!"

Sod off—"go away"

Speaking Welsh—throwing up

Spliff—marijuana cigarette

Steaming—drunk

Stitched up good and proper—conned, fooled

Ta—"thanks"

Take a reddener—get embarrassed

Take the piss—mock or satirize

Tara, or t'ra!—"good-bye"

Tidy—"this is satisfactory"

Titchy—very small

Trollied—drunk

TTFN—"tata for now"

Twee—cardigan-wearing cupcake fan (a mocking term)

Upswallow—throw up

Up the duff—pregnant

Wazzock—idiot (affectionate term)

Wet—ineffectual or soppy, as in "wet nelly"

Wotcha—"hello"

WHAT TO SAY: Any of the above.

WHAT NOT TO SAY: French stuff. You'll only confuse people.